INSTITUTE OF INTERNATIONAL STUDIES
YALE UNIVERSITY

The Soviet Image of the United States

A STUDY IN DISTORTION

The Soviet Image of the United States

A STUDY IN DISTORTION

Frederick C. Barghoorn

KENNIKAT PRESS
Port Washington, N. Y./London

THE SOVIET IMAGE OF THE UNITED STATES

Reissued in 1969 by Kennikat Press by arrangement
Library of Congress Catalog Card No: 70-85983
SBN 8046-0599-8

Manufactured by Taylor Publishing Company Dallas, Texas

To My Mother

Contents

Acknowledgment

WHATEVER merit this study may possess, it owes in large measure to the inspiration, insight, and information from which I have benefited in my association with other students, both academic and official, of Russian problems and of international relations in general. To them, and in particular to the Director of the Yale Institute of International Studies, Frederick Sherwood Dunn, and to the Associates and staff of the Institute I am grateful for the encouragement and help which made preparation of this book possible. Needless to say, the sins or defects of omission or commission from which this study surely suffers are entirely my responsibility.

For permission to quote from works published by them I am indebted to Doubleday and Company, Inc., Harper and Brothers, Oxford University Press, and Viking Press.

Introduction

What the Soviet Propaganda Picture of America Signifies

THE thesis of this study is that Soviet propaganda against the United States is one of the main instruments of the Kremlin's aggressive foreign policy. It follows logically that one of the principal tasks of American policy is the analysis, exposure, and ideological annihilation of Soviet propaganda. The Kremlin's Korean war underlines the importance and urgency of this task. Moscow's handling of the propaganda and political warfare aspects of the Korean operation constitutes the latest and most intense phase of a ferocious hate campaign which the Soviet leaders have been conducting for several years.

Soviet propaganda presents the Korean war as a struggle for national liberation against American "imperialist" aggression. This line exemplifies two of the major Communist propaganda objectives discussed in this work. One is the attempt to mobilize the peoples of Asia and other economically underdeveloped areas against European and American "imperialism." The other is the exploitation of the world's yearning for peace and fear of war in the interests of Soviet expansion. But the Korean propaganda and the other Soviet political maneuvers and propaganda lines accompanying it, in particular the campaign for signatures to the so-called "Stockholm petition" demanding the outlawing of atomic weapons and branding as war criminals the first national leaders who might use such weapons in time of war, illustrate a still more fundamental characteristic of Soviet propaganda.

This characteristic is the attribution to America and other free, non-Soviet nations of the motives and tactics typical of

Soviet Communism. While talking peace, the Kremlin wages war. It may also be said that in the postwar period the West, by and large, has lived and acted peace while occasionally—in the person of some of its politically inept spokesmen—talking in a misleading warlike tone, which was sure to be skillfully exploited by Soviet propaganda. A number of Soviet refugees with whom I have talked describe Stalin's policy as the "Stop Thief!" policy. According to them, the Soviet leaders act like a thief, who with his hands in the pocket of his victim shouts "Stop, Thief!" at the top of his lungs to distract attention from his own actions.

Aggression against the freedom of nations is not the only trait of Soviet Communism which its leaders attribute to their opponents. The same phenomenon of projecting one's own motives to others prevails in most areas of Soviet life and policy. As a result the meaning of words such as "democracy," "sovereignty" or "liberty," not to mention "peace," has been strangely transformed. And now, in connection with Stalin's recent pronouncements regarding the nature of language, we find the Soviet press emphasizing the necessity of freedom of scientific inquiry. All of this brings to mind the words of Isaiah Berlin in his article in *Foreign Affairs* for April, 1950: "There is a persecution not only of science but by science and in its name . . ."[1]

President Truman has called for a "campaign of truth" against Soviet propaganda. The United States government has stepped up its foreign information program. This is all to the good, but in a democracy such as ours the task of setting straight the distorted image of America conveyed by Soviet propaganda cannot be left to government alone. Indeed, it cannot be performed successfully by government alone. The government's "truth campaign" can be successful only against the background of an informed, enlightened public opinion.

Such enlightenment can be achieved only by the broadest possible public study of the specific content and techniques of Soviet propaganda and political strategy. It is necessary to

[1] *Foreign Affairs,* Vol. 28, No. 3, p. 382.

analyze in some detail the stream of communications by which the Soviet leaders seek to implant in the minds of peoples under their control the image of an America which seeks, they allege, to enslave or destroy them, and whose nefarious designs must therefore be foiled by all available and feasible means.

In this book I seek to assist Americans to visualize the picture of American life, thought, and action presented to the Soviet and other peoples by the Soviet propaganda machine. I began to gather the material on which it is based during more than four years of service in the American Embassy in Moscow from December, 1942, to March, 1947. During approximately the first three years of this period it was possible for a foreigner to talk far more freely with Soviet Russians than it became after the Kremlin had restored and intensified the controls over its subjects which had necessarily been somewhat relaxed during the war for survival. The material I gathered and the insights I gained by personal contacts with Russians, as distinct from official publications, are presented mostly in Chapter XI of this study. As I indicate there, this firsthand experience furnished a bright and hopeful spot in an otherwise somber picture. For it became clear to me that the Kremlin had by no means succeeded in turning the Russian people into robots or intellectual shadows. The critical attitude of many Russians toward the Soviet regime and their friendly curiosity and admiration concerning America made me feel that one of the principal tasks of American policy must be to convince the Russian people that America could assist them in realizing their aspirations for peace, prosperity, and human dignity which the Kremlin was thwarting.

Such convictions and such hopes were fortified by dozens of surprising and often heart-warming experiences which befell me on my travels and wanderings. I shall never forget a conversation on the Trans-Siberian railroad with a Soviet school teacher who exclaimed with admiration that America was the center of world civilization, nor the day when in a suburban town near Moscow a barefoot Russian lad told me he wanted me to take him to Moscow where the Americans would take care of him.

But of course such experiences, though common enough, had to be viewed against the background of obstruction, suspicion, and hostility revealed in the actions and published utterances of the Soviet government. It is to the analysis of the latter material that this study is mostly devoted. The principal sources used in preparing it were Soviet daily newspapers, such as *Pravda,* and political journals, such as *Bolshevik.* Radio broadcasts, transcripts of public lectures, books and pamphlets have also been used. I have described certain methods used by Soviet propagandists, such as repetition, the blending of facts and symbols into propaganda themes, and the attempt to associate these themes in the mind of the audience with emotional reactions which the Kremlin wished to stimulate.

But this book is not primarily a study of propaganda techniques. It is a study of the propaganda itself, with appropriate attention to "doctrine," "opinion," and "attitudes." By propaganda I mean the stream of communications issued through the Soviet propaganda media to influence persons who can be reached thereby inside or outside the U.S.S.R. In this study I emphasize Soviet propaganda for domestic consumption. By "doctrine" I mean the body of thought and belief regarding the nature of human society, and particularly of international relations, to which Soviet policy-makers adhere. "Attitudes" I use in a still more general sense to include vague and intangible psychological factors such as a general state of anxiety and tension, which mold the mentality of the Soviet leadership. "Opinion" I define as a more or less rational estimate drawn up by the Soviet leaders of any given political situation, for example, the probability of war with the United States at any given time. Finally, I occasionally employ the term "ideology" more or less synonymously with "doctrine." This word is sometimes used by the Soviets as synonymous with my use of the word "doctrine," but sometimes in the sense in which I here define "propaganda."

Propaganda is one of the chief instruments employed by Soviet policy-makers to assist them in achieving their objectives.

Soviet statements and actions indicate clearly the vast importance attributed by the Soviet leaders to propaganda and ideology, terms often used almost interchangeably by the Soviet press. For example, Stalin's statement at the eighteenth Party Congress (1939) to the effect that nine-tenths of all problems could be solved by "ideologically tempering" Soviet "cadres" is frequently quoted.

Soviet propaganda operates within rather narrow limits imposed by a number of factors. One of these is the basic doctrines of Marxism-Leninism, which describe the world, define values, and prescribe ultimate goals. It is important, however, to keep in mind that Marxism-Leninism is a rather flexible doctrine, imposing upon its adherents continuous, complex problems of interpretation. Although, for example, it postulates the ultimate decline of capitalism, it is vague regarding the time factor in this process. The aspects of Marxism-Leninism most relevant to this study are those which emphasize the class struggle within each capitalist state and the antagonism between the Soviet Union and the non-Soviet world.

While Marxism-Leninism prescribes the ultimate goals of Soviet policy, it permits considerable flexibility of interpretation; at any given time the Soviet leaders are likely to be guided by expediency as well as by doctrine. That they themselves are consciously very practical in their application of doctrine is indicated by the frequency of such statements as the following: "The propaganda of Marxist-Leninist theory which our Party tirelessly carries on . . . is always subordinated to the basic tasks confronting the Party at this or that historical stage." [2]

A second factor shaping Soviet propaganda is the concentration in the U.S.S.R. of decision-making power and responsibility, in all spheres of politics, economics, and culture, in very few hands. This power monopoly is paralleled in the propaganda field. Given the coexistence of sovereign states, of which the U.S.S.R. is one, this situation tends to impose upon Soviet propaganda the task of justifying Soviet policies before world public

[2] Quoted from leader in Central Committee journal, *Party Life*, No. 8, April, 1947. This organ has since discontinued publication.

opinion. It seems also that whenever there exists any substantial amount of discontent with Soviet institutions or policy among the domestic population, there is an unusually strong tendency to find or create scapegoats, particularly foreign ones, upon whom to heap blame for the real or imaginary evils of Soviet life. Since the citizen living in a highly centralized polity and under a planned economy must tend to blame his troubles on the government, the leaders must in turn seek to divert discontent away from themselves.

A third important factor in shaping Soviet propaganda is the existence of differences between the Soviet way of life and standard of living and those of the United States and other Western countries. This factor can, of course, operate upon the people of Soviet Russia or of other countries only to the extent that they are aware of it. Soviet propaganda has always sought to utilize this fact to its own advantage abroad. But at home, at least up to the present, Soviet leaders have feared open competition between the Soviet and the bourgeois, particularly the American, way of life. They have combated foreign influence by closing channels through which it might reach the Soviet population and by physically excluding alien agents. And they have sought to render their people immune to the attractions of capitalist culture by painting what for their purposes was an expedient description thereof.

The ways in which the Soviet regime deals with the problems of "cultural competition" are not unique. They are, for example, strikingly similar to, though much more extreme than, those employed by the Government of the Russian Empire throughout most of its history.

A fourth major factor basic to Soviet attitudes and propaganda is historical experience, both pre-Soviet and Soviet. Both Russian and Soviet leaders and peoples have had to deal with an international environment far less favorable than that, for example, in which the United States has developed. Particularly during the Soviet period, life for both the state and the individual has been a grim struggle for survival. It is not surprising that the Soviet leaders regard politics as a life-and-death struggle, in which the only rules are those imposed by circumstances, nor that they should seek to communicate this attitude to their people. Nor is it surprising that Soviet Russians, whatever their attitude toward the regime, are unusually suspicious both of their fellow countrymen and of foreigners.

Finally, there is one other major factor shaping attitudes and propaganda regarding international relations in both the U.S.S.R. and the United States. This is what roughly one may call "bipolarity," the existence of two "super-powers," in a world of sovereign states which tend to orient their policies toward one or the other of the two giants. This situation need not, one may hope, lead to catastrophe, but it does tend to cause both giants, and especially their policy-makers, to think of the other as a nuisance, a rival, or an enemy.

I have listed above what I consider the main factors that determine Soviet political thought and are reflected in Soviet propaganda. Not all possible factors are listed. For example, no mention is made of Russian national character, not because I do not consider it important but because I feel that its influence on the subject discussed in this book cannot be analyzed with sufficient precision to justify its inclusion. Its influence is general, and could probably not profitably be considered in respect to one aspect of opinion or propaganda. More important, national character has far less scope for expression in the field of propaganda than it may have in a freer society such as the United States. There is, however, one aspect of Soviet propaganda which may perhaps be explained by reference to Russian character or to a Soviet intensification of a Russian trait. This is its extreme vituperativeness.

In part this seems to reflect a certain intellectual naïveté which finds it difficult to credit an opponent with other than the blackest of motives. Russians, especially Soviet Russians, seem to think in terms of extremes and to overlook nuances. This trait was reflected by Lenin in the polemical tone of his political writing, and has become a part of the Bolshevik tradition.

I linger on this relatively minor point because I think Americans sometimes fail to remember that language which strikes us as extremely belligerent may seem quite calm to a Soviet

Russian. While I was in Moscow, I was often impressed by the capacity of Russians to endure from one another insults which in this country would almost certainly have led to violence. The Soviet Russians seem to have learned to inflict verbal damage upon an opponent without necessarily thinking in terms of physical combat.

In general, I feel that the ideological and power-political factors are the major determining forces in Soviet propaganda regarding the foreign policy and the economic condition of capitalist countries. But Soviet attempts to deflate the prestige of Western culture, though in part, and in a general sense, derived from Marxism-Leninism, have been powerfully reinforced by the fear of the Soviet leaders that the minds of their people would be poisoned by its influence. This I hope to demonstrate by appropriate quotations from the Soviet press and by reference to my own personal experience in the U.S.S.R.

During and more especially since World War II, interpreting America to the Soviet public has been perhaps the most important and difficult task facing Soviet propaganda. During the war this leading democracy had to be presented as an ally without arousing too much sympathy. Since the war, it has had to be presented as a rival without arousing too much fear. Marxist-Leninist doctrine and the Kremlin's interpretation of the postwar power situation prescribed these tasks.

In this study I outline briefly Russian and Soviet attitudes toward America before World War II. In more detail, the wartime situation is discussed. Then follow chapters on Soviet propaganda regarding American foreign policy, war and peace, atomic policy, and the postwar American domestic scene. All of these are based on Soviet official sources. In the next to the last chapter, however, I have sought to sum up my personal impressions.

Finally, in the concluding chapter I have discussed the implications for American policy of the pattern of attitudes and beliefs contained in the Soviet propaganda themes, which now, in Korea and elsewhere, serve partly as the basis for and partly as the justification of ominous actions.

The Soviet Image of the United States

A STUDY IN DISTORTION

PART ONE

Before World War II

I. The Evolution of a Symbol

THE attitudes of nations toward one another—somewhat like those of individuals—present a bewildering and ever changing complex of myth and reality. This has been true even when proximity and similarity have made for familiarity, though not necessarily for friendship, as in the case of France and Germany; it has been even more true in the relations of America and Russia.

America has meant many things to many Russians, and the Russian image of America has undergone kaleidoscopic changes. Here I can set forth only the bare outlines of Russian attitudes toward America prior to World War II when our detailed analysis begins.

In the now dim days before the communist revolution America represented to Russians more than to any other people a promised land. Particularly to Russian liberals, and also to most Russian radicals, the United States symbolized human dignity, the pioneer virtues, and dazzling material progress. This appeal diminished somewhat after about 1890, in an era when a still unsophisticated capitalism was flaunting its achievements in America and was bringing to Russia the harsh unease of the early stages of the industrial revolution. After the October revolution America was cast in the negative role of the greatest capitalist power. But the United States continued after 1917 to be regarded as a model of technological progress. Moreover, a surprising degree of good will toward America persisted even under the Bolsheviks, especially among Soviet citizens who did not belong to the new ruling Party.

The attitude toward America of pre-Marxian Russian radicals such as the Decembrists, the leaders of the abortive palace revolution of 1825, Herzen, Chernyshevski, Dobrolyubov, Pisarev and other Russian thinkers, was undeniably favorable. In general, the pre-Marxian radicals believed that America had made vast progress toward the goals for which they themselves were fighting in their struggle against Russian serfdom and despotism. More important was the absence in America of evils which they deplored in both the Russian and Western European social and political orders. Both the moderate wing of the Decembrists, headed by Nikita Muravev, and the radicals, headed by Pestel, were greatly influenced by American political institutions and practice. Muravev's draft of a constitution for Russia lifted long extracts unchanged from the American constitution.

The most gifted literary artist among Russian radicals and one of the most influential Russian pre-Marxian socialists, Alexander Herzen, regarded America, together with Russia, as the only countries capable of realizing his ideals of human welfare. Herzen set forth this attitude in numerous statements such as the following: "If reaction and absolutism finally vanquish the revolution in Europe," even Russia "perhaps . . . will perish." In that event "progress will pass to America."

Michael Bakunin, greatest of anarchists, and the embodiment of what he himself called the "creative force" of destruction, repeatedly characterized America as "the classic land of political liberty." To the most profound thinker and scholar and noblest character among the Russian pre-Marxians, Nicholas Chernyshevski, America—at least "the free Northern states"—was "the land that was almost the living embodiment of his desires." [1]

These men were not only anti-capitalist but anti-industrialist. Another highly influential publicist, D. I. Pisarev, the leader among the radical youth in the later 1860's, favored an en-

[1] For this statement and for the quotations and remarks on Herzen, Bakunin, and Chernyshevski, see David Hecht, *Russian Radicals Look to America, 1825-1894*, Harvard Univ. Press, 1947, pp. 1-121.

lightened industrial capitalism. He derived his ideas from the American economist, Henry Charles Cary.[2]

A certain disillusionment with the United States set in among Russian intellectuals after the American Civil War with the rise to dominance of "industrial capitalism and the ruthless captain of business enterprise . . ." This trend was intensified after about 1890 when "the Russian revolutionary movement turned more and more to Marxism, and concomitantly tended to lose its lingering illusions in regard to the United States." [3] As America came to be more and more regarded as the classic land of capitalism, negative attitudes toward this country grew stronger among radicals and also among conservative anti-capitalist intellectuals like Dostoevski. As early as 1869 in Dostoevski's novel *The Possessed,* the character Shatov expressed his disgust with America and its exploitation, lynch law, and commercialism.

Though perhaps with gradually diminishing intensity, a relatively favorable attitude toward American, and even British, political life and institutions, in contrast to those of continental Europe, persisted among Russian radicals until, roughly, the period of the Russian Civil War of 1917-21 with its foreign, including American, intervention. This fact seems to indicate that the Russian radical thinkers were not indifferent to political freedom. They were hostile to what they regarded as use of slogans of political liberty to deprive the masses of socialist organization, without which in their opinion mere parliamentary democracy was a sham.[4] Their attitude probably contributed to the Leninist criticism of "formal" democracy. On the whole, broad sections of the Russian intelligentsia continued to hold a sympathetic attitude toward America. The vast

[2] Cf. my articles "The Russian Radicals of the 1860's and the Problem of the Industrial Proletariat," *Slavonic and East European Review,* American Series, March, 1943, pp. 57-70; "D. I. Pisarev: A Representative of Russian Nihilism," *Review of Politics,* April, 1948; "Russian Radicals and the West European Revolutions of 1848," *Review of Politics,* July, 1949.

[3] Hecht, *op. cit.,* pp. 218-20.

[4] Cf. my article cited above in *Review of Politics* for July, 1949, for additional observations on this point with special reference to Herzen.

Russian Jewish emigration to the United States and the American condemnation of pogroms in the early twentieth century were important factors in this situation. America down to 1917—and later—remained in the eyes of many Russians a promised land. Another factor which aroused much sympathy among Russian liberals and radicals was American condemnation of the absolutist institutions and practices of the Imperial Russian Government. This was expressed, for example, in George Kennan's well-known book, *Siberia and the Exile System*. Another of many factors making for mutual Russian-American sympathy, at least on a nongovernmental plane, was the vast popularity of American literature in Russia, especially the writings of Mark Twain and Jack London. As Robert Magidoff wrote in his fascinating article, "American Literature in Russia," in the *Saturday Review of Literature* for November 2, 1946, Russian admiration of American literature fostered before 1917 and to a surprising degree even after 1917 an "almost universally accepted conception of the United States as a man-made paradise, and of Americans as muscular, upright, free, and happy demigods."

On the official level, Russian-American relations were on the whole friendly and even cordial throughout most of their pre-1917 history.[5]

The Mayor of Vladivostok said to me in May, 1946: "American and Russian troops have never fired on one another." Certainly he was correct if he meant that they have never fought in large-scale engagements. This is surely remarkable in the relations of great powers. The two countries fortunately were geographically and politically remote throughout most of their history, and during most of the nineteenth century had in Britain a common or potential enemy.

Particularly interesting is Lenin's pre-1917 attitude toward American political institutions and the possibility of achieving

[5] See Foster Rhea Dulles, *The Road to Teheran*, Princeton Univ. Press, 1944, and for a study in a less optimistic, more realistic vein of a specific aspect of Russian-American relations, Edward H. Zabriskie, *American-Russian Rivalry in the Far East*, Univ. of Pennsylvania Press, 1946.

socialism without a cataclysmic revolution. Until 1917, Lenin seems to have believed it possible that America and Britain might achieve socialism without violent revolution. At any rate, it was not until that year that he explicitly argued in *State and Revolution* that the British and American states had become police machines which must be smashed in order to carry out a "people's revolution." He wrote that the Anglo-Saxon democracies, formerly free of "militarism and bureaucracy" had fallen during the years 1914-17 into the "bloody swamp of bureaucratic institutions." [6] Lenin, on this point, revised both his Russian pre-Marxian predecessors and Marx himself. Marx, in a speech at Amsterdam in 1872, had affirmed that there were certain countries, including the United States and England, in which the workers might hope to achieve their aims by peaceful means, and Engels in 1886 in his preface to the first English translation of *Capital* had echoed this opinion.[7] It is interesting that one of the leading Soviet ideologists, P. F. Yudin, went out of his way in a lecture delivered and published in 1946 to remind his audience of Lenin's revision of Marx on this point.[8]

The social-economic basis for Lenin's early exception of America from the necessity of a violent revolution was the distinction he drew between the American and the Prussian types of capitalist development. In the former type of economy a multitude of independent farmers assured high purchasing power and a basis for political democracy. The latter was the Junker economy, in which owners of large estates held economic and political predominance.[9]

[6] Quoted from *Gosudarstvo i Revolyutsiya* (*State and Revolution*) as published in V. I. Lenin, *Izbrannye Proizvedeniya,* 2 vols., Moscow, 1943, II, 143. This work is available in numerous Russian and translated editions.

[7] For interesting comment on this point, see Sidney Hook, *Towards the Understanding of Karl Marx,* Day, 1933, pp. 291-93.

[8] *Sotsializm i Kommunizm,* Moscow, 1946, pp. 6, 7.

[9] Lenin developed this distinction most fully in his *The Agrarian Program of the First Russian Revolution, 1905-07,* first published in 1908 and republished in 1917 and subsequently.

The First World War and the Russian Revolution intensified the extremist tendencies of Lenin's thought. Before 1914 he had emphasized the revolutionary aspects of Marxism and had condemned the moderate Marxist parties both in Russia and Western Europe. However, he had apparently believed that the capitalist system still retained a certain vitality. The "Imperialist War," as he called the First World War, simultaneously deepened his rage against the capitalist system and raised his hopes that the destruction of the established order was imminent. His horizon, hitherto confined mainly to Russia, was widened to include the whole world. He came to feel that world capitalism was a unified system and that it probably would collapse as a unit. These trends found expression in a number of his works written in Western Europe, particularly in *Imperialism, the Highest Stage of Capitalism*. They were still further intensified when the February revolution offered the prospect that in backward Russia, where Lenin had thought a bourgeois revolution must precede the proletarian revolution, the latter was at hand. Thus Russia would take the lead in the destruction of world capitalism. Lenin registered this feeling in his *April Theses* of 1917.

By this year there had crystallized a body of concepts and attitudes which constituted for Lenin a fanatical political religion and which determined the policy and propaganda of Soviet Russia toward the non-Soviet world. The most important concept was that the Russian Revolution had opened a new and wonderful era in the social development of mankind and that it would inevitably and speedily spread to other capitalist countries. It was logical that the countries which were the main bulwarks of world capitalism, France, Great Britain, and the United States, should be regarded as the enemies of the vanguard land of world social revolution, Soviet Russia.

At first, the Bolsheviks were confident that the revolution would spread quickly to at least all of continental Europe. When this did not occur, they had to face the problem of the existence of their socialist state in what they assumed was a decaying but mortally hostile capitalist world. To deal with this situation, Lenin prescribed both the building of a Soviet state machine sufficiently strong to withstand the expected onslaught of the capitalist powers and the exploitation in the interests of Soviet Russia of divisions among the capitalist countries. He and his lieutenants sought by every means to exploit and inflame the internal "contradictions" within the capitalist camp as a whole and within each individual capitalist country.

The Bolsheviks approached the capitalist world with implacable hostility rooted in unbending dogma, but they permitted themselves flexibility of tactics in the interests of the survival of Soviet Russia. The allied intervention in Russia as well as the conduct of the Germans during and after the Brest-Litovsk peace negotiations naturally deepened the Bolsheviks' hatred, fear, and suspicion of all capitalist governments. At the same time the violent subversive actions of the Communists through the Comintern, organized in March, 1919, confirmed and deepened the fears of established governments and most of their citizens that Soviet Communism was a potentially fatal menace to order and civilization. Thus occurred the schism of the world into two mutually distrustful camps whose experience seemed to confirm each side's prejudices regarding the other.[10]

An impressive array of quotations could be marshaled from Lenin's writings after November, 1917, to indicate his feeling that the world was now divided into two irreconcilably hostile camps. Some of these we shall examine presently. But first it will be helpful to recall briefly the history of relations between Soviet Russia and the outside world from 1917 to 1941. The policies and propaganda of the Soviets have conformed with remarkable consistency to the long-range objectives formulated by Lenin. However, the Soviet leaders were forced by circumstances to transform their utopian revolutionary program into

[10] For facts and narrative regarding Soviet-Allied and Soviet-American relations and attitudes of the various governments toward one another see: Louis Fischer, *The Soviets in World Affairs*, 2 vols., London, 1930; and Dulles, *op. cit.* Dulles covers cursorily the period to Teheran in 1943, Fischer in great detail to 1930. Max Beloff's scholarly study, *The Foreign Policy of Soviet Russia* (2 vols., Oxford Univ. Press, 1947-49), takes up where Fischer leaves off and brings the story up through 1941.

practical domestic and foreign policies which would assure survival during what was conceived to be the interim period between the Russian Revolution and similar revolutions elsewhere. Their attitude during this period, which increasingly assumed the character of permanence, has been a combination of rigidity of professed ends and strategy, and flexibility of means and tactics.

From 1921 to 1928, the internal weakness of the U.S.S.R. dictated a relatively cautious Soviet policy. Fortunately for the Bolsheviks, these years of recovery from the effects of World War I and the Civil War coincided with what Soviet leaders regarded as, or at least often termed, a "breathing spell," a "temporary stabilization" of world capitalism. Internally, this was the period of partial and temporary concessions to capitalism known as the N.E.P. (New Economic Policy). Externally, it was characterized by establishment of diplomatic relations with Great Britain, France, Italy, Japan, and lesser powers. Several major trends became apparent in Soviet foreign policy in the N.E.P. period. One was the attempt to expand economic relations with the leading capitalist countries, which included the granting of a number of concessions to foreign firms, such as the permission granted to the Harriman interests for exploiting the manganese deposits of Georgia. These were liquidated in connection with the self-sufficiency drive of the Five-Year Plans.

Another major theme of Soviet policy in this period of recuperation was neatly summed up by Louis Fischer: "Moscow today submits the proposition—embodied in a Soviet resolution, for instance, at the International Economic Conference in Geneva in May, 1927—that the capitalist and Communist worlds may live side by side in peaceful co-existence."[11] This line was doubtless intended mainly for foreign consumption. It implied no repudiation of the long-range goals of the revolution, allegiance to which continued to be pledged in program speeches of Stalin and other leaders to party meetings. How-

[11] Fischer, *op. cit.*, II, 823.

ever, it furnished a basis for a *modus vivendi* with a capitalist world almost as hostile in this period to the Bolsheviks as the latter were to its "ruling classes."

Finally the Kremlin remained faithful to the Leninist injunction to play the capitalist powers against one another. Beginning at Rapallo in 1922 it aligned itself—but did not ally itself—with the other pariah power, Germany. The attempt to play off the Germans against the "Versailles" powers did not, of course, inhibit the Soviets from abetting, through the Comintern, the forces of revolution in Germany.

Certain characteristics of Soviet policy which took shape in the 'twenties remained among its basic traits. Two of these stood out as most important. One was the conscious, calculated dualism of Soviet foreign policy represented by the Foreign Office and the Comintern. The other was the Kremlin's permanent mobilization to deal with multiple contingencies. This was embodied in simultaneous pursuit of the policy of "coexistence" and that of world revolution. The two sets of instruments and their accompanying policies and propaganda lines were manipulated with the flexibility of which only a tightly centralized regime is capable. They were employed variously, in blends and proportions appropriate to shifting circumstances. Then, as now, the Janus-like quality of Soviet foreign policy created confusion, irritation, and justifiable anxiety among Western statesmen.

With the adoption of agricultural collectivization and planned industrialization in the U.S.S.R., Soviet policy and propaganda toward the capitalist world returned in part and for a time to the aggressiveness of the 1917-21 period. The great depression of 1929-33 increased the confidence of the Soviet leaders that disintegration was proceeding in the capitalist system and added immensely to the prestige of the U.S.S.R. in wide circles of world opinion.

A new phase of Soviet policy and propaganda was inaugurated as the result of the rise of Hitler in Germany and the increasingly menacing German attitude toward Soviet Russia, paralleled by the growing threat of an aggressive Japan.

When the Kremlin in 1934, after a period of hesitation and of hopes either for an early collapse of the Nazis or for some sort of accommodation with them—the latter lingered stubbornly—finally decided upon an aggressive anti-Nazi policy, it abruptly changed its whole foreign policy. The new policy included joining the League of Nations, formerly anathematized as a world committee of imperialists, and forming an alliance with France, formerly denounced, as in the sixteenth Party Congress in 1930, as the most aggressive of all the imperialist powers. The new policy also prescribed certain changes in the immediate objectives and tactics of the Comintern with the aim of converting the whole international revolutionary apparatus temporarily at least into an anti-Nazi weapon.

Maxim Litvinov ably presented this so-called "collective security" policy before the international forum of Geneva. Perhaps Moscow in carrying out this policy went somewhat beyond the limits of Lenin's warning that "to support one [capitalist] country against another would be a crime against Communism," but the over-all tone of Soviet propaganda and behavior in this period and subsequently indicates clearly that the Kremlin considered the "united front" policy an application of Lenin's accompanying advice to "use one country against another." [12] This is not to deny, of course, that the policy offered advantages not only to Moscow but to the Western democracies as well.

The Soviet-German Pact of August 22, 1939, also fits logically into the Leninist-Stalinist pattern of diplomacy, which David Dallin in his book *Soviet Russia's Foreign Policy* [13] called the diplomacy of the "third power." With characteristic flexibility the Kremlin turned off its anti-Axis propaganda and directed its fire against the Anglo-French "warmongers" who were now accused, together with their American supporters, of seeking world domination.

[12] For these and additional similar quotations see David Shub, *Lenin*, Doubleday, 1948, appendix pp. 389 ff.

[13] *Soviet Russia's Foreign Policy, 1939-1942*, Yale Univ. Press, 1942.

Shocking as it was to idealistic liberals in the West, the Pact must have seemed to the Kremlin a rational adjustment to the developing situation in the capitalist camp. As in the pre-Hitler period, it again seemed more profitable to do business with the Germans than with the Western powers. The shift reflected what had become a tradition: Soviet policy was not oriented in any direction except the interests of the U.S.S.R. as defined by the Politburo. The spirit of Soviet policy in this period was typified by an article in *Bolshevik* for April, 1941, according to which the world was divided into two camps—the imperialist, which was engulfed by war, and the Soviet, which remained at peace.

The position of the United States in Soviet policy and propaganda throughout the entire pre-1941 period was slightly paradoxical. Although the United States, together with Great Britain, was the core of the world capitalist system, and therefore according to Marxist-Leninist logic the greatest potential enemy of world communism and Soviet Russia, it was safely remote geographically. Moreover, it was the world model of technological progress and industrial efficiency. Finally, it often acted in a manner which did not indicate conscious or determined pursuit of its interests as the center of world capitalism. And so the negative attitude toward the United States prescribed by Leninist doctrine was slightly modified. Moreover, if popular opinion as distinct from official Communist Party doctrine with which we have been concerned is taken into account, the Soviet attitude toward America becomes still more favorable. I will touch briefly on this point toward the end of this chapter.

Let us now examine briefly Soviet policy and propaganda toward the United States throughout the period 1917-41. In general, they focused on two main problems. The United States was viewed as a hostile capitalist power and thus a major factor in the international situation. At the same time, and this point became increasingly important with the building of a great Soviet industrial state, it was regarded as the chief rival of the U.S.S.R. in a world struggle of social systems.

The numerous statements in which Lenin pictured the entire world as the arena of struggle between socialism and capitalism included by inference the United States. Lenin stated in 1918: "International imperialism . . . could not under any circumstances . . . live side by side with the Soviet Republic . . ." Also in 1918 he said, "Of course, the final victory of socialism in a single country is impossible. Our unit of workers and peasants which is supporting the Soviet government is only one of the units of the great world army. . . ." One of Lenin's best known formulations of this theme was his statement that "we are living not merely in a state but in a system of states and the existence of the Soviet Republic side by side with imperialist states for a long time is unthinkable."

In his last published work, which appeared in *Pravda* for March 4, 1923, Lenin wrote that the Western imperialists had succeeded in splitting the world into two camps. They had enslaved Germany. Ranged against them were the Soviet Union and the peoples of the East, comprising together the majority of mankind. But in order that the Soviet Republic might "assure our existence until the next military clash between the counterrevolutionary imperialist West and the revolutionary antimilitarist East . . . it was necessary to construct a strong efficient Soviet state."[14]

A number of Lenin's statements in this period applied more directly to the United States. He wrote as follows:

> Wilson's glorified republic proved in practice to be a form of the most rabid imperialism, of the most shameless oppression and suppression of weak and small nationalities. The average democrat in general, the Menshevik and the Socialist-Revolutionary, thought: "Who are we even to dream of a superior type of government, a Soviet Government? We'd be thankful for at least an ordinary democratic republic!" And, of course, in "ordinary," comparatively peaceful times such a "hope" would have lasted for many a long decade.
>
> But now . . . there is no *other* alternative left. Either the Soviet government triumphs in every advanced country in the world, or

[14] Lenin, *Izbrannye Proizvedeniya*, II, 774-85.

the most reactionary imperialism triumphs, the most savage imperialism which is out to throttle the small and feeble nationalities and to reinstate reaction all over the world; this is the Anglo-American imperialism which has perfectly mastered the art of using for its purposes the form of a democratic republic.

One or the other.

There is no middle course.[15]

Lenin's "A Letter to American Workers," written in August, 1918, and published in the December, 1918, issue of the radical magazine *Class Struggle*, was a furious diatribe against the "beasts of prey of Anglo-French and American imperialism" whom he accused of prolonging the "imperialist slaughter" and of profiting more than any other "imperialists" from the war. The Soviet newspapers in 1917 and 1918 abounded in statements like the following: "The American President Wilson, adopting the tone of a Quaker preacher reads . . . a sermon . . . but the people know . . . that Americans came into the war because of the interests of the New York Stock Exchange."[16] In a work included in all editions of Lenin's collected writings and republished in *Pravda* for August 22, 1940, Lenin excoriated American domestic as well as foreign policy, and predicted that the American workers would "be with us for civil war against the bourgeoisie." Soviet optimism regarding the probability of revolution in the United States reached its height early in the summer of 1919. Speaking in Petrograd in September of that year, Zinoviev hailed the birth of the American Communist Party as "the first swallow which foretells the coming of a world-wide Communist spring."[17]

In a number of his pronouncements, Lenin applied to the United States his injunction to Communists to take advantage of conflicts among the imperialist powers. Again and again he stressed the contradictions between the United States and Japan or the United States and Britain. To these contradictions Lenin

[15] Quoted by Shub, *op. cit.*, p. 391.

[16] *Izvestiya*, December 22, 1917.

[17] Quoted by Martin Ebon in *World Communism Today*, Whittlesey House, 1948, p. 19.

attributed the survival of the Soviet Republic. Thus in a speech made in November, 1920, Lenin said that "what had saved" Soviet Russia was the fact that Japan did not wish to pull chestnuts out for America. The basic rule for Russia was to exploit the conflicting interests of the capitalist states, to "dodge and maneuver."[18] The spirit in which Lenin approached these rivalries is indicated by his words in Moscow in 1920: "If we are obliged to tolerate such scoundrels as the capitalist thieves, each of whom is preparing to plunge the knife into us, it is our direct duty to make them turn their knives against each other."[19]

Stalin has followed Lenin's conception of international relations as essentially a struggle between Soviet Russia and her foreign supporters and a capitalist camp usually wracked by contradictions. Typical of his formulation of the basic principles governing international relations was an assertion in his report to the Tenth All-Russian Congress of Soviets in December, 1922, which adopted the first constitution of the U.S.S.R. He stated that "since the time the Soviet Republics were formed the states of the world have split into two camps: the camp of socialism and the camp of capitalism."[20] The concept of this world split was explicitly written into the 1924 Soviet constitution, which was in effect until 1936. In 1925, Stalin, in his speech at the fourteenth Party Congress, made his well-known observation that "two chief but opposed centers of attraction are being formed, and, in conformity with this, two directions of gravity toward these centers throughout the world: Anglo-America . . . and the Soviet Union . . ." He presented a similar analysis to the American labor delegation which visited him in 1927.

Stalin, following in Lenin's footsteps, has consistently opposed tendencies to regard the United States as in any sense immune from the "laws of social development" which are leading to the disintegration of capitalism everywhere. However,

[18] David Dallin, *Russia and Postwar Europe*, Yale Univ. Press, 1943, p. 73.
[19] Shub, *op. cit.*, p. 393.
[20] Stalin, *Sochineniya*, Moscow, 1946, V, 152.

he has also recognized that American capitalism is stronger than that of any other country. For example, in speaking to American Communist Party representives in 1929, he attacked them for "rightist-factionalism" and stated that "it cannot be denied that American life offers an environment which favors the Communist Party's falling into error and exaggerating the strength and stability of American capitalism." Again in 1929 Stalin declared: "When a revolutionary crisis has developed in America, that will be the beginning of the end of all world capitalism."

In the period following the rise of Hitler, Stalin soft-pedaled the threat of revolution within at least the Western democratic powers. This was logical, since he hoped that these powers might be useful allies of the Soviet Union against the Fascist powers. He even made a series of statements, particularly in his interview with Roy Howard in 1936, in which he revived the thesis of the desirability of co-operation and the possibility of peaceful coexistence between the capitalist and socialist systems. However, even in his interview with Howard, Stalin went out of his way to point out that the capitalist and Soviet systems could not evolve toward similarity.

Meanwhile, in a steady stream of statements intended mainly for Soviet and foreign Communists, Stalin and official Soviet publications continued to pledge allegiance to the ultimate goal of world communism. This goal is proclaimed, for example, in the foreword to the official history of the Communist Party published in 1938 and attributed to Stalin. These statements, together with a number by Stalin and other Soviet leaders regarding the unimportance of ideology in Soviet relations with the Fascist states, indicate that the Kremlin regarded "coexistence" as a temporary tactic. Both Stalin and Molotov proclaimed that Fascism in Germany and Italy was no obstacle to good relations between the U.S.S.R. and those countries. In a word, it would appear that the Soviet leaders saw no essential difference between the democracies and the Fascist powers. This point was to be strongly, if implicitly, re-emphasized in Stalin's conversation with Harold Stassen in April, 1947, by Stalin's denial of any difference between the Nazi and United States economies.

A further indication of this attitude was furnished in a series of statements, applicable to all capitalist countries, made by Stalin regarding "capitalist encirclement" and the danger to the U.S.S.R. of foreign spies. In a speech in March, 1937, Stalin stated that America was swarming with Japanese spies and Japan with American spies. Why, asked Stalin, should it be supposed that the bourgeois states should be "milder and more neighborly" toward the Soviet Union than toward their bourgeois fellows. Shortly after this, millions of pamphlets were distributed to the Soviet population explaining the diabolical methods of intimidation and blackmail used by the intelligence services of bourgeois states "not only in the struggle with probable adversaries but also against so-called friendly states." [21]

But while a general attitude of suspicion against all capitalist countries was thus maintained and even intensified during the middle and late 'thirties, Soviet propaganda at the same time ceaselessly enjoined the Western democracies to join with the U.S.S.R. in collective action against Nazi Germany, Fascist Italy, and Japan. From early in 1934 down to and including Stalin's report delivered on March 10, 1939, to the eighteenth Party Congress, this was the line taken by the Soviet leaders and press.

The newspaper and magazine propaganda to this effect was supplemented by books such as Lisovski's *The U.S.S.R. and the Capitalist Encirclement,* released for publication in February, 1939. This book developed in detail the thesis set forth at about the same time in Stalin's report. Arguing for a U.S.S.R.-British-French-U.S. grouping to check German-Japanese aggression, it attacked the "ruling class" of the Western democracies, particularly Britain and France, for allegedly seeking a war between Soviet Russia and Germany which would exhaust both. Both Stalin's report and Lisovski's book gave as an additional reason for the irresolution of "bourgeois politicians" to-

[21] For an exhaustively documented analysis of Stalin's views on America see Historicus, "Stalin on Revolution," *Foreign Affairs*, January, 1949.

ward Fascist aggression the fear of revolution within their own countries. Reflecting the collective security line, Lisovski's book took a rather favorable attitude toward the foreign policy views of Roosevelt and Churchill.

After the Nazi-Soviet Pact, of course, the line changed startlingly. Molotov, at the session of the Supreme Soviet ratifying the Pact on August 31, 1939, referred to reports in the Anglo-French and American press regarding alleged plans of Hitler for seizing the Soviet Ukraine and said: "It looks as if the object of this suspicious hullabaloo was to incite the Soviet Union against Germany . . . and to provoke a conflict with Germany without any visible grounds." [22]

In his report on the foreign policy of the Soviet Union to the Supreme Soviet of the U.S.S.R., October 31, 1939, Molotov criticized the President of the United States for allegedly considering it proper "to intervene in these matters" (Soviet-Finnish peace negotiations) and said that "one finds it hard to reconcile this with the American policy of neutrality." He compared Soviet relations with Finland, which had long ago obtained freedom and independence from the Soviet Union, with the United States' relations with Cuba and the Philippines, which had long been demanding "freedom and independence" from the United States and could not get them.[23]

Molotov's report of August 1, 1940, to the Supreme Soviet of the U.S.S.R. was bitterly critical of the U.S. He said flatly:

> I shall not dwell on our relations with the United States if only because there is nothing good to say about them. . . .
>
> Imperialist appetites are growing not only in far-off Japan but also in the United States. . . . All this carries the danger of a further extension and inflaming of the war, of its conversion into a world imperialist war.[24]

Numerous other official Soviet statements of the Pact period cast the U.S. in the role of one of the chief warmongers.

[22] *Pravda*, March 11, 1939, and September 2, 1939.

[23] *Pravda*, November 1, 1939. See also New York *Times*, same date.

[24] *Pravda*, August 2, 1940.

A similar attitude was expressed in the *Political Dictionary*, an authoritative handbook for party and government officials published in 300,000 copies in 1940. This work stated, *inter alia:* "From the beginning of the second imperialist war in Europe, the United States of America assumed a position of false neutrality, seeking to derive profit from trade with the warring states, Britain and France."[25] It accused "French ruling circles" of waging war for world hegemony. Its article on Fascism did not mention Hitler, but did state that the "difference between so-called bourgeois-democratic and Fascist states" had been disappearing since the beginning of World War II.

Needless to say, this view of international relations during the Pact period was echoed by the American and other Communist parties throughout the world.

The negative line taken by Stalin and the Soviet press before June 22, 1941, toward America as a factor in world politics was supplemented by a similarly derogatory view of American social institutions, life, and culture. In this sphere too, Lenin furnished a basic pattern, which was followed by Stalin and the entire Soviet propaganda and educational mechanism.

Lenin and his followers believed, as is well known, that the foreign policy of capitalist states was inevitably aggressive because it reflected the interests of the predatory economic and political dictatorship of the bourgeoisie within each capitalist country. In order to maintain their profits, as well as to divert the discontent of their native proletariat from themselves to external enemies, the bourgeoisie of each country engaged in foreign expansionist policies and eventually in war.

Partly as a result of this reasoning, one of the major tasks of Soviet scholars and propagandists since the establishment of the Soviet regime has been to study the internal economic and political situation of capitalist countries and to demonstrate the connections between their domestic situation and their foreign policies. Such analysis has been regarded as an essential part of the necessary orientation of Communist Party members, and in-

[25] *Politicheski Slovar,* Moscow, 1940, p. 524.

deed all Soviet citizens, toward a complex and dangerous international situation. Together with a constant stream of warnings regarding the policies of foreign countries, it has helped in the psychological preparation of Soviet citizens for war against the "encircling" capitalist lands.

But economic and political analysis of foreign countries has also served other important purposes of Soviet domestic and foreign policy. By seeking to prove that Soviet culture and institutions are unique and superior to those of the bourgeois world, it has tried to stimulate the enthusiasm and sustain the morale of both Soviet and foreign Communists and fellow travelers. The Soviet people have been forced by their rulers to endure hardships and deprivations in building socialism. Soviet propaganda has sought to convince them that the lot of the masses elsewhere was worse than theirs, and that their own hardships were temporary sacrifices required for the building of a better world. It has also, by arousing moral indignation and contempt for the decadence of bourgeois civilization, attempted to inoculate Soviet people against the disturbing influences emanating from the outside world or transmitted from the older to the younger generation within the U.S.S.R. The steady stream of depreciation of bourgeois life and culture which flowed from Soviet presses during the years before 1941 was not, however, entirely or even mainly a manufactured, synthetic product. It was the logical result of the application of Marxist-Leninist doctrine and a rationalization and justification of the policies of Stalin and his associates. Its strident dogmatism reflected the rawness and lack of sophistication of a new and insecure elite, as well as the latter's appalling ignorance of the real facts about the non-Soviet world.

Over the years, Soviet propaganda portrayed America as a plutocracy ruled by a handful of ruthless, selfish, and wasteful monopolists, who held in poverty the vast majority of the population. It dilated on unemployment and exploitation in the United States. The unfavorable contrast between the American and Soviet social systems took a new turn after the adoption of the first Five-Year Plan in the U.S.S.R., and was intensified as a result of the American depression.

An interesting example of this propaganda comparing the Soviet and non-Soviet economic systems is contained in Chapter II of a book published in the U.S.S.R., under the title *The Story of the Great Plan,* to popularize the first Five-Year Plan. This book was published in the United States in 1931 as *New Russia's Primer* in a translation by George S. Counts and Nucia P. Lodge. The chapter referred to is entitled "Two Countries." With considerable skill it contrasts the anarchy, waste, exploitation, and economic insecurity rampant in America with the planned production for the welfare of the community in the U.S.S.R. The essence of the chapter may be read in the following statement: "We increase production. In America they reduce production and increase unemployment. . . . We make what is essential. In America hundreds of factories consume raw materials and power in order to make what is altogether unnecessary."

The propaganda of the Five-Year Plans admitted that the U.S.S.R. lagged behind the United States but had surpassed other leading capitalist countries in technological and industrial development. The goal of overtaking and surpassing America in *per capita* industrial production was officially proclaimed. In 1938 it was announced that this goal would be achieved in some fifteen years. The Soviet leaders held out to their people the hope that they would relatively soon enjoy a standard of living higher than that of America and unmarred by the social ulcers of American capitalism.

Progress toward fulfilling these aspirations was reported confidently in Molotov's "Report on the Third Five-Year Plan for the Development of the National Economy of the U.S.S.R.," delivered March 14, 1939, to the eighteenth Party Congress. "We shall," he said, "make the U.S.S.R. the most advanced country in the world in all respects." After stating that the problem had arisen "of developing economic competition between the U.S.S.R. and the leading capitalistic countries," he expressed supreme confidence that the U.S.S.R. would win. He poked fun at the "poor, wretched apologists" of the capitalist system, which, he said, had now become "in many cases the strangler of progress in science, art and culture." [26]

Many other vital Soviet speeches as well as such authoritative handbooks as *The U.S.S.R. and the Capitalist Countries* (1938 and 1939) expressed similar confidence that the U.S.S.R. was winning the battle of social-economic systems.

An important and characteristic claim of Soviet propaganda, particularly after the Five-Year Plans had been launched, was that only in the U.S.S.R. was it possible to employ modern technology in the interests of the community. This claim has become habitual in Soviet propaganda and has gradually been extended to a vast range of not only technological but also scientific and other fields. The publishing house of the Young Communist League in 1937 published 100,000 copies of a Russian translation of a book by Paul de Kruif entitled *Must They Die?* The work contained a special introduction pointing out that while under American capitalism the masses could not avail themselves of the benefits of medical science, the Soviet people were solving this problem.

A vast literature of books and articles published in the U.S.S.R. in the 1920's and 1930's echoed a similar tone. The charges brought by this literature against American society were unfortunately partly justified. However, Soviet criticism of American life was so extreme and so lacking in objectivity that it amounted in most cases to caricature. Above all, it refused to recognize any defects on the Soviet side. The all too real imperfection of the foreign world was contrasted with the boasted but non-existent perfection of the U.S.S.R.

The best and most famous of all Soviet books on the United States was Ilya Ilf's and Evgeni Petrov's travel book, *One Story America*, published in 1937, and translated into English under the title *Little Golden America*. It illustrates the scope and tone of Soviet criticism of American society. Written by two of Soviet Russia's most gifted authors, in a brief period of rela-

[26] *XVIII Sezd Vsesoyuznoi Kommunistichskoi partii* (18th Congress of the All-Union Communist Party), Moscow, 1939, pp. 282-314.

tively friendly political relations during which the Soviets hoped to line up America against Japan and Germany, the book is somewhat less a mosaic of clichés than most similar accounts. It is much more colorful than the usual dull, statistical Soviet handbooks on foreign countries. It was published in several editions in the U.S.S.R. and was immensely popular. Presumably it exerted considerable influence in shaping Soviet attitudes toward America in the immediate prewar years. During my period of service in the American Embassy from 1942 to 1947, I found that most of my Soviet friends were delighted with this book.

Ilf and Petrov cast their story in the form of an account of a transcontinental round trip motor journey in the U.S. with a certain "Mr. Adams." This device enabled them to comment on many aspects of the American scene. Their analysis of American social institutions and mores conformed to the usual Soviet pattern. America was a country of extreme contrasts of wealth and poverty. Class and racial stratification and discrimination were rampant. The authors reiterated the standard Soviet expressions of horror at the position of Red Indians and Negroes in America, and the usual partially justifiable but exaggerated expressions of sympathy for their plight and admiration for their talents.

Another characteristic theme of Soviet propaganda regarding America in this book is its admiration for American Communists and fellow-traveling intellectuals. "Mr. Adams" is presented in a highly sympathetic light as typical of the progressive forces in America. A scion of a wealthy family who has cast in his lot with the Communists elicits the authors' praise. While what they described was in large measure true to the American life of the period, Ilf and Petrov took pains to conform to the stereotypes of Soviet propaganda and presented them in a highly conventionalized manner. Thus, in describing the activities of a Communist labor leader, they had him refer to the shooting of strikers as if that were a normal, everyday occurrence in American labor disputes.

Despite its negative appraisal of the American system, *One*

Story America probably had a positive effect on Soviet opinion of America. This was certainly the impression I received from my conversations with numerous Russians regarding it during my residence in Moscow. There was enough of the genuine writer in this gifted pair to force them willy-nilly to allow some of the color and vitality of American life to break through the strait jacket of stereotypes imposed upon Soviet authors describing capitalist countries. In general, America emerges from their pages as not only a technological wonderland and consumers' paradise of super-highways, snack bars, drug stores, skyscrapers, and a hundred other amenities unknown to Sovietland, but as a country of fantastic and superabundant energy, ingenuity, and good will. It certainly would be risky for a Soviet writer in our present somber era to produce such a book.

Other Soviet prewar books regarding America presented the same general picture as that sketched by Ilf and Petrov, although with far less talent. Among them were V. Lan's scholarly—discounting for ideological limitations—handbook *The U.S.A.* (1939), which, characteristically, contained an introductory note informing readers *inter alia* that it described the role of the Communist Party in "consolidating the progressive forces of the country." Less scholarly, but equally typical was Alexander Hamadan's *American Silhouettes* (1936) which bore on its cover a picture of a forlorn hobo set against the New York skyline. Its theme was the social decadence of technologically progressive America. It was packed with evidence of unemployment, poverty, misery, racial prejudice and persecution, and moral and cultural barbarism.

As I suggested above, Soviet criticism of America in this period embraced all aspects of life. One of its major themes was the alleged denial of opportunity for the masses in America to obtain education. An official Soviet *Handbook for Elementary School Teachers,* of which 75,000 copies were published in February, 1941, stated: "In fact, in the U.S. as in other capitalist countries the majority of pupils are deprived of real knowledge. In elementary school, children are taught only reading, writing and arithmetic because in the opinion of the American bourgeoisie this is enough for the children of the toilers."[27] This handbook did, however, assert that the elementary schools of America were more democratic than those of other capitalist countries.

Unemployment and racial discrimination remained, however, the chief and all-pervasive themes of Soviet attack on American capitalist society. The passages for translation from English to Russian in a Soviet secondary school English text published in 1938 included a long item headed "Mister, Buy an Apple," certainly calculated to arouse sympathy for the American toilers and satisfaction that one was not in their shoes. The same textbook describes the unhappy plight of American plantation Negroes.[28]

To this same period belongs the extremely popular Soviet motion picture "Tsirk" (The Circus), which I attended with a Soviet friend in Moscow in 1944. It was the story of an American Southern white girl who fled to the U.S.S.R., where she found happiness, after having been ridden out of her home town because her baby's father was a Negro.

Some of the anti-American propaganda of this period had a grimly amusing aspect. To this category belongs the Soviet picture of American prison life presented in *Belomor*, published in Moscow in 1934 and translated into English in 1935. This is an official account of the construction by "correctional" (forced) labor of the White Sea–Baltic Canal. Here a Soviet thief, who allegedly served time in Sing Sing, is made to say: "I remembered that devilish island (sic!) and the work shops where we made bolsters for 6c a day. And the soup—five spoonfuls to a person."

He says further: "In Sing Sing, even the solitary confinement cells have steam. . . . They lock you in and smother you with steam, like a rat."

Such a description of American prison conditions in a work

[27] *Spravochnaya Kniga Uchitelya Nachalnoi Shkoly*, Moscow, 1941, p. 45.

[28] See Eric Ashby's delightful *Scientist in Russia* for these excerpts, Penguin, 1947, pp. 246-47.

prepared by the Soviet secret police, to which leading Soviet writers such as Gorki—as well as Zoshchenko, purged in 1946—contributed, would be amusing if it did not serve as a rationalization of the Soviet slave labor system. This type of propaganda belongs to a vast mass of material which, as we shall see later, seeks to divert attention from evils at home to the capitalist scapegoat. One wonders if it does not also in at least some degree reflect the existence of a sense of guilt even among the hardened secret police.

The official Soviet interpretation of American political institutions prior to World War II was as negative as its picture of American society. The Soviet attitude toward Roosevelt and his New Deal is particularly interesting. We have already seen that the Kremlin looked with great suspicion on American foreign policy even under Roosevelt. But even more striking was the Soviet attitude toward Roosevelt's domestic policies. On the whole it was negative and derogatory. Its general tone was set by Stalin in an interview with H. G. Wells published in the Soviet press in September, 1934. While indicating admiration for Roosevelt's personality and character, Stalin expressed the opinion that his program would fail because it was essentially an attempt to do the impossible, that is, to cure the evils of capitalist society within a capitalist institutional framework. If Roosevelt went too far, according to Stalin the capitalists would replace him with another president.

The line followed by the Soviet press and publications toward Roosevelt's administration throughout most of the period before the Nazi-Soviet Pact was considerably less favorable than that taken by Stalin in his interview with Wells.

Foreign Armies, a handbook for Red Army officers, released for publication in November, 1934, stated that, "The measures undertaken by the Roosevelt government . . . are directed against the toilers and constitute an attempt to emerge from the crisis by intensifying the exploitation of the industrial proletariat and the working farmers." This handbook noted with satisfaction the growing influence of the American Communist

Party and the increasingly revolutionary temper of the American proletariat.[29]

The magazine *Bolshevik* stated in 1936:

> Roosevelt is a bourgeois politician the same as all his conservative and reactionary adversaries. . . . Roosevelt's New Deal policy . . . has indeed the objective of opening up to American capitalism additional possibilities for worming its way out of the crisis. . . . Government interference which was going on under the slogan of "driving the money changers out of the temple" . . . meant in reality that the banks and corporations should be saved.[30]

World Economics and World Politics for August, 1936, stated:

> Fascist tendencies have undoubtedly grown in strength under the Roosevelt regime and Roosevelt has made no serious attempt to fight the forces of reaction. All this has brought it home to the broad masses of the American proletariat that they have nothing to hope for from the old political parties and that the Democratic Party when in power protects the interests of capitalism in the same way as the Republican Party.

Such was the interpretation of the New Deal presented to the Soviet public even before the Nazi-Soviet Pact. During the latter period, of course, the United States was lumped with other capitalist states, in all of which, it was maintained, a terroristic dictatorship of the bourgeoisie prevailed.

During both the 20's and 30's the only real exception made by Lenin and Stalin and the Soviet press to this negative attitude toward America was admiration for American technology and efficiency. Lenin had, for example, despite the poverty of the new Soviet regime, advocated importing certain U.S. films to teach such American efficiency methods as "Taylorism."[31]

Two features, said Stalin in 1924, make for a proper style in Party and state work: "the wide outlook of the Russian revolutionist" and "American practicality." Russian revolutionary scope, said

[29] *Inostrannye armii*, Moscow, 1934, p. 239. Fifty thousand copies were printed.

[30] *Bolshevik*, December 1, 1936, No. 23, p. 52.

[31] See *Partiya o Kino*, Moscow, 1938.

he, is an antidote against routine, mental stagnation, and a slavish following of ancestral traditions. It awakens thought, pushes forward, breaks with the past. But the chances are that in practice it will degenerate into "empty 'revolutionary' phrase-mongering," unless it is combined with American practicality in work. American practicality is an antidote to such phrase-mongering and "flights of 'revolutionary' fancy." It is "that indomitable force, which knows and recognizes no obstacle, which by its businesslike perseverance washes away all and every impediment, which simply must go though with a job begun even if it is of minor importance, and without which any serious constructive work is impossible." But American practicality, Stalin maintained, runs the risk of degenerating into narrow and unprincipled commercialism, unless it is fused with the wide outlook of the Russian revolutionist. Only a combination of both, he concluded, produces "a finished type of Leninist worker, the Leninist style of work." [32]

In an interview with the German writer Ludwig in 1931, Stalin praised American "businesslike co-operation in industry, technology, literature, and life." Perhaps reflecting the fear of the Soviet leaders that admiration for American efficiency tended to be extended to American life and civilization as a whole, Stalin in this interview was careful to say: "We never forget that the United States is a capitalist country." In this interview Stalin also touched on another positive aspect of the Soviet attitude, even on the official level, toward the United States. He expressed appreciation of the "democratic simplicity" of American manners. While a relatively minor theme, this attitude, which reflected the Soviet-Marxist view that America, though thoroughly capitalist, was free except in the South from "remnants of feudalism," helped to furnish the basis for the Soviet line during World War II regarding American democracy.

What were the attitudes toward America of the "common man" in Soviet Russia during this pre-1941 period? Was there a popular as distinct from official opinion? It is difficult to answer these questions with much assurance or precision. The pic-

[32] As described by Julian Towster, *Political Power in the U.S.S.R. 1917-1947*, Oxford Univ. Press, 1948, p. 396.

ture would be unclear even if favorable conditions had prevailed for the observation and study of public opinion, such as an uncontrolled press and freedom of contact between Soviet citizens and foreigners. They did not, and the evidence available on this subject is fragmentary and inadequate. Nevertheless, a few general observations can justifiably be ventured, and significant trends pointed out.

The evidence afforded, often indirectly, by official Soviet sources, supplemented by the observations and comments of foreign travelers in the U.S.S.R., indicates that there was much good will toward and admiration for America among the Soviet people throughout the period under discussion. In part this popular attitude reflected the fact that even official Soviet sources presented some aspects of American civilization in a favorable light. The admiration implicit in the Soviet program of "overtaking and surpassing" America industrially and technically fostered respect for America. The Soviet Union was in a vulnerable position in its cultural competition with America. After all, despite the official Soviet depreciation of American civilization, the latter in large measure furnished the model which the Soviets emulated. In myriad ways, the Soviet people and even their highest leaders were daily engaged in imitating America.

To mention a trivial but symptomatic example, when Politburo member Mikoyan, then Minister of Food, returned in 1936 to the U.S.S.R. after a trip to the United States, he caused such typically American food products as cornflakes and tomato juice to be placed in production and sold in Soviet food stores. He also had an automat opened in Moscow which was very like its American counterpart except that it sold vodka. In a speech at the eighteenth Party Congress in 1939 Mikoyan said: "We have learned a lot already and have still to learn a few things from Americans." He added that the U.S.S.R. was "employing American methods" but not on a sufficiently large scale.[33] Eskimo pie, which Soviet people ate even during World

[33] See *The Land of Socialism Today and Tomorrow*, Foreign Languages Publishing House, Moscow, 1939, pp. 368-70.

War II at 20 degrees below zero, became popular. "Amerikankas," booths with high-topped tables at which one ate standing, were introduced. I remember sharing bread and vodka with a shoeless Soviet lad in one of them in the suburban town of Podolsk in 1944. Learning that I was an American he "adopted" me and insisted on returning with me to Moscow.

While the Soviet people were assured that they would one day outstrip their American competitors, the fact remained that this goal was still some years in the future. Having made a fetish of technology, the Soviet Communists rendered their people—and perhaps themselves—dangerously susceptible to the attractions of a culture which had already achieved so many of the goals toward which the Soviet Russians were being lashed by their rulers.

When Emil Ludwig in his well-known conversation with Stalin in 1931 observed that there appeared to be among the Soviet people an admiration for everything American, Stalin went out of his way to assure him that this was not the case.

The testimony of other foreign travelers and journalists suggests that Ludwig's observation was correct. Eugene Lyons points out in his book, *Assignment in Utopia,* that when he and his wife had been in Soviet Russia a short time, in 1928, they discovered that "Americans, in particular, were infinitely fascinating to Russians. For the older generation nurtured on democratic hopes, America was the land of vast freedoms and individual opportunities. For the younger people, thrilling to the vision of an industrialized future, it was the land of marvelous technique."

Lyons' observations were similar to those of many other foreigners who were in Soviet Russia in the 20's or 30's. Some of them pointed out that the fascination of America for Soviet people extended in large measure even to Communists. Paula Lecler, who worked as a correspondent in Moscow, describes Max, a Soviet tourist guide and police agent who "affected the American" in dress and appearance. According to her, Max both detested and idolized America: "Hourly he engaged us in unwitting 'socialist competition' with Russia, in which America was always worsted . . . but remained the measure and model for Soviet progress!"[34]

The speeches of Soviet leaders and the periodical literature were not the only sources shaping Soviet popular attitudes toward the United States. American literature was even more widely disseminated under the Soviets than before the revolution. To be sure, it was employed as an instrument of anti-capitalist propaganda. Huge editions of Dreiser's and Upton Sinclair's novels, and the works of minor "proletarian" writers like Michael Gold were widely distributed. Even during the war, in 1944, I saw a Soviet film strip on America in which Gold and Richard Wright were stated to be the two leading American writers. But favorites such as Mark Twain, Jack London, Poe, and Walt Whitman also received increased distribution. The net effect of the widespread dissemination of American literature was probably to increase good will toward the American people even if much of it painted a black picture of contemporary American civilization.

Personal contacts between Americans and Russians were also an important and on the whole positive influence. Their very infrequency in some ways intensified this effect, as there was complete absence of the friction and animosity often resulting from too close contact between widely differing peoples. Among the channels of personal contact were American tourists' visits to Russia and the occasional American tours of highly trusted Soviet writers such as Ilf and Petrov. A number of Soviet workers studied engineering in the U.S. Some of them, such as V. V. Kuznetsov, now the head of the Soviet Trade Unions, obtained advanced technical degrees. In 1937, the Soviet aviators, Chkalov, Belyakov, and Baidukov, flew from Moscow to the U.S. The first ranking American to greet them upon landing was General George C. Marshall. In May, 1939, Kokkinaki and Gordienko flew to America. In 1937, an American naval squadron visited Vladivostok. Many American scientists visited Russia in the prewar years, especially during the International Geological Congress held in Moscow in 1936.

[34] "The Dead Hour," in *As We See Russia*, Dutton, 1948, pp. 94-95.

Probably by far the most important opportunity for personal contact between Russians and Americans resulted from the presence and work in the U.S.S.R., over a period of many years up to about 1937, of hundreds of American engineers and technicians. As Isabel Cary Lundberg remarked in an article in the December, 1948, *Harper's Magazine:*

> What tends to be too completely overlooked in all discussions of the United States *versus* the Soviet Union is the embarrassingly primary observation that without the technical know-how supplied by the United States, the Union of Socialist Soviet Republics would never have achieved its present stage of industrialization, inadequate as it is.

Mrs. Lundberg's observation touches on a vast field which awaits and deserves extensive research. Some basic facts are, however, well enough known. American engineers, under the direction of Col. Hugh Cooper, played a major part in constructing the famous Dneprstroi power dam. Incidentally, even in the postwar reconstruction of this dam some of the turbines used were American. The American engineer, John Littlepage, was a key adviser to the Soviet gold trust. His book, *In Search of Soviet Gold,* written in collaboration with Demaree Bess and published in 1937-38, sheds fascinating light on the ruthless but dynamic process of Soviet industrialization and the role played in it by hundreds of American engineers.

Eric Johnston has written that Stalin told him in a conversation in June, 1944, that about two thirds of all the large industrial enterprises in the Soviet Union had been built with American material aid or technical assistance. Stalin said, among other things, "The Soviet Union is indebted to Mr. Ford. He helped build our tractor and automobile industries." [35] "Fordism" became synonymous in Soviet Russia not only with efficiency, but also paradoxically with the ruthless speed-up of labor which according to Soviet propaganda was characteristic of American industry. Significantly the Soviet leaders have them-

[35] Eric Johnston, *We're All in It,* Dutton, 1948, p. 81.

selves been introducing "Fordism" on an increasing scale, while it has been disappearing in the United States.

American engineers and executives also made an important contribution to the development of transport in Russia, without which the Five-Year Plans would have been much more difficult to carry out. Beginning as early as the period of the Provisional Government in 1917, American railway engineers under John F. Stevens helped put the Russian railways in commission. Their work in the Russian Far East is described in General William S. Graves' *America's Siberian Adventure*. This railway building, together with the construction of buildings in Vladivostok which were still, when I visited the city in May, 1946, among its finest, helps to explain why the American part in the intervention not only created less resentment among all groups in Soviet society than that of any other power but in some ways even created a favorable impression.

During the first two Five-Year Plans, Ralph Budd, president of the Great Northern Railway, was an important adviser to the Soviet engineers charged with the reorganization of railway transport.[36] American engineers became symbols of efficiency to Soviet Russians. It is probably largely because of the impression they made on the Soviet mind that American efficiency and American punctuality became proverbial.

Our engineers even became a character type in Soviet literature. Ina Telberg in her interesting article, "Heroes and Villains of Soviet Drama," in the *American Sociological Review* for June, 1944, refers to American engineers who were characters in two Soviet plays. She writes that "they were efficient, matter-of-fact technicians with a good sense of humor, who knew how to give and receive sarcastic remarks about theirs and the Soviet social order."

Of course, the appearance of only two American engineers in plays covering the period 1926-41 was in fact niggardly recognition of their role in building Soviet industry. But an extreme playing down of the Soviet debt to Western industrial

[36] For additional detail see Department of State Publication 3480, "Cultural Relations between the United States and the Soviet Union," Washington, 1949.

civilization, even in technological fields, has always been characteristic of Soviet propaganda. This makes all the more significant the occasional, usually highly laconic and heavily qualified acknowledgments or reflections of American influence on Soviet life to be found in Soviet sources for domestic consumption. This grudging tone may be heard in a sketch of life in 1926 in the manganese town of Chiaturi, Georgia, written by Marietta Shaginyan, and republished in her book *Soviet Transcaucasia.*[37] Shaginyan describes the introduction of "cultured" foreign technology and the people of "American appearance" one met in Chiaturi, but she paints a black picture of the policies of the American concessionaires then operating the mines. In the 1946 edition she is also careful to point out that her observations refer to the period of the "American concession" and that the defects described were remedied after the liquidation of the concession.

Actually, no amount of censorship or propaganda could conceal from hundreds of thousands, even millions of Soviet people knowledge of either the work done in the U.S.S.R. by American engineers, or the importance of the American turbines, printing presses, stamping machines and other products of American industry imported by thousands during the Five-Year Plans.

When the first Soviet ambassador to the United States, Troyanovski, presented his credentials to President Roosevelt, he stated: "There is among the people of my country a most natural feeling of sympathy, respect and admiration for your great country, which they associate with high technical and scientific progress and which they regard as an immense creative force."

Making due allowance for the element of diplomatic courtesy reflected in this statement, it is fair to say that it summed up the favorable aspects of Soviet reactions to acquaintance with American engineers, technicians, and scientists.

Another important and now little-known American effort which created great popular good will in the U.S.S.R. was the

[37] Erevan, 1946, see pp. 332-36.

extensive relief activities carried on by the American Relief Administration during the famine of 1921-22 and by the Near East Relief in the Soviet Caucasus as late as 1928.[38] Henry C. Wolfe has described the gratitude of rank-and-file Russians for the ARA's work. Despite official suspicion—and obstruction—it was so successful that even Kamenev, then one of the top Soviet leaders, expressed gratitude for its "tremendous, utterly unselfish efforts" which saved millions.[39] A distinguished American student of Russia who was there about 1930 tells me that peasants he talked to then discussed whether, in view of their Government's "rudeness," America would help them again "next time." A similar influence was the activity of the Jewish Relief Agency and the American Joint Distribution Committee, described in Markoosha Fischer's book, *My Lives in Russia.*

All these and other channels of communication, such as correspondence between Soviet people, particularly Jewish people and relatives in the United States, helped to keep alive good will and in many cases admiration for America. It would be ingenuous, of course, to assume that no negative attitudes developed among the Soviet people toward the United States or that the barrage of anti-capitalist propaganda did not create suspicions or contempt. A certain touchy pride, reflecting the insecurity and inferiority feelings of the new intelligentsia which grew up in the Soviet period, also soured the Soviet attitude toward the United States and other capitalist countries. This attitude is perhaps most typically reflected in the extremely popular poem by Vladimir Mayakovski entitled "Verses on a Soviet Passport," which says, "I am delighted with New York, but I do not take off my cap. Soviet people have their own pride: we look down upon the bourgeois." [40] Bumptious Soviet pride, combined with isolation from the non-Soviet world, created in some Soviet minds, probably mainly among party

[38] See James L. Barton, *Story of Near East Relief,* Macmillan, 1930.

[39] See Wolfe's "We Intervened in Russia," in *As We See Russia,* cited above, pp. 247-60.

[40] Quoted from a 1947 edition of 100,000 copies published by the Komsomol Publishing House.

members, a feeling that the Soviet Union was the only country which was progressing. The available evidence regarding Soviet attitudes and opinion indicated, however, that there was also widespread consciousness that the U.S.S.R. still had a great deal to learn from the United States, at least in respect to the material aspects of civilization.

Much can be drawn from this background sketch that will help in an understanding of the nature of Soviet propaganda and opinion during World War II. Both the Communist elite and the Soviet masses, each in appropriate ways, had been conditioned for the "Anglo-Soviet-American coalition." It was not difficult to "sell" America, especially to the Soviet people. They were prepared to accept joyfully the United States as a mighty ally. The Communist veterans on the other hand had been seasoned in Marxist-Leninist doctrine which taught them to make use of any instrument necessary to assure the salvation of the Soviet fatherland as the embodiment of the world revolution.

Neither the Soviet leaders nor their people, however, had any real understanding of American life, institutions, and policies. Isolation, ignorance, and Marxist-Leninist dogma had created a great wall of suspicion and misunderstanding between Soviet Russia and the West. The wartime partnership offered a great opportunity to break down this wall. Would the Soviet leaders make the best of this opportunity? Would they modify their hostile attitudes toward the capitalist world? Many hints of how these questions were to be answered were furnished by the way in which Soviet propaganda handled the major problems of Soviet-Allied relations during the war. The next four chapters are devoted to an analysis of the wartime Soviet line toward America. They help to explain why the hopes and desires of American leaders to see Russia brought into friendly partnership with the other nations of the world were frustrated.

PART TWO

The Coalition War

II. The Concept of the Coalition

HITLER'S attack of June 22, 1941, forced Stalin to seek all possible aid in a ferocious struggle for survival against his erstwhile ally. The Kremlin and its world Communist apparatus swiftly claimed leadership in a war to save humanity from Fascism. Simultaneously, they moved to organize a "fighting alliance" with the Western democracies against Germany. The British and American governments and their leaders responded with amazing celerity and generosity to Moscow's appeal for help. On the Soviet side, Stalin, in his crucial speech of July 3, 1941, acknowledged Anglo-American assurances. Beginning with his November 6 speech on the 24th anniversary of the October revolution, he referred to the relations among Britain, America and Russia as the "Anglo-Soviet-American Coalition."

The world was soon facing the spectacle of an alliance between Communist Russia and the leading capitalist powers. Membership in this alliance posed most difficult problems for Soviet policy and propaganda. The Politburo's conception of the nature of these problems must have been somewhat as follows: how to achieve the maximum of exploitation of the allies without losing either ideological prestige or freedom of political action abroad, without weakening the institutional structure or the ideological discipline at home.

The Soviet leaders were surprisingly successful in dealing with these problems. In fact, in the propaganda field at least, their performance was masterly. By clever and well-planned symbol manipulation, they succeeded in achieving tremendous influence over public opinion in Britain, America and other countries, while simultaneously allaying the well-grounded fears of the Allied governments as to the nature of Soviet war aims. At the same time their presentation of the story of Allied aid to Russia was calculated to sustain the morale of the masses without arousing fraternal emotions or stimulating ideas dangerous to the Kremlin. To be sure, the Politburo did not achieve this last aim with as complete success as it desired. As we shall see in later chapters, the relaxation of ideological discipline forced by the war had certain subversive effects. However, there occurred no mellowing or modification of the Soviet system as many in the West had hoped.

Let us now examine those aspects of Soviet wartime propaganda regarding America which help to explain why what seemed to many to be the beginning of a new era in Soviet-American relations was only a deceptive interlude. In this chapter I shall deal mainly with the Soviet propaganda presentation of America's role as a member of the coalition against Nazi Germany. In subsequent chapters of this section, I shall explore the related subjects of the American war effort, American domestic developments during the war and the Soviet attitude toward the shape of things to come in the postwar world, which all participants in World War II realized would differ radically from the prewar configuration.

What was the over-all Soviet conception of the nature of the coalition? This question was answered much more explicitly and frankly by Soviet leaders in the postwar period than during the war itself. Stalin in his election speech delivered on February 9, 1946, declared that World War II arose as the inevitable result of the "Second Crisis" of capitalism. It was a war between two camps of the capitalist world. However, the bourgeois-democratic countries were defending themselves against the threat of Fascist enslavement. Thus the war from its beginning was an anti-Fascist liberating war. The "entry" of the Soviet Union into the war, according to Stalin, intensified this anti-Fascist liberating character.

A member of Stalin's Politburo, N. A. Voznesenski, who has

since dropped from sight, in a book published at the end of 1948, wrote:

> The Second World War revealed in sharp form the contradictions in the camp of the capitalist countries between the bloc of bourgeois-democratic states and the bloc of Fascist states. These contradictions constituted a peculiar reserve of the Socialist state; their utilization in the interests of smashing Hitlerite Germany and subsequently in the interests of defeating Japanese imperialism constituted the greatest victory of the U.S.S.R.'s foreign policy.[1]

In other words, the Soviet leaders remained faithful during the war to Lenin's injunctions to play one group of capitalist countries against the other, to enhance the power of the U.S.S.R. and the cause of world communism. Naturally it would have been inexpedient to have admitted this fact at a time when the Kremlin was seeking to mobilize all possible forces against Germany. The concept of the coalition of democratic and peace-loving countries against the Nazis furnished Stalin with the formula he needed to rationalize what Major General John R. Deane, who worked for two years in Moscow with top-level Soviet military leaders, called the "strange alliance." [2]

This formula permitted the Kremlin to continue to pursue its own aims and at the same time to persuade influential elements in America and Britain that Moscow's aims, aspirations and values were similar to those of London and Washington. These objectives were realized despite the fact that by inference at least Moscow's propaganda during the coalition period continued to view world politics from the traditional Marxist-Leninist point of view.

This fact was concealed from all but expert eyes by Moscow's aggressive and voluble adherence to "democracy," "progress" and other lofty principles. Soviet propaganda claimed world

[1] N. Voznesenski, *Voennaya ekonomika U.S.S.R. v Period otechestvennoi voiny* (*The War Economy of the U.S.S.R. during the War for the Fatherland*). There are two English translations of this work, one prepared under the auspices of the American Council of Learned Societies, the other by International Publishers (both 1948).

[2] John R. Deane, *The Strange Alliance,* Viking Press, 1946.

leadership in championing these principles. To be sure, it included the Western powers in the "democratic" camp, but it made it clear that Soviet democracy was superior to that of the West. Stalin laid down the wartime line on this point in his speech of November 6, 1941. Here he ridiculed Nazi propaganda, which branded the political systems of the United States and Britain as "plutocratic" regimes. He stated that in England and the United States there were "elementary democratic liberties"—there were trade unions and liberal parties and a parliament. The Hitlerites had deprived the working class of Europe of these elementary liberties and rights.

After 1942, Stalin almost ignored this problem of the difference of political systems between the Anglo-Americans and the U.S.S.R. He touched on it briefly, however, in his November 6 speech of 1944, in which he predicted that the differences revealed at the Dumbarton Oaks Conference held in August that year would not prevent agreement on postwar security. Here he said, not without demagogy, that differences occurred even among people in the same party. They were all the more bound to occur between representatives of different states and representatives of different parties. In this speech Stalin also stated that the alliance of the Big Three was founded not on casual short-lived considerations but on vital and lasting interests. Thus Stalin presented the coalition as the alliance of genuine Soviet democracy with inadequate bourgeois democracy, the latter being superior, however, to fascism.

Stalin's speeches and the Soviet press reinforced these expressions of democratic solidarity, formulating the war aims of the coalition in a fashion calculated to make a favorable impression in America and Western Europe. Stalin's speech of November 6, 1942, proclaimed as the aims of the coalition the restoration and maintenance of the sovereignty and integrity of nations and of democratic rights and liberties. Such reassuring statements were supplemented by Soviet adherence to the Declaration by United Nations in January, 1942, by Molotov's statement when Soviet troops crossed the Rumanian border in April, 1944, that the U.S.S.R. intended to eschew interference in the internal affairs of other countries, and by numerous similar acts and declarations.

The success achieved in the West by these tactics is illustrated by the fact that Wendell Willkie at a Toronto mass meeting on November 28, 1942, told cheering crowds that Stalin in his November 6 speech, cited above, had given an exact definition of the war aims of the United Nations. The abolition of the Comintern and Stalin's wartime concessions to religious freedom evoked similar responses. Stalin's assertions, echoed by Soviet propaganda and by well-wishers and wishful thinkers abroad, that ideological and institutional differences among countries were no obstacle to co-operation, also soothed foreign fears. The real meaning of such assurances was only understood by the few experts who recalled that Stalin and his lieutenants had for tactical reasons frequently made similar statements in the past, for example, shortly after the Nazi-Soviet Pact of 1939.

Thus, however disingenuously or reluctantly, Soviet propaganda fitted the Western Allies into the general framework of the coalition. In addition, and this was perhaps of even greater importance in impressing foreign opinion, the Soviet leaders and their propaganda machine greeted every major event in the development of the coalition with a fanfare of skillful publicity. The Hopkins, Harriman-Beaverbrook and Harriman-Churchill visits of 1941-42, the Anglo-Soviet Alliance and the Master Lend-Lease Agreement of. 1942, the Moscow and Teheran conferences of 1943, the Normandy invasion of 1944, and the Dumbarton Oaks Conference of the same year—these and many other events were hailed by Moscow as evidence of the growing strength of the coalition and the increasing closeness of collaboration among the Big Three. This publicity, together with the lavish hospitality on state occasions, of which only the Soviets are capable, created an impression that the Kremlin was indeed anxious for full co-operation and that ideological considerations were unimportant.

And, finally, we must not forget that the power of Soviet propaganda was multiplied many times by the heroic and grand campaigns of the Red Army. The Kremlin regarded World

War II as an episode in Moscow's march toward Communist world rule. Its war and that of the Western democracies were parallel, or even separate, wars. But to the peoples of the West, especially Britain, great, and sometimes it seemed, irresistible, force was lent to Soviet protestations of sincerity in the common cause by the mighty Soviet war effort.

In the next chapter, we shall see how Soviet propaganda exploited the Red Army's heroism and depreciated the Allies' military contribution. Now I should like to point out briefly the several ways in which Moscow balanced the lip-service to the idea of co-operation outlined above.

In the first place it should be emphasized that nothing in Stalin's speeches or in the vast volume of Soviet wartime propaganda could be construed as repudiating the aims or the basic principles of Marxist-Leninist doctrine. True, as I shall point out later in some detail, Soviet propaganda held out the possibility that wartime co-operation might be continued after the war. There were some indications that the Anglo-American war effort might have caused the Kremlin at least to revise upward its estimate of the strength and survival power of bourgeois democracy. Thus, for example, the most important article on social and economic theory appearing during the war, pointed out that imperialism was "dying" but not "dead" capitalism.[3] It reiterated Stalin's point regarding the superiority of "bourgeois democratic" to "fascist" political institutions, and it admitted that the capitalist states had during the war achieved a limited measure of "planning" of their economies. This article was erroneously interpreted by many in America as a tendency in Soviet economic thinking to a return to capitalist principles. Actually the reverse was true. The article as a whole signalized a campaign of reindoctrination in the basic tenets of Lenin's theory that imperialism is the last stage of capitalism and the eve of the socialist revolution.

I have dwelt at some length on this article to illustrate three

[3] "Some Problems of the Teaching of Political Economy," *Under the Banner of Marxism* (*Pod Znamenem Marksizma*), No. 7-8, 1943.

points. First, the coalition line furnished a theoretical framework for a guarded and arms-length co-operation, or at least, coexistence of the Soviet and Western capitalist systems. Secondly, American opinion was overly optimistic in interpreting Soviet propaganda regarding this point. Finally, such few formal concessions as were made in the presentation of Soviet ideology were embedded in a context which offered no hope that a fundamental revision of Soviet ideology had begun.

It is true that some basic traditional themes of Soviet propaganda regarding capitalism were muted. They never disappeared entirely, however, even from the newspaper press. A few days after the outbreak of the war in June, 1941, one of the leading Soviet experts on ideology, E. Yaroslavski, published an article in which he referred to the great difficulty the Soviet state had always experienced in surviving under conditions of "capitalist encirclement." P. Yudin, in an article in *Pravda* on January 21, 1942, in connection with the eighteenth anniversary of Lenin's death, pointed out that Lenin had told the Soviet workers and peasants that the Soviet state could not long survive without a mighty army since "the Soviet people building a new life under the conditions of capitalist encirclement have many enemies." Victor Kravchenko, in his *I Chose Freedom*, cites Yudin as one of the principal propagandists, one of whose important tasks was to keep alive in the minds of highly placed party and government officials suspicion of the American "ruling classes," including President Roosevelt.

Occasional reports of talks by professional agitators in Moscow and at the American "shuttle bombing" base in the Ukraine which have come to my attention confirm Kravchenko's account. One very reliable American, who was an officer at the Poltava base, told me that political officers were warning Soviet troops at the time of our Normandy invasion that America would not long be Russia's ally. One of the friendliest Soviet publications appearing during the war, I. A. Startsev's pamphlet *America and Russian Society*, included a quotation from Stalin to the effect that although Soviet people admire American businesslike qualities, they never forget that the U.S.A. is a capitalist country.[4]

In the period after the Stalingrad victory, which assured the Soviet leaders not only survival but also prospects of great expansion of their power, the general propaganda of Marxism-Leninism with all its somber implications for any long term collaboration between socialist and capitalist countries, was steadily intensified. Intensification of Marxist-Leninist indoctrination was accompanied by a trend toward chauvinistic nationalism which boded ill for the long-term prospects of the coalition. An interesting indication of this trend is furnished by comparison of the 1942 and 1944 editions of the syllabus used in teaching modern history in Soviet secondary schools. The paragraph in the early version regarding the historic tradition of friendship between the Soviet and American peoples was omitted in 1944. So was a statement expressing appreciation of the traditions of non-Soviet people. Beginning on a grand scale in 1944, a vast program of reprinting individual booklets of Lenin's works got under way.

A highly significant statement of the type so often made by Soviet leaders, seemingly harmless but actually full of hidden meaning, was made by Molotov in February, 1944, at the meeting of the Supreme Soviet which amended the constitution of the U.S.S.R. by reorganizing the Ministries of Foreign Affairs and Defense from all-Union to Union-Republican commissariats. On this occasion, Molotov stated that this step would increase the significance of the Soviet Union for "the peoples of East and West." Although few in America realized it at the time, this statement was strikingly reminiscent of passages in Lenin's last published work, "Better Less, Yes, Better," which had appeared in *Pravda* in March, 1923, and in which Lenin had viewed the world as an arena of struggle between Anglo-American imperialism and the vast masses of colonial peoples of the East and the industrial proletarians of the West. A great many such statements, the implications of which were disquieting, were made from time to time during the war.

[4] I. A. Startsev, *Amerika i russkoe obshchestvo*, Moscow, 1942, p. 29.

It must also be remembered that, although it was soft-pedaled, the Soviet conviction that the United States and Britain were not united internally, but were the arena of struggle between progressive and reactionary forces, never disappeared entirely from the Soviet press and particularly from the statements made by agitators at party and other meetings. For example, in February, 1942, a political lecture given in Kuibyshev and attended by an American pointed out that class differences existed within the individual capitalist members of the "democratic front" and also between socialist and capitalist members of that front. The lecturer, to be sure, stated that these differences were subordinate to the struggle between the Axis forces of destruction and the democratic forces of civilization. Nevertheless, the fact that this idea was kept alive is significant. It helps us to understand the wary and guarded nature of the Soviet propaganda line, which always kept the Soviet public mind prepared for unpleasant surprises.

From time to time, references were made to "white guard" and foreign interventionists during the U.S.S.R. civil war, as in the editorial on the front page of *Pravda* for March 8, 1943, commenting on Stalin's appointment as Marshal of the Soviet Union. The most outstanding warning not to trust the Western Allies was the famous "Cairo rumor" published in *Pravda* for January 17, 1944, only about a month after the Teheran Conference. A "special correspondent" reported from Cairo that separate peace negotiations were said to be proceeding between the Germans and the British. Such tactics probably reflected the Soviet view that there were powerful forces in the U.S. and Britain seeking to sabotage the war against Nazi Germany, which might in the future gain control over the foreign policies of the Western powers. They also undoubtedly reflected concern lest dangerous thoughts be stirred in the minds of Soviet people by the friendly attitude of the capitalist allies toward the U.S.S.R.

To put it bluntly, the content of Soviet wartime propaganda toward the Western Allies was suspicious and reserved. The effect produced by its content was heightened by its presentation and tone. Although the American and British story was told in great volume, it was nevertheless minimized. Throughout the war, especially in 1943 and 1944, the Anglo-Americans or "Allies," as they were usually called, received an average of about half of the space devoted to foreign news by the four-page Soviet dailies. However, this material was almost always published on the back pages. During the first desperate months of the war, when the Soviets had nothing but defeats to report from the front, American or British news occasionally made the front page. But after the Soviet victory in the battle of Moscow, which reassured the Kremlin, Anglo-American items disappeared from page one as if by magic. Even before this, most items consisted of expressions of solidarity with the Soviet cause by "progressive" groups or individuals. For example, Negro American writers were quoted to the effect that the Russians were fighting the battle of the colored peoples of the world. Material of this character was calculated to raise the morale of the Soviet people by making them feel that "progressive" mankind sympathized with their cause. It was not, however, likely to give them a clear conception of British or American policies and attitudes, or the role of the Allies in the coalition.

Extremely few editorials or signed articles were devoted to the Allies. Editorials and all other press devices for heightening the importance of an article were reserved almost exclusively for the policies and achievements of the Communist Party and Soviet Government. When they were mentioned editorially, the Allies were treated almost as appendages to the Soviet Union. Often they were omitted entirely from accounts of events in which they had played a central role. One editorial on the front page of *Pravda* for December 31, 1944, performed the extraordinary feat of reviewing all the political and military events of the year without once mentioning America or England.

Another peculiar and significant aspect of the reporting of the coalition war in the Soviet press was the overwhelming emphasis placed upon a few key figures in the allied countries. The Soviet reader was given the impression that the friends of the U.S.S.R. consisted of a handful of powerful leaders such as

Roosevelt, Harry Hopkins, Henry Wallace, and a few others in the United States, and Churchill in England. These men were presented as the mouthpieces of the "progressive" forces in these countries. They received hundreds of times as much space as any other foreign leader.

When Hopkins, Harriman, or Beaverbrook, or more especially Eden, Hull, Churchill, or Roosevelt, came to the Soviet Union or engaged in conferences with Soviet leaders, their photographs were published in the newspapers and a tremendous fanfare of publicity resulted for a few days. The major speeches and policy statements of Roosevelt and Churchill were copiously reported in the Soviet press, although portions of them which conflicted with the Soviet propaganda line of the moment were deleted. Such a personal presentation of international affairs was not surprising in the press of so absolute a regime as that of the U.S.S.R. At the same time, it must have made the Soviet people wonder what would happen to Soviet-American relations if these key leaders lost power or changed their attitudes.

An interesting example of this kind of thinking came to my attention during the American presidential campaign of 1944, when several of my Soviet acquaintances told me that unless Roosevelt was re-elected they would probably never see me again. Perhaps still more significant is the fact that almost nothing was published which might arouse favorable emotional responses toward America or the American people. Somehow, presumably for purely selfish motives of self-preservation or profit, the Americans were involved in the war against Fascist Germany. But little indication was given to the Soviet people that Americans of all ranks and kinds were fighting and working against the Fascist enemy with motives similar to those of the Soviet people. Words like "heroic," which were used so frequently to describe the Red Army, the Yugoslav partisans, or even the resistance movements in France and other European countries, were almost never applied to the Americans or British.

It is not unfair to conclude that the Soviet public, insofar as it was within the power of the Soviet propaganda machine, was given the impression that the united front against Nazi Germany was inspired from Moscow and only its Soviet and, perhaps, its foreign Communist contingent, was actuated by firm principles and noble ideals.

III. The American War Effort

MOSCOW'S reserved and calculating attitude toward its allies was manifested vividly in the Soviet presentation of the American and British contribution to the anti-Fascist war. Niggardly and grudging in recognition of allied efforts, this presentation was vehement in criticism of allied shortcomings. Above all, it never concealed its authors' suspicion of allied motives. Both in what was said and what was left unsaid it contrasted sharply with the warmly generous and too often naïve recognition accorded Soviet war achievements by the bulk of the Anglo-American press.

In essence, the Soviet story of the war was as follows: America and Britain have vast resources, material and human. Their full mobilization and use are essential for the swiftest possible victory over the reactionary Nazi enemy. However, since these forces are not being fully utilized, the Soviet people are forced to bear the brunt of the struggle and to do more than their share of working, fighting, and dying for the common cause. The U.S.S.R. is fully capable of carrying this unjustly heavy burden because of the heroism of its people and the superiority of its social system. But in return for its decisive role in the war it is entitled to play the major part in the construction of a progressive postwar order in which the economic and social causes of fascism and war will be eradicated.

This simple formula, reflecting Soviet ideology and ancient Russian suspicion of the Anglo-Saxons, was adapted and modified to meet changing circumstances. As the power of the coalition increased and the prospect of a vast expansion of Soviet power grew ever brighter, Moscow increasingly emphasized the role of Soviet arms and the superiority of the Soviet social order. What had been mainly an instrument for mobilizing Soviet and non-Soviet resources for the Kremlin's war of survival was increasingly converted into a weapon of a renewed Soviet political offensive against the West.

The Soviet interpretation of America's role in the war can most logically be discussed under three main topics: American capabilities, particularly scientific, technical, and economic; American governmental and private economic and material aid; and American military operations.

The emphasis on the American—and British—war potential was greatest during the very early months of the war. During this period, when Moscow had nothing but defeats to report from the front, the presence in the Soviet camp of mighty allies had incalculable value for sustaining Soviet morale. This early and truly desperate period may be divided into two parts. The first ended with the defeat of the Germans before Moscow in November and December, 1941. It was only during this brief span that British bombings of Germany, and American and British scientific and industrial prowess were reported in a fashion calculated to make a powerful impression on Soviet readers. For it was only during these few months that news items relating to these topics were published on the front page of the four-page Soviet newspapers. After the fall of 1941, the allied war effort disappeared almost entirely from the front page, which was now devoted mostly to recording the Red Army's campaigns.

It was also only during this period that any substantial number of the numerous photographs of British or American military equipment or war production activity available to Soviet publications were used. At best, the use made of them was insignificant in comparison with the big play given in the American and British press to Soviet photographs. Moreover, for the most part they were published only in the provincial papers.

Typical of the Russian line in this short first period was a statement by the president of the U.S.S.R. Academy of Sciences, Vladimir L. Komarov: "The United States, the country of Franklin and Edison, has become the industrial base of the world anti-Nazi front." In the same speech, which was broadcast by short-wave radio, Komarov stated: "During the years of the technical reconstruction of the Soviet economy American technology was assimilated on a grand scale in the Soviet Union." [1]

A few signed articles in *Pravda* and *Izvestiya* in the early months of 1942 developed further the line taken in Komarov's address. The physicist, Academician A. N. Frumkin, in *Pravda* for May 11, 1942, referred to America as a "country of mighty technology." Like Komarov, he emphasized the historic admiration of Russian scientists for their American colleagues.

The latter theme, though with diminishing emphasis, remained a feature of Soviet propaganda during the war. In 1944, the leading physicist Kapitsa, in accepting the medal of the Franklin Institute of Philadelphia, emphasized the theme, as well as the friendly relations and solidarity of interests among American and Soviet scientists. This concept was kept alive throughout the war by publication of friendly messages exchanged by Soviet and American scientists. It received its most dramatic expression at the 220th anniversary celebration of the Soviet Academy of Sciences held in Moscow a few days after V-E Day. After Stalingrad, and more especially with the launching of a campaign in 1943 and 1944 against undue emphasis on Russia's cultural debt to the West, this theme was increasingly balanced by counter-propaganda.

The theme was, however, an essential part of the Soviet line that the preponderance of power was on the side of the anti-Nazi coalition. Stalin himself in his November 6, 1941, address stated that World War II was a "war of motors" and that the coalition would win because its motor-producing capacity was thrice that of the Axis. I have been told by persons who attended the first Moscow conference in September, 1941, that Stalin

[1] For this and similar statements see the brochure *The Patriotic War and Science* (*Otechestvennaya voina i nauka*), Moscow, 1942.

there had privately made a similar statement. Later at Teheran he was to admit eloquent recognition of the role of U.S. and allied machines in winning the war, but not for publication in the Soviet press.

The economic-industrial might of America continued throughout the war to be the subject of news items in the daily and periodical press and a major theme of the few special monographs on the U.S. published in Soviet Russia during the war. Most of the news items reporting on American war production or developments in engineering and war equipment were brief and severely factual. Occasionally, especially in 1941 and 1942, there appeared a signed, cautiously interpretive article such as that by N. Sergeeva in the June 21, 1942, *Pravda,* entitled "America Gathers Speed." Sergeeva, who was to distinguish herself after the war by her vitriolic anti-American articles, lauded the American government's mobilization of American resources for war. As is well known, the venerable Soviet economist Eugene Varga was to be criticized and demoted after the war for attributing efficiency and leadership to the U.S. government in this field.

The monographs *The United States of America* (*Soedinennye Shtaty Ameriki*), *Countries of the Pacific Ocean* (*Strany tikhogo okeana*), and *Why the United States is Fighting Hitlerite Germany* (*Pochemu Sha voyuyut protiv gitlerovskoi germanii*), all of which appeared in 1942, contained extensive factual material designed to prove that the U.S., and especially the U.S. and Britain combined, were overwhelmingly superior industrially and economically to Germany and also to Japan.

Even after 1942 and indeed to the end of the war a considerable volume of such material continued to appear. That it received a considerable circulation is indicated by a curious item published in *Pravda,* November 12, 1944, entitled "Hackwork in the Guise of a Dissertation." The item pilloried a hapless Comrade Ivanenko who in 1943 submitted a doctoral dissertation to the Moscow Pedagogical Institute on "The United States of America and Its Resources in the Struggle against Fascism." The article charged Ivanenko with plagiarizing his material from a number of Soviet textbooks and periodical articles, but in retrospect one wonders if he was not a victim of the incipient stage of what was to become, after the war, a gigantic campaign of depreciation and vilification of America's war effort.

As we have seen, recognition of the American economic potential diminished during the summer of 1942, and was reduced still more after the turn of the tide at Stalingrad. Apparently, the Kremlin was more confident of the outcome of this second crucial test of strength than it had been during the days still referred to by the Soviet people who lived through them as the "Moscow panic." Even though mobilizing all forces for a last-ditch stand against the invader, Soviet leaders were increasingly preoccupied with political questions. They doubtless looked forward to a day when it would be inconvenient if either Soviet or foreign public opinion retained the impression that allied aid had played any significant role in saving Russia. This reasoning was unquestionably stimulated by reports reaching the Politburo of the psychological impact on Soviet people, particularly officers and men of the armed forces, of the steadily increasing flow of American military equipment and other supplies. In December, 1944, I talked to a very young Red Army Air Force Colonel who had fought at Stalingrad who told me of the tonic effect on Red Army morale produced by the arrival of American tanks and planes during this great battle. If the Politburo had approached its allies in the same spirit as they did Russia, such a reaction as that of the young aviator would have been welcomed. But the Kremlin's attitude was far too opportunistic and suspicious to permit normal sentiments of gratitude for American and British aid to develop unchecked among its people.

The Soviet presentation of American material aid to Russia was extremely grudging and inadequate. No major Soviet policy statement during the war accorded more than carefully qualified recognition of the value to the Soviet cause of what eventually amounted to more than eleven billion dollars in lend-lease supplies and hundreds of millions in private relief.

It is true that Stalin in his July 3 and November 6, 1941, speeches thanked the U.S. for its assurances of aid. But neither here nor later did he or other Soviet leaders suggest the possibility that this aid might be a major factor in assuring Soviet survival. This restraint was in sharp contrast to frequent official and private statements made in America and Britain regarding the role of Russia in saving democracy from destruction by the Nazis.

After the first few months of the war, having aroused expectations and hope of arrival of American material, Soviet propaganda rendered only a perfunctory, almost formal account of the ever swelling volume of U.S. aid. One of the most striking proofs of this is the fact that neither the May Day nor November 7 slogans issued during the war ever mentioned American material aid. Now these slogans, issued by the Bolshevik Party's Central Committee in connection with these major Soviet holidays, are almost as important political directives as the annual November 6 speech. Had the Kremlin been so minded, it could and would have included in these slogans cordial recognition of the value and good intentions of American assistance.

The Soviet propaganda machine confined its treatment of this subject largely to a combination of more or less ceremonial reporting of official conferences, such as that of September-October, 1941, concerned with American-British supplies to Russia, and publication, in whole or in part, of official American releases regarding lend-lease shipments. On the occasion of the ratification by the U.S.S.R. Supreme Soviet in June, 1942, of the Master Lend-Lease Agreement between the U.S. and Russia, Molotov referred to prospects of increased shipments from the U.S. Stalin in his message summing up the results of the first year of the war stated cautiously that the Agreement "brings the defeat of Germany nearer." Similarly cautious statements were made in 1943, 1944, and 1945 on the anniversaries of the signing of the Agreement. In the 1945 statement addressed to President Truman, Stalin said that American lend-lease shipments "played an important role and to a substantial degree assisted the successful completion" of the war against Hitlerite Germany. In 1946, the anniversary went unnoticed. Later, the Soviet press was to take the line that American aid was of insignificant magnitude and that anyway America had enriched itself by participation in the war.

The handling by the Soviet press of American private aid to Russia was even more niggardly than that accorded lend-lease. Private aid was, of course, on a far smaller scale, but its scope was nevertheless considerable and the warmth of feeling with which it was given might be considered to have justified something more than the near silence with which it was received.

Ambassador Standley's famous press statement in March, 1943, protesting against the failure of the Soviet press to report American private relief seems to have been well grounded. It is true that an occasional two- or three-inch news item had been published regarding Russian War Relief and other American aid activity. Even these inconspicuous items must have startled the occasional attentive Soviet reader. For they reported the activities of governors and mayors, of bankers and industrialists in raising funds to assist America's "socialist" ally. The Ambassador's statement may have erred slightly in detail, but basically his was a healthy reaction against the Kremlin's policy even during the war of preventing the development among Russians of any feeling of kinship or fellowship with their allies.

Although coldly factual news reporting of Russian War Relief and American Red Cross shipments—and especially of lend-lease—increased somewhat after Admiral Standley's statement, the Soviet press never gave editorial recognition to American nongovernmental aid. This truly extraordinary record can be explained mainly by the desire of the Soviet leaders to prevent the development of gratitude and admiration for America. There is probably another reason. I learned from conversations with Soviet people during and after the war that the American gifts intended by their donors for distribution among ordinary Soviet folk found their way mainly to the pockets of high party and police officials. Extensive publicity given to the receipt of these goods in Russia might have aroused public curiosity of a kind the Kremlin habitually seeks to prevent.

Although understatement and omission were the Kremlin's main techniques in dealing with the question of American material aid, they were supplemented covertly by private talks by agitators depreciating its importance and casting doubt on U.S. motives. For example, a Soviet musician, now dead, told me in 1944 that the "political worker" attached to his orchestra had told its members that American aid in food to Russia up to that time had been sufficient to feed Moscow for only a few days. Other Soviet friends expressed indignation regarding the "profits" which agitators had told them America was making from lend-lease. Political workers at the front attempted to dampen Red Army enthusiasm regarding American equipment by telling the officers and men that America was sending Russia only its obsolete equipment.

If Soviet propaganda dealt with American lend-lease and other aid mainly by inadequate and deprecatory reporting, it followed rather different tactics in regard to American—and other Allied—military operations. Geographic factors imposed upon the Soviet people the main burden of the land fighting in Europe. Soviet propaganda exploited this fact to the fullest possible extent. Its major weapon was the "second-front" campaign.

Before describing this campaign in detail, however, I should like to point out that the second-front theme, though the most important, was only one example of the slanted and distorted Soviet interpretation of America's military contribution to the war. The vast Allied naval and air efforts received extremely slender treatment. To be sure, they were mentioned from time to time in Stalin's speeches or in the May Day and November 7 slogans, but they were treated as a useful but definitely minor supplement to the central core of the anti-Axis war waged by the Red Army. Perhaps the most striking indication of this treatment is the fact that during the war in the list of fifty-odd slogans issued for key national holidays mention of the Allies was reserved for fifth place or lower, and on each such occasion they were allotted not more than one or two slogans.

One of the most extraordinary examples of the playing down of the Allies' war role was the Soviet press treatment of the war in the Pacific. Stalin did not even mention this vast and bitter conflict until his speech of November 6, 1944, in which he identified Japan as the "aggressor" against America and Britain. Following this statement, preparation of the Soviet public mind for possible entry into the war against Japan was accelerated. There followed a flood of material, including Stepanov's nationalistic novel, *Port Arthur*, and atrocity stories relating to the Japanese occupation of the Soviet Far East during and after the civil war. After final agreement had been reached at Yalta regarding Soviet entry into the war, the U.S.S.R. in April, 1945, denounced its neutrality pact with Japan on the grounds, about which silence had hitherto reigned, that Tokyo was Germany's ally, helping the latter in its war against Russia. The official statement denouncing the pact added that Japan was at war with the U.S.S.R.'s allies, America and Britain.

Prior to the summer of 1945, when the U.S.S.R. began its three weeks' war against Japan, military operations in the Pacific had usually been reported in brief and inconspicuous news despatches a few column-inches long. The Pacific war had been treated as a separate story, unrelated to the European war. Strict neutrality was observed in covering it, though this did not prevent David Zaslavski, one of the most vitriolic of Soviet journalists, in *Pravda*, December 30, 1941, from excoriating General MacArthur for "Petain methods" in declaring Manila an open city.

Occasional interpretive review articles, and such monographs on the Pacific area as *Countries of the Pacific Ocean* harped steadily on the theme of Japan's inferiority in strength to the Allies.[2] These publications viewed the Pacific war as a struggle

[2] The same thesis was presented in Kh. Eidus' *Japan and the U.S.A. in the Pacific War* (*Yaponiya i SShA v voine na tikhom okeane*), Tashkent, 1943.

between Japanese expansion and the established interests of Anglo-American capital. They expressed no favorable sentiment regarding the Allies, and were full of admiration for the "heroic Chinese people."

Despite the lip-service paid to the Allies in the denunciation of the Soviet-Japanese Pact and the Soviet declaration of war, the separateness of the Soviets and her allies was in effect reemphasized after Russia entered the war. Hundreds of times as much space was devoted to Soviet as to allied war operations. The Soviets refused to accept Japan's surrender at the same time as the Allies, delaying until they had completed their occupation of the vast territories marked out by Soviet strategy for economic and political exploitation. Finally, when Stalin on September 2 announced the signing of the act of capitulation by Japan, he went out of his way to assert that Japan in 1918 had been able to occupy and plunder Soviet Far Eastern territory by "utilizing" and "relying upon" the hostile attitude of the U.S. and Britain toward the U.S.S.R. No indication was given in the Soviet press that the atomic bomb might have had anything to do with Japan's defeat.

The thin and ungracious Soviet coverage of the Pacific war stands out all the more strikingly when one recalls what precious aid was rendered to the U.S.S.R. by American war operations which probably prevented Japan from attacking Russia. In this connection, the curious fact is worth noting that a member of the American Embassy staff heard an agitator state in the summer of 1943 that Japan would not dare attack Russia because American bombers would retaliate from Soviet bases and an American fleet would operate from Petropavlovsk on Kamchatka.

The second-front theme in Soviet wartime propaganda was introduced in radio broadcasts by Litvinov, the first of which was delivered on July 8, 1941. Stalin on November 6 authoritatively explained the reverses of the Red Army by the absence of a second front in Europe. These official statements were, of course, conspicuously reported in all Soviet propaganda media, and their effect was heightened by the prominent reporting of meetings in Allied countries demanding the early opening of a second front. The second-front agitation in England and America became a powerful weapon of Soviet policy from 1942 to 1944, as the prestige of the U.S.S.R. soared among the British and American public.

In the early months of 1942, particularly after the Germans launched the offensive which was to lead them as far as Stalingrad, Soviet second-front propaganda became tense, urgent, and bitter. In April, 1942, Litvinov delivered a speech in Philadelphia in which he emphasized that time was not necessarily on the side of the anti-Nazi coalition. Pointedly he declared that "the complete destruction and final defeat of Hitler requires the definite united efforts of the Soviet Union and Britain and increased aid from the United States." Germany, he insisted, could not be defeated by blockade or bombing. The main field of battle was the Soviet Union where the overwhelming majority of German forces were concentrated and would continue to be concentrated. This speech was typical of the Soviet position throughout the whole period prior to the allied invasion of Normandy in 1944. It was the main single theme of the Soviet press during most of the war. It was endlessly repeated and voluminously developed and disseminated. Numerous variations appeared, often highly unfair and sometimes unscrupulous, such as the report in the Soviet press in March, 1944, that the British, with the connivance of the Americans, were releasing medically fit German war prisoners who soon returned to the Soviet-German front. Many times during the war the Soviet press reported that military units were being withdrawn from the German forces in the West and transferred to the Soviet-German front. Such reports, in fact, accompanied every major Red Army offensive, even after the invasion of Normandy.

The full fury and effect of the second-front campaign was unleashed after Molotov's visit to Washington, following the issuance on June 11, 1942, of the joint Anglo-Soviet-American communiqué which stated that "in the course of the conversations full understanding was reached in regard to the urgent tasks of creating a second front in Europe in 1942." At the meeting of the U.S.S.R. Supreme Soviet in June, 1942, to ratify the Anglo-Soviet treaty of alliance this phrase was repeated again and again by Molotov and other deputies. The possibility of a second front was the major subject of interest at the meeting. Although Molotov himself and most of the other speakers kept to the careful phrasing of this announcement, one deputy declared that it furnished "proof of the determination of the great democratic powers of the world to open a second front in Europe in the nearest future and to finally destroy Hitler's war machine in 1942." In this connection it must be borne in mind that Stalin in his speech of the previous November had predicted that in no more than a year Hitlerite Germany must fall under the weight of its crimes.

The extremely difficult situation of the U.S.S.R. in 1942, and the fact that Stalin himself, seconded by other leaders such as Kalinin, in his 1942 New Year's message had promised victory in that year, made it inevitable that the United States and Great Britain would be used as the scapegoats for Russian defeats and sufferings. It appears obvious in retrospect that the joint communiqué referred to above played into the hands of both domestic and foreign Soviet propaganda. When no second front developed it appeared that the Allied governments were failing to fulfill their obligations.

It seems likely that the Soviet leaders had forced the British and American governments to place themselves in this disadvantageous situation. Alexander Werth in his perceptive study, *The Year of Stalingrad*, states that Wendell Willkie while in Kuibyshev in October, 1942, told him that Roosevelt had supported Molotov in regard to this communiqué while Churchill had opposed it.[3] According to a review of R. H. Bruce Lockhart's book, *Comes the Reckoning*, published in the London *Times Literary Supplement* for February 14, 1948, the key phrase quoted above from the communiqué was brought back by Molotov from Washington and its use virtually forced by Molotov upon the British Foreign Office.

[3] Werth, *The Year of Stalingrad*, London, 1946, p. 260.

General Deane writes:

> The Russians had some reason to question the sincerity of our intentions in the matter. We had at one time decided on a small scale invasion to establish a bridgehead on the continent in the fall of 1942 . . . when the African operations were undertaken in the fall of 1942 the invasion had to be postponed until the fall of 1943. When it was decided to exploit the African successes by invading Sicily and Sardinia, OVERLORD receded into 1944.

Deane declares that after each big Roosevelt-Churchill conference one of the last items of business was to prepare a message to Stalin telling him of decisions which had been reached. These decisions, he states, were in terms which perhaps gave the Russians more hope of a second front than was justified.[4]

Historical truth regarding this second-front question will not be established until documents not now available have been studied. It is clear, however, that Stalin and his propaganda machine seized upon the second-front question as a means of explaining to the Soviet people why the Germans were able to tear across the South Russian plains in the summer and fall of 1942. They also utilized it to assist them in mobilizing public opinion in England and America to force the Allied governments to render maximum assistance to the U.S.S.R. Finally, the skillful exploitation of the 1942 conference was of incalculable value to Soviet diplomacy in the closing period of the war and in the early postwar period to justify Soviet political and territorial demands.

Alexander Werth in *The Year of Stalingrad* describes with copious and vivid detail the way in which the second-front question was presented to the Soviet people in the summer and fall of 1942. He points out that as the summer wore on there were more and more frequent references in the press to German divisions sent to the Soviet front from the west. He writes: "The firm conviction was being built up that if things were going badly on the Soviet-German front it was very largely

[4] John R. Deane, *The Strange Alliance*, Viking Press, 1946, pp. 16-17.

through the Allies' failure to fulfil the promise of the Second Front communiqué."[5]

Early in October, 1942, Stalin, in reply to the AP correspondent Cassidy's letter, stated that as compared with the aid the Soviet Union was giving to the Allies by drawing upon itself the main force of the German armies, the aid of the Allies to the Soviet Union had been of little effect. He added that to improve this aid it was necessary only for the Allies to fulfill their obligations fully and on time. In mid-November, however, in reply to a second letter from Cassidy, Stalin acknowledged the "considerable" significance of the Allied invasion of North Africa. He stressed that the military initiative had now passed into the hands of the Allies and that the military and political situation in Europe had changed radically in favor of the Anglo-Soviet-American coalition.

With the further development of the war in Africa, the Mediterranean, and Italy, and the steadily increasing tempo of air bombings of Germany, the Soviet line toward Allied military operations settled down to a routine. The Allied struggle was presented only indirectly in the form of news items and the reprinting in whole or in part of British or American communiqués. With occasional exceptions, the front page editorials continued to view the war as almost exclusively a Soviet-German struggle. Throughout 1943, prior to the Teheran Conference, the press from time to time published material reminding the Soviet public that such success as the Germans had enjoyed on the Soviet front was due to the lack of a second front in the West. A rare example of editorial recognition appeared when *Pravda*, on April 26, 1943, in commenting on the slogans issued by the Central Committee of the Communist Party for May Day, referred briefly to the expulsion of the Axis from Libya and stated that it was also being driven from Tunisia, "the last strong point of the Italo-German coalition on the African continent." Similar editorial statements were made in connection with the celebration in June, 1943, of the first anniversary of the Lend-Lease Agreement.

[5] Werth, *op. cit.*, p. 139.

The press fairly frequently published items on the growing military power of the Western Allies, indicating that as this potential was brought into action it would help to assure the defeat of the Germans. But on the whole, the emphasis upon the growing Allied military potential had an accusatory overtone, for it seldom failed to imply that the potential was not being translated with sufficient rapidity into action. This impression was intensified by the fact that Soviet comment on Allied offensives constantly attributed their success to the operations of the Red Army. Stalingrad was constantly cited as the turning point of the whole war. The surrender of Italy was attributed to the Red Army's summer offensive, which began in July in the Belgorod, Orel, Kursk area. During this offensive numerous military surveys in the Soviet press demanded that the Western Allies adopt strategy similar to that of Foch in 1918 and boldly use their accumulated reserves to crush the enemy.

After Teheran, a new and temporarily more favorable phase began in Soviet presentation of the Allied war role. Frequent references were made to "agreed" military decisions reached by the Big Three, and an air of anticipation of coming great events pervaded the press. "Hitler's European fortress before the Storm," the leading editorial in *War and the Working Class* for January 15, 1944, pointed out that the year began under circumstances especially favorable to the anti-Hitler coalition. But like most reviews of the military situation, it emphasized that the fullest exertion of all the efforts of the anti-Hitler coalition was necessary to achieve speedy victory over Germany. It stressed the crushing blows being delivered by the Red armies and criticized the slowness of the Allied advance in Italy. The tone of the Soviet press in the winter and spring of 1944, and of Stalin's May Day order, was one of confidence tempered by a sense of urgency and by continued suspicious anxiety as to whether the Allies would fulfill their military obligations. In his May Day order Stalin emphasized that "joint blows" must be delivered from the east by Soviet troops and from the west by Allied troops in order to finish off the "German beast" in its own lair.

In the spring of 1944, American military operations enjoyed the best press that they had received in the Soviet Union since the beginning of the war. A typical article, "The Persian Gulf during the War," appearing in *War and the Working Class* for May, 1944, not only expressed admiration for the scope and efficiency of the activities of the Persian Gulf Command but also showed appreciation for the friendly attitude of Americans toward Russians. The author, Orestov, even went so far as to refer to United States posters urging speed in getting shipments to "Uncle Joe" as an example of the sympathy for Comrade Stalin among Americans. A few days before the beginning of the Normandy invasion several Soviet newspapers, particularly the Red Army's paper *Red Star*, published friendly articles regarding the American "shuttle bombing" operations based on Soviet and Allied air fields.

The Normandy invasion itself was acclaimed by Stalin on June 13 as "an achievement of the highest order." Stalin pointed out that the Allies had succeeded in doing what neither Hitler nor Napoleon had been able to accomplish. During the first week after the invasion began it received over half of all the foreign news space in *Pravda* and *Izvestiya*. The Soviet newspapers published President Roosevelt's prayer broadcast in connection with the invasion. *Pravda* even published a few photographs of American military equipment.

The enthusiastic Soviet attitude toward the invasion and subsequent Allied operations in the West did not long persist. In the thousands of pages devoted to war operations from June, 1944, to May, 1945, the old tendencies to minimize the allied contribution to the war and overemphasize the Soviet share quickly reasserted themselves. Beginning about the middle of July the press began to assert that the Allied invasion was made possible by the fact that the Soviets were pinning down the principal German forces in the East. As was true throughout the whole war, extremely inadequate recognition was given to the Allied air and naval operations. Many factors doubtless played a part in shaping this sour and niggardly attitude toward the Allied role in the war after D Day. The interests of the Communist Party's prestige and the morale of the war-weary Russian people impelled the Soviet propagandists to present the relative Soviet and Allied war efforts in this distorted light. When in the fall of 1944 and again in the spring of 1945 the rapid Allied offensive seemed to overshadow the Red Army's operations, such motives must have become irresistible.

I suspect that the warm, friendly reaction of the Soviet people toward the Allies evoked by the materialization of the long-awaited second front must have aroused great anxiety in the Kremlin. Americans in Moscow during the summer of 1944 were lionized by their Soviet friends, and the favorable response evoked by the invasion of France apparently extended even into official circles. During the fall of 1944, I visited on business several high officials of the Ministry of Education of the R.S.F.S.R. who assured me that Russians since June 6 had taken a "very special interest" in America and that study of the English language was growing by leaps and bounds.

Unfortunately, during this same period there were problems creating tension between the Soviets and the Allies, tension which was reflected in an increasingly unfavorable presentation of the Allied role in the war. It is only by keeping in mind the fact that both military and political questions, particularly in the minds of the anxious and suspicious Soviet leaders, were more and more viewed as twin aspects of a power rivalry thinly concealed by the coalition that we can understand the almost bizarre reporting of the Allied operations from the fall of 1944 until V-E Day. For example, the Soviet press in the week of August 28 to September 3 attributed the liberation of Paris mainly to the activities of the "French Partisans" and the Red Army. This seems all the more strange if it is recalled that the Soviet press at the same time maintained that it was criminal of General Bor to instigate the Warsaw uprising because partisans could never carry out a major military operation. During the last two months of the war the Soviet press published many items indicating that the Germans, while continuing to fight fiercely against the Red Army, were surrendering without resistance to the Allies. It is now known, from the memoirs of former Secretary of State Byrnes and other sources, that Stalin in the spring of 1945 cast aspersions of bad faith upon Roosevelt in connection with the surrender of the German forces in Northern Italy and that a sharp exchange of communications took place between the two men. Stalin's suspicion was unquestionably reflected in the Soviet press coverage of the closing weeks of the war.

Toward the very end of German resistance the tone of the press improved somewhat. However, eloquent evidence that the Soviet leaders wanted to keep alive in the minds of their people the feeling that the Soviet-German war was separate from the Allied-German war, and the conviction that Russia had played the predominant role in defeating Germany, was furnished by the way in which they announced V-E Day. The Soviet press and radio gave the impression that the surrender of the Germans to the British in Rheims was only incidental to the Berlin ceremonies. V-E Day was celebrated in the U.S.S.R. on May 9 instead of May 8. And only two years later, in the postwar campaign to erase from the mind of the Soviet people all memory of Allied aid in Russia's struggle for survival, a decree was issued abolishing this holiday.

IV. Wartime Glimpses of American Life and Culture

HISTORY may record that the Kremlin's greatest crime was its failure to permit the Russian people to grasp the hand of friendship extended during World War II by the American people. Circumstances were extraordinarily favorable for the establishment of cordial personal relationships and for an exchange of intellectual and cultural output upon which a long period of fruitful postwar collaboration might have been founded. The American government and enlightened American opinion were almost pathetically eager to pierce the Chinese wall separating the Russian people—and the Russian mind—from the world community. The story of frustration of the efforts, public and private, by which Americans sought to establish normal human contacts with the people of the U.S.S.R. is too well known to need retelling here.

My main purpose in this chapter is to draw attention to evidence unknown to most Americans which indicates that on the Soviet side also there existed a desire for closer personal and cultural relations. The very existence of this evidence perhaps demands a slight qualification of our strictures on Soviet cultural isolationism, for it cannot be denied that Soviet-American cultural relations during the war were not quite a one-way street. A handful of trusted Soviet citizens were authorized to associate with Americans. Several thousand Soviet people made business trips to the United States. A few of these were permitted, or more probably commissioned, to write of their experiences in the strange and exciting "transatlantic republic." Contrary to the impression of some Americans, a good deal of unofficial mingling took place, not always dangerous to the Soviet persons involved, especially where, as at Murmansk or Archangel, an attempt was made for a time to make a favorable impression on foreigners. Still, even in the favorable weeks following the Teheran Conference, a number of friends of Americans were called into the offices of the dreaded political police and warned either to discontinue their acquaintance or to prepare regular reports on the attitudes and actions of their friends.

Finally, the Soviet leaders permitted a thin trickle of new American films, plays, music and books, insignificant in volume compared to the flow of Simonov novels and Shostakovich symphonies to America, but important enough to warrant in the postwar reaction a vast ideological disinfection campaign.

It seems to me that these slight concessions to cultural internationalism were rather similar in character to Soviet wartime concessions to religious freedom. Abroad, they helped camouflage the Kremlin's basic hostility and mistrust of its allies. At home, they at least partially satisfied the yearning of Soviet intellectuals—I am using the word in its specific Soviet sense of mental as distinguished from manual workers—for a change from its heavy diet of propaganda. I feel also that the enthusiastic response to this foreign fare reflected the desire of the Soviet intelligentsia for closer cultural relations with the West.

Wartime articles and lectures by Soviet aviators, artists and journalists describing their experiences in America furnished a refreshing contrast to the normal propaganda boilerplate. To be sure, these accounts had been carefully sifted by the censors. They had to hew closely to the political line laid down in Stalin's speeches. They carefully skirted ideological problems. They refrained from dangerous speculation about the fantastic and fascinating world which they described. Moreover, their authors were after all themselves products of a culture in many ways alien to that of the classic land of individualism. They wore the intellectual blinders which had prevented even Ilf and Petrov from grasping the true quality and essence of America. In general, they presented America, in conformity with the traditional Soviet conception, as a country of technological and material progress which could teach the U.S.S.R. little or nothing in the social or moral spheres.

And yet some of the observations about America by Soviet travelers or other intellectuals written during the war had a personal quality which makes them engaging and provocative. To a certain extent, they represented a genuine individual human response to the paradox of the alliance between capitalist America and Soviet Russia. On the whole the published accounts of Russians who traveled or worked in America during the war were more favorable to the American scene than the official propaganda line carried in the press. At the same time these Soviet travelers displayed in their observations certain negative reactions which were carefully avoided in the main stream of propaganda, for example, their shocked emphasis on the easy life of ordinary Americans as indicated by the abundance of food and consumers' goods available despite the war.

The well-known Soviet airman, Georgi Baidukov, published in *Pravda* during December, 1941, an account of his experiences in the United States in the fall of that year. Baidukov's articles were republished early in 1942 in a booklet in 100,000 copies entitled *American Impressions*. Baidukov and the other members of his party were received at the War Department by General Marshall and in the White House by President Roosevelt. They also visited Dayton, Ohio, and nearby Wright Field. The Soviet aviator's account is a curious mixture of impressions: gratitude for the cordial hospitality accorded his group, admiration for American aviation techniques, and bewilderment at certain phases of the American system, such as the difficulties imposed by private property rights on the powers of the government. He described President Roosevelt as a splendid conversationalist, competent in military problems and possessed of a hearty sense of humor. He was tremendously impressed by American civil aviation, with its "enormous network" operating with clock-like precision. However, he was apparently astonished by the fact that the President had to resort to special powers in order to establish a military airfield in Washington. Baidukov was fascinated but rather appalled by the hustle and bustle of America. He observed that the "struggle with noise" in American cities was a serious problem. He could not sleep in our hotels.

Like most Russians who have traveled in the United States, he had the impression that there was much in common between the American and Russian characters. He wrote: "Like the Russian, the American is friendly, talkative, and sociable." About the only unfavorable comment on Americans was his statement: "From my observations of the life of American soldiers and officers I draw the conclusion that they are so accustomed to comforts that they have carried them into the army." He added that he did not consider that it was possible to maintain these comforts in military operations and therefore considered dependence upon them harmful. These observations were made in connection with his description of American military installations in Alaska, the efficiency, comfort, and cleanliness of which he clearly admired. He was, incidentally, pleased and touched by the thoughtfulness of his American hosts in preparing a Russian meal for him at Nome.

Another Soviet pilot, A. Shtemenko, wrote an even more interesting account of his American trip, in the literary magazine, *Oktyabr*.[1] Shtemenko was Molotov's pilot on the latter's official visit to the United States and Britain in 1942. It is curious that more than two years passed before his piece appeared in *Oktyabr*. It belonged to a flurry of relatively friendly items regarding American life published either shortly before or shortly after the Normandy invasion.

Shtemenko referred to the cordial, almost embarrassingly friendly hospitality with which he and his fellow crew members were received in Washington. His article vividly reflected the deep impressions made upon him by the vigor and energy of America. And like almost all Soviet Russians who have been in a position to record their impressions of the United States, he was impressed by its wealth and prosperity. There is something naïve but at the same time keenly perceptive in his observa-

[1] Number 6, 1944, pp. 57-88.

tions. Of Washington he wrote that he had expected it to be a "heap of skyscrapers" but he found that it was not a city but a park. The only typically American feature he saw in Washington was the astounding number of automobiles. Shtemenko described the "fantastic activity" of American photographers and newsreel men, and he was amazed that it was possible to have a uniform cleaned and pressed in a few hours. The time spent in Washington would remain in his memory not only because his party was so hospitably received but "because something worth remembering" had been observed in the "unusual setting of America," with its "peculiar and specific culture."

Although his account was wholly positive, like Baidukov, he had exercised a great deal of restraint. Neither visitor permitted himself to draw any general conclusions from his experience regarding the character of American life or institutions. Probably both of these travel sketches were carefully edited by competent political authorities, for both displayed a tendency to interpret American institutions in terms of Soviet patterns. For example, Shtemenko wrote that when his party visited the White House they were greeted by a member of its "apparat." The flavor of this word certainly suggests to a Soviet reader an organization far more formal and formidable than anything attached to the White House.

A characteristic feature of Soviet life is the great number of public lectures organized by the government. Some of these lectures during the war were delivered by Soviet intellectuals who had been in America. I attended a characteristic one on April 21, 1944, given by the famous Soviet Jewish actor, Solomon Mikhoels. Shortly before his public lecture, Mikhoels had contributed two articles on his American journey to *War and the Working Class*. The articles were in a somewhat sharper and more negative tone, probably reflecting the influence of the editors. In general, Mikhoels' observations on America were a mixture of admiration and ridicule. Following the established official line, he portrayed America as a nation of dollar-chasers where the materialist interests of the individual predominated over any community interests. On the other hand, he maintained that there were strong progressive forces in the United States and there was great admiration for the U.S.S.R. He also paid the usual tributes to American technical proficiency, and he eloquently described the vast scope of American war production.

Mikhoels' approach was that of a prominent Soviet intellectual hewing closely to the party line. The impressions he received of American life were certainly highly distorted. He followed the conventional Soviet political formula which selected and exaggerated the least appealing aspects of American life while overlooking and probably not understanding its major currents. It was obvious from his account that during this tour of the United States he had associated mainly with Communists and fellow travelers. In one important respect his impressions were probably sincere and personal. He was not at all impressed by the impact of the war on the lives of Americans, and he indicated that they were not making sacrifices comparable to those experienced by the Soviet people.

Another typical Soviet lecture I attended, entitled "America during the War," was delivered by a young journalist, B. P. Vronsky, at the House of Savants in Moscow on November 15, 1944. Naturally, Vronsky, like Mikhoels, had to present his observations within the framework of the current Soviet propaganda line, but his lecture contained some fresh personal reactions. In general, he emphasized that as a result of the war public opinion in the United States had evolved away from isolationism and toward international co-operation, particularly with the U.S.S.R. He also placed great stress on the economic mobilization of America for war. In a somewhat facetious vein he described the difficulties experienced by Americans when for the first time they had to deal with such problems as rationing. Like many Russians who have been in the United States, Vronsky regarded with a mixture of amusement and irritation strange misconceptions he had encountered among Americans regarding the Soviet Union. He said, for example, that one American geography textbook stated that the chief form of transportation among the Russians was the *troika*. He told a story about several Russians living in an American hotel who were regarded as abnormal because they did not have long beards or drink vodka.

The audience reaction to lectures on the United States was always interesting to me. In general, a mood of exceedingly eager and friendly curiosity prevailed. At the Mikhoels and Vronsky lectures, the audience seemed to shrug off or laugh at the unfavorable remarks regarding the United States and to show enthusiasm for those statements which could be regarded as praise. I remember with special vividness a scholarly-looking, elderly gentleman criticizing Vronsky's lecture indignantly to a friend as the audience was leaving the lecture hall. The old man thought that Vronsky had greatly underestimated the recognition given in the United States to Russian literature and music.

In both tone and content such accounts and lectures were fresher, more personal, and more favorable to American life and culture than official handbooks and similar media. The handbook, *The United States of America,* contained a considerable amount of material on American music, literature, and other aspects of American culture. Unfortunately, it followed the schematic Soviet platitude that in the United States the few struggling progressive intellectuals had to fight a hard battle against the crushing weight of conservative and reactionary forces and institutions. The handbook took the position that unless a writer or artist was a Communist or fellow traveler he was of no significance, and it emphasized the role of intellectuals who painted a negative and critical picture of American life. The stereotyped distortions of this publication concerning American life and culture can best be seen in the following excerpt:

> Immediately after the first world imperialist war, the novel received wide distribution in America. A whole pleiad of writers came forward, who quickly gained world recognition. The most outstanding among them was Theodore Dreiser. In his novels, *The Financiers* and *The Titan,* Dreiser gives a critical picture of the activity of the representatives of big finance capital. In the *American Tragedy,* Dreiser gives a fresh version of the traditional theme of success in

American literature, showing that the path to it is not equal for all (which was the basic proposition of the school of "tender realism"). Dreiser is closely associated with progressive public activity in America and is a friend of the Soviet Union. Sinclair Lewis gives in his novel, *Babbitt*, a satirical but fully realistic composite figure of the American bourgeois. In *Arrowsmith* Lewis shows the position of the learned man under conditions of capitalism while in *Main Street* he debunks the figure of the average American. However, Lewis's creative work is very uneven. He writes novels (*A Work of Art* and *Dodsworth*) which are an apology for capitalist enterprise. In them we see figures of benevolent businessmen; he also creates novels of pure entertainment whose artistic significance is very slight.

An outstanding master of contemporary American literature is Ernest Hemingway. He holds first place in the group of writers of the so-called "lost generation" of the postwar intelligentsia (Dos Passos, MacLeish, and others). The war of 1914-1918 disillusioned this generation and it no longer believes in capitalist civilization and flees from it (*A Farewell to Arms*).

The sharpening of social contradictions in America brought about the appearance of revolutionary literature, the clearest representatives of which are Michael Gold, Erskine Caldwell, and others. The works of these writers, in particular Michael Gold and Caldwell, are sharply distinguished from the accusatory literature of America by realistic depth of artistic representation and by the appeal to the unity of the labor movement, and to practical struggle. Recently the talented Steinbeck, the author of the very popular novel, *The Grapes of Wrath*, has adhered to progressive literature. In 1935 there was founded the League of American Writers, which unites the most outstanding writers and poets of America. The progressive weekly *New Masses* has great significance in the development of American literature. It is the center of gravity of all progressive writers, artists, and scientists of America.

A particular place in the literature of the United States is held by the literature of the American Negroes, which is rightfully considered the outstanding literature of the whole Negro race. The beginning of Negro literature in the United States is in folk lore. Negro folk tales, created in America, are founded on African tales. The most characteristic and popular among them, the so-called *Tales of*

Uncle Remus, were written down by Joel Chandler Harris from the words of Negro slaves.

The form of African music is characteristic for Afro-American folk songs, but their content is related to the life of the Negroes in the United States. The first spirituals were composed in the period of slavery. Behind the splendid melodies of the spirituals there is hidden the tragedy of an enslaved people seeking salvation in religion. Sometimes in these songs there is perceived a note of protest, concealed behind Biblical terminology.[2]

A similar impression of American literature was given by a carefully prepared handbook, *The Best Representatives of English and American Literature*, published in 1942 by the State Library and Bibliographical Publishing House of the RFSSR. In some ways the handbook was an excellent production. Under American literature it listed works of Irving, Cooper, Poe, Longfellow, Harriet Beecher Stowe, Walt Whitman, Bret Harte, Mark Twain, O. Henry, Jack London, Dreiser, and Upton Sinclair. Brief notes on these writers followed the same familiar line as the handbook described earlier.

In this period, there was less criticism of American intellectuals in the Soviet press and publications than in the later period of the war. The shift to a more critical attitude, though one which still remained within the ideological framework of the anti-Hitler coalition, was reflected in an article published in the literary magazine *Znamya* in April, 1944. This article, by Vladimir Rubin, was entitled "The War Theme in American Literature." Rubin was sharply critical of American writers for their alleged neglect of the war. He quoted a Czech anti-Fascist writer to the effect that the spirit of American literature was "business as usual." Even the works devoted to the war, such as Steinbeck's *The Moon is Down,* he considered inferior since they made the enemy appear too "complicated and humanized."

Rubin's criticism went somewhat beyond the war theme. He took the position that in general American literature was un-

[2] *The United States of America* (*Soedinennye Shtaty Ameriki*), Moscow, 1942.

able to maintain the creative heights which it had reached in the past. American writers, he maintained, were not in touch with the masses and they were afraid to express either deep convictions or strong feelings.

The line taken by Rubin was further developed in other articles and publications, among them a scholarly brochure entitled *Contemporary English and American Writers*, published by the same agency as *The Best Representatives of English and American Literature*. This pamphlet was written in 1944 but did not appear until March, 1945. It contained brief descriptions of the work of some twenty American novelists and poets, from Sherwood Anderson to Stewart Engstrand. Among these writers were the two Negro novelists and poets, Richard Wright and Langston Hughes. Paul de Kruif was also included. Both the selections of writers and the critical comment followed the same line as the other sources cited above, but the ideological tone of the booklet was a little sharper than that of Rubin's article.

A striking fact reflecting the cautious attitude of the Soviet authorities toward anything which could be considered "selling" the American way of life even during most of the war was the almost complete lack of Soviet books, plays or films about America. One cannot help contrasting the absence of American characters on the Soviet stage and screen with Hollywood's efforts to tell the Russian story in such films as *Song of Russia* or *North Star*.

The most notable exception to this rule during the war was what now seems—by way of contrast with the postwar flood of Soviet plays and novels portraying Americans as grotesque and repulsive—the amazingly friendly play by Alexander Korneichuk, *The Mission of Mr. Perkins to the Land of the Bolsheviks*.[3] This play appeared for the first time in Moscow in the fall of 1944 and ran for a few months. It was the story of Perkins, a "millionaire from Chicago," who came to the U.S.S.R. with the avowed intention of finding out whether it

[3] Published in 300 copies by All-Union Administration for Safeguarding Authors' Rights, Moscow, 1945.

was possible to do business with Stalin. Perkins was accompanied by his secretary Miss Down, and by Hemp, a journalist from Chicago. Hemp was intended to symbolize the American "Yellow Press." In contrast to Perkins, who represented an unsentimental, hard-boiled but open-minded businessman, Hemp found in all his experiences in Russia confirmation of his prejudices. His mentality as a matter of fact was uncannily similar to that of Soviet journalists visiting the United States. For example, at the beginning of the play Hemp said in loud tones, "How fine Moscow is," and then whispered to Perkins, "Agents of the GPU are listening to us everywhere. Speak in a whisper." He reminded Perkins of his series of newspaper articles, *Secrets of Moscow.*

During their stay in the U.S.S.R. these three were involved in a variety of adventures as a result of which Perkins and his secretary became convinced that it was possible to get along with the Soviets while Hemp retained his original opinion. They visited a collective farm and also the Ukrainian front. On the collective farm Perkins made friends with the fifteen-year-old daughter of the woman president of the farm. There was an amusing scene in which two girls, members of the Young Communist League, after first protesting that they would not sit at the same table with a "real live bourgeois," became convinced that Perkins was not a bad fellow after all. For his part, Perkins, although constantly boasting about the superiority of America to every other country, ended up by saying that the only weakness of the Soviet people was that they were not fully aware of their abilities and achievements. While at the front he even helped some soldiers to carry boxes of ammunition.

This play probably represented the most effective expression of the idea that the Soviet Union and the United States could "do business." It can best be understood against the background of the recently opened second front and the feeling which existed in certain circles in both countries that there would be political collaboration as well as extensive trade between Russia and America after the war. It also indirectly reflected the strong desire among many Soviet intellectuals for closer cultural relations between Russia and America. Korneichuk, its author, although a convinced Communist and ardent Soviet patriot, was at this time friendly to the United States.

The only other Soviet play known to me in which an American played an important and positive role was *Immortal*, produced in 1943, in which an American newspaperman joined a Russian guerilla band and fought against the Nazis.

A small-scale effort was made during the war to make available to the Soviet people American literature, drama, films, and music. Far less was done than American official and private agencies desired. However, the picture was not entirely black. Probably the most significant field of communication was films. A number of American films, such as *North Star*, *Song of Russia*, *Mission to Moscow*, some Walt Disney films and some films starring Deanna Durbin were shown in Russia during or within a year or so after the war. The American film *Edison*, starring Spencer Tracy, was very successful. Even though these films were carefully selected for their ideological and political points of view, they undoubtedly created good will and admiration for America.

Some of these films, by their effort to present Soviet life favorably, aroused amusement. I saw *North Star* with a Russian friend who was convulsed with laughter at the magnificence of Ukrainian peasant cottages à la Hollywood. The apologetic line of *Mission to Moscow* probably won little respect for America among Russians. On the whole, however, Soviet people not only enjoyed the American films they saw during the war, they appreciated and responded warmly to the friendly message they conveyed. The best indication of this fact was the immense popularity of our films. They were well liked by the masses—when they could see them—and by intellectuals. Special showings at the American Embassy and in Soviet organizations, to a select few, were usually crowded. In 1943, 1944, and 1945, Soviet newsreel films fairly often used fragments of the American or British commentaries supplied by the Ministry of Information or the OWI. Among the most popular newsreel films which contained such material were those on the Crimea and Potsdam conferences in 1945. A number of Soviet presentations or adaptations of American plays also ran in the U.S.S.R. during the war. These were either left-wing ideological dramas, including several by Lillian Hellman, or pure entertainment. In the latter category belonged a Soviet version for the stage of the American movie *It Happened One Night.*[4]

In the field of music, beginning with a special "concert of American music" sponsored on July 4, 1943, by the All-Union Society for Cultural Relations with Foreign Countries, serious American music, as well as several jazz pieces, received considerable distribution in the U.S.S.R. In this field, just as in literature and drama, little was done by comparison with efforts in the United States to popularize Russian culture. Wide sections of the Soviet public would have liked more. There was tremendous demand for American musical scores among Soviet orchestras, but it was met to a very limited extent. Even so, old American jazz standbys, such as "Alexander's Ragtime Band," and the war song, "A Tavern in the Town," were among the most popular Soviet jazz tunes during the war. In the restaurant of Moscow's leading hotel American jazz predominated.

At that time these developments seemed to represent promising beginnings of closer cultural and intellectual relations between the U.S.S.R. and America. While they seem very remote at present, I feel certain that the demand for access to Western thought and culture among the Soviet public continues to exist. Hundreds of thousands, perhaps millions, of Soviet teachers, engineers, doctors, and intellectuals of all sorts responded eagerly to the wartime opportunity to learn more about the outside world. There was a widespread desire for Russia once again to be brought into the international cultural community and freed from her paralyzing isolation from intellectual contacts abroad. In general, to the extent that rigid official regimentation permitted it, Soviet intellectuals and spe-

[4] Presented as *The Road to New York,* by the Leningrad Comedy Theatre. I saw it in Moscow in July, 1944.

cialists took eager advantage of opportunities to enter into closer contact with their opposite numbers in America and England. Librarians, directors of medical institutions, musicians, and many other groups did what little they could to establish relations, either personally or by correspondence, with their foreign colleagues.

The friendly attitude of Soviet intellectuals and specialists was reflected in the following quotation from an official but semi-restricted publication of the State Lenin Library:

> Cultural relations among the allies have become much closer. This is indicated especially by increased book exchange with America and Britain and by the great interest of Soviet librarians in the courageous work of English and American libraries. . . .[5]

Unfortunately, the Soviet government permitted only a thin trickle of communications in the cultural relations field. It restricted and distorted the flow of information about America and still more severely the importing of American literary or other works into Russia except, of course, those which followed the Soviet political line; it was infinitely more severe in its restrictions on personal contacts. The standoffish attitude of the Soviet authorities was brought to my attention during the war when it was one of my duties at the Embassy to obtain Soviet publications and arrange for exchange of Soviet and American material. The Soviet publications officials genuinely desired to help the Embassy, but their zeal was tempered and often paralyzed by politically inspired restrictions and by fear of incurring the disapproval of higher authorities.

Three typical incidents, two of them out of my own experience, may serve to illustrate the difficulties involved. In October, 1942, it was reported in the bulletin of the Soviet Embassy in Washington that a series of lectures and reports on the United States and a number of exhibits had been arranged in Soviet cities in honor of the 450th anniversary of the discovery of America. One would have expected that Americans in Mos-

[5] *Eighty Years in the Service of Our Country's Culture and Scholarship*, Moscow, 1943, 1000 copies.

cow would be invited to this exhibit, which was held in the Moscow public library. Such was not the case, and the American official personnel stationed in Moscow in fact experienced great difficulty in obtaining any information on the exhibit. In the spring of 1945, one of my Embassy colleagues read in the *Moscow News* that one of the city schools was putting on a special program on America. We telephoned to this school seeking permission to visit and discuss this program. However, we met with the usual run-around. Despite repeated telephone conversations, we found that the personnel who would have been able to furnish information regarding this program were unavailable, all having developed mysterious illnesses. Another trivial but vexatious example of evasion and obstruction was the failure of the Embassy in the spring of 1945 to obtain from the Moscow public library copies of the New York *Times* which it had itself a few weeks before presented to the library.

All of this, however, certainly does not mean that nothing was accomplished, at least during the war, in stimulating interest in American life and culture among Soviet people. While the individual reactions of Soviet people regarding the United States, as far as I was able to observe them, are discussed in detail in the last chapter of this book, it seems appropriate to conclude this chapter by referring to a conversation which I had in August, 1944, with a Soviet professor of history, now dead. The professor was very optimistic concerning the development of closer cultural relations between Russia and the Anglo-Saxon countries. It was his opinion and his fervent desire that what he called the "Chinese Wall" which had sealed Russia off from the rest of the world was beginning to break down. All groups of the Russian people, he said, from the simplest factory workers and peasants to the intellectuals, wanted to know more about America and England. The professor himself was scheduled to give a series of lectures on Anglo-Saxon democratic institutions at a Soviet university. There can be little doubt that in his desire that the wartime collaboration between

Russia and the Anglo-Americans be not merely continued but immensely strengthened after the war this man was typical of a considerable section of Soviet opinion. But as I shall point out in the next chapter, the Kremlin did not share his confidence regarding the possibility or desirability of such a trend.

V. Looking Toward the Postwar World

THE main task of Soviet propaganda during the war was, of course, the mobilization of human and material resources against the Fascist enemy. This task was symbolized, especially during the first two years of the conflict by the slogan "everything for the front." At the same time, the Kremlin's propaganda machine performed another important operation, the significance of which increased as political problems obtruded upon the consciousness of both Allied and Soviet policy-makers. This was the preparation of Soviet and non-Soviet opinion for Kremlin policy in the postwar world. What was the shape of things to come in the Kremlin's crystal ball? To answer this question we must first examine the analysis of domestic American political and social forces presented by Moscow through its propaganda media. Only within the framework of this presentation do Soviet wartime pronouncements regarding international relations and international organization make sense. For Soviet doctrine has always emphasized that a country's foreign policy reflects its domestic policy and social structure.

Soviet wartime propaganda clearly reveals that the Kremlin cherished some hope of eating its cake and having it too. It hoped vastly to expand Soviet power by establishing friendly governments in a broad belt of contiguous countries; at the same time it hoped to persuade and cajole a shrunken capitalist world to assist in the reconstructing of the war-shattered Soviet economy. To achieve the latter objective, Soviet leaders intended to join an international security organization, to exploit the immense prestige won by Soviet arms in World War II, to play up fear of a Nazi resurgence, and to utilize the widespread hope of a new deal for the common man. They hoped to exploit also American fears of a postwar economic crisis. If the Americans and British refused to pay the high price of collaboration on Soviet terms, the Kremlin was prepared to revert to its prewar policy of outright ideological warfare against capitalism.

If one surveys Soviet wartime coverage of United States internal politics, it will be apparent that little attention was paid to the American domestic scene prior to 1943. A virtual moratorium on the class struggle interpretation of American politics prevailed. One striking indication of this fact was the almost complete disappearance of news concerning American Communism in the Soviet press. Even President Roosevelt's release of Earl Browder from prison was reported inconspicuously. It was made clear to the Soviet public that Communism was not an important factor in U.S. politics. In fact, a negative appraisal of the Communist movement in America was suggested by occasional quotations from leading Americans to the effect that the American people were in principle opposed to Communism. The Soviet newspapers for November 26, 1942, reported Averell Harriman's statement in London that the American people opposed Communism and understood that aid to Russia implied no change in American official opposition to Communism. The comprehensive Soviet reporting of Eric Johnston's visit to Russia in June and July, 1944, played down, however, Johnston's blunt warnings to Soviet leaders that exporting Communist ideology to America would sour United States-Soviet relations. The reporting of Johnston's and Henry Wallace's overlapping journeys emphasized the two men's optimistic statements about rosy prospects for postwar Soviet-American economic collaboration.

Even the official organ of the Comintern, *Kommunisticheski Internatsional* (abolished in June, 1943), made only infrequent references to the American Communists. These references, however, were couched in language conspicuously different from that of publications available to the broad Soviet public.

Typical of them was a review published in January, 1943, of Earl Browder's book, *Victory and After.* Signed by "J. Brown," it portrayed the Communist Party as leader of the patriotic forces in the United States and its opponents as members of the Hitlerite "Fifth Column." From this point of view it presented Browder's views on the domestic and foreign problems of America as a member of the anti-Hitler coalition. Being a capitalist country, America could not achieve the patriotism and unity enjoyed by the Soviet Union. Soviet patriotism grew out of a Socialist society; in America, unity could be "attained only by compromise between . . . capital and labor."

The review listed Browder's recommendations for achieving unity, including the establishment of a central planning authority to direct the economic phases of the war effort, and discussed the role of trade unions and the American Communist Party as the vanguard of all-out mobilization. It contained a long attack on so-called "appeasers," stigmatizing the Dies Committee as their leader.

Almost all of the attention paid by Soviet propaganda to American politics was devoted to the two major parties. Roosevelt and his supporters were presented as progressives, and received the lion's share of publicity. The conservative Republicans and the anti-Roosevelt Democrats were branded as reactionaries and isolationists, and prior to the 1944 presidential campaign were relegated to near oblivion. A more favorable view was taken of the Willkie wing of the Republican Party.

The criterion by which political parties, groups, and movements in the United States were judged was, of course, that of their attitude toward the Soviet Union, and particularly toward all-out military and economic support for the U.S.S.R. against the Germans. For this reason great stress was placed upon the problem of isolationism. A distinction was drawn between traditional isolationism, which the Soviets viewed as a petty bourgeois radical attitude, and alleged big business isolationism, which they branded as covert encouragement to Fascism. While this line was not openly or prominently manifested in the Soviet press until 1944, it was a subdued theme even in the first war years. *Pravda,* April 23, 1942, in reporting the Republican Party Congress in Chicago, emphasized the struggle between the "extreme isolationist" position of Taft and that of the Willkie supporters. This Tass dispatch was slanted against the Republicans in general and the isolationists in particular. It emphasized that the resolutions adopted at the Congress did not take a clear position on the necessity for the United States to fight the war to final victory or to assume definite obligations toward its allies.

Increasing interest was displayed during 1943 in American internal political problems. References to pro-Fascist elements in the United States gradually became more frequent. The Central Trade Union newspaper, *Trud,* played up the 1943 race riots in Detroit and attributed them to American Fascists. Only in 1944, however, did extensive and serious coverage of American politics begin. The Soviet propaganda machine was mobilized in support of Roosevelt and against Dewey. It proclaimed that Roosevelt's policy was that of a vigorous war effort and postwar collaboration with Russia. The Republicans, including Dewey himself, were accused of concealing big business imperialism behind a façade of verbiage about international co-operation. Ranged against the Republicans were the mass of the population, the progressive intellectuals and many influential businessmen who realized the necessity of Soviet-American co-operation and trade.

Typical of the numerous newspaper and magazine articles in this vein was one by N. Sergeeva in *War and the Working Class* for September 15, 1944, entitled "American Isolationism at the Present Stage." Sergeeva emphasized that there had been a sharp turn away from isolationism in the United States. Public opinion now realized that the safeguarding of American interests was a complex matter requiring an active international policy. However, isolationism was not dead. Since the isolationist wing of the Republican Party had been victorious over the Willkie wing, it had, in fact, acquired a new significance. Whereas throughout the war the isolationists had taken a defeatist attitude, now they were working for a "soft" peace for Germany. Powerful business interests, such as Du Pont, Ford, and others, took this attitude toward Germany because of their interests in the German economy. Sergeeva in this article attacked Senators Vandenberg and Wheeler and a number of other leading American political figures as anti-Soviet and in fact pro-Nazi. She declared that there were relatively few isolationists in the Democratic Party but that one could not overlook such important figures as Senator Reynolds.

The Soviet line toward American isolationists and alleged pro-Fascists was reinforced by warnings which began to appear in 1943 and 1944 regarding the danger of a third world war if the isolationist forces in the United States should gain control. One of the earliest of these was a very prominent report in *Pravda*, March 12, 1943, of a speech by Henry Wallace, who was quoted as criticizing numerous concealed and dangerous forms of isolationism, which if victorious might lead directly to a third world war. This anxious note was frequently reiterated in Soviet coverage of the 1944 American elections.

Despite its undertone of alarm the press during the campaign took on the whole an optimistic view of American political trends. It expressed confidence that Roosevelt would be re-elected and that his policies would be continued. It particularly emphasized the activities of the CIO Political Action Committee as indicative of the growing strength of progressive forces. An interesting and characteristic feature of the election campaign coverage was the publication of Roosevelt's speeches in whole or in large part, and the almost complete ignoring of Dewey's except when individual points were selected for direct or implied criticism.

On the eve of the election *Izvestiya* published a fantastic editorial, prophesying that the Republicans in desperation might be ready for an "adventure." It referred to alleged reports that the Republican "staff" was preparing a false attempt on Dewey's life which would be blamed on the Communists, and attempted to establish a parallel between this possible stratagem and the burning of the Reichstag by the Nazis. Like the famous Cairo rumor, this editorial gave a startling indication of the suspicion regarding the potential behavior of their allies which seems always to have lurked in the minds of the Soviet leaders. Moreover, like many statements or actions even during the period of the coalition war, it exemplified their tendency to project to foreign political leaders their own political morality. This editorial was only the most striking of a number of strange and disquieting notes sounded in the Soviet press regarding American public figures who dared to criticize Soviet policy. Another surprising one was the vicious Zaslavski attack on Willkie in January, 1944, for mildly criticizing Soviet policy toward Poland. Willkie had been a friend in Soviet eyes in 1942. In 1944, he was told to keep his nose out of Soviet business.

The Soviet press expressed satisfaction with Roosevelt's re-election, and in this connection took a hopeful view of the possibility of continued friendly American policy toward Russia, although it also issued warnings in post-election editorials regarding the continued strength of anti-Soviet forces in the U.S. A typical example of the Soviet reaction to the fourth term election was an article by Khavinson in *Bolshevik*, November, 1944, which viewed the triumph of the Democrats as a victory for the anti-Hitler coalition. The "Hitlerite brigands," said Khavinson, had staked their hopes on the election; they had counted on Roosevelt's defeat. They hoped that some of their "American advocates" would help to extricate them from their hopeless position. The attempt of the Hitlerites to use the American election to split the anti-Nazi coalition had suffered failure. Roosevelt's re-election was vivid proof of the will and determination of the American people to win victory and to organize a stable peace in alliance with the U.S.S.R. and Britain.

Khavinson attributed Roosevelt's victory to his attitude toward the U.S.S.R. He indicated by considerable detail the continued strength of isolationism and reaction in the Republican Party, pointing out at the same time, however, that progressive elements among the Republicans were growing stronger. He took a mildly favorable attitude toward such Republicans as Saltonstall, Austin, Ball, and a few others.

Two lectures delivered on July 28 and November 25, 1944,

by Doctor of Juridical Science Levin presented a somewhat more favorable picture than the press accounts of the American political scene and institutions. Levin's lectures, entitled "The State Organization of the United States," and consisting mainly of a description of the American political system, were largely factual in content and friendly but cautious in tone. In both lectures Levin commented on the American elections, but did not differ essentially from Khavinson. He made the usual attacks on isolationists, naming Hoover, Lindbergh, Hearst, and others. Mention of Hearst was characteristic, it may be noted parenthetically, in criticism of reactionary forces in the United States from 1944 on. Zaslavski earlier in the year had written two scorching editorials branding him as an agent of Hitler. Levin stated that the isolationists in America, whose attitude was really one of isolation from the freedom-loving nations, hoped to save Germany from complete defeat.

The most notable feature of Levin's lectures was his account of the American political system. This was surprisingly objective, although it stayed within the framework of Soviet ideology. He emphasized that the state organization of the United States was a striking embodiment of bourgeois democracy. Democracy, he said, had struck roots in the psychology of the average American. The man in the street had a deep aversion to any authoritarian form of state organization, such as fascism. There was no indication in Levin's lectures that any basic change was likely to occur in the near future in the American political system. He made no mention whatever of the American Communists. In discussing American political parties, he pointed out that they were not organized on class lines but that each party contained both reactionary and progressive elements. Levin also stated that boss rule was on the decline.

Levin naturally emphasized that Soviet democracy was superior to American because it was based on a socialist economy but echoed Stalin to the effect that differences of institutions could not impede growing understanding and co-operation between Russia and America. Levin's lectures probably represented the attitude of patriotic but relatively unpolitical Soviet intellectuals. Their optimism was certainly greater than that of the Communist Party leaders.

The 1944 line toward political forces in the United States persisted, but with increasingly pessimistic qualifications, until after the failure of the first London Conference of Foreign Ministers in September and October, 1945. This line presented American domestic and foreign policy as that of a progressive capitalist administration which was forced to contend against powerful reactionary forces seeking to change American policy. After the London Conference, the Soviet propaganda line more and more identified American government policy with that of the reactionary forces.

But though the distinction between American administration policy and the political hostility of anti-Soviet forces continued to be maintained after Roosevelt's re-election, there was a tendency, particularly after Roosevelt's death on April 12, 1945, to publicize increasingly the existence and activities of groups or persons who criticized or opposed this or that aspect of Soviet policy. These were considered by definition to be reactionary elements. The death of Roosevelt must have been a serious blow to the Kremlin and it certainly was to the masses of the Soviet people. With it came doubt in both the official and popular mind of the possibility of continuing even the arm's-length collaboration which had developed during the war.

The Russian masses were grief-stricken by the American leader's death. Many wept in desolation. Among them were some of my own Russian friends. Rightly or wrongly, the Russian common people, like their American fellows, felt they had lost a warm and generous friend. I think that they had a somewhat similar reaction to the death about a year later of their own "president" Kalinin, the only popular member of the Politburo, who was replaced by the colorless functionary Shvernik.

Now it should not be supposed that the hard men of the Kremlin shared the grief of the Russian masses. They had probably always viewed the architect of the New Deal as a far-sighted politician, trying to postpone the collapse of capitalism. Their interests and his had for a time coincided. He had served their propaganda as a symbol of democracy, which they astutely manipulated against reactionary forces. Even in death he was a useful instrument. Soviet propaganda reported his passing in a manner shrewdly calculated to suggest that an era had ended. He was eulogized as a champion of peace and democracy. Although brief accounts were published of his successor's career, and although Mr. Truman was identified as a Roosevelt man, the impression was given that a "wait and see" attitude would now be taken. Truman himself was expected to prove that he would continue to pursue progressive policies. It is interesting that although the Soviet government had decided not to send Molotov to the forthcoming San Francisco Conference Stalin changed his mind after Roosevelt's death. Molotov may well have been sent to the United States mainly to size up the new President.

As we have learned since the end of the war from an impressive body of sources, including articles or books by former Assistant Secretary of State Adolph Berle, and former Secretary of State Byrnes, and Robert Sherwood's *Roosevelt and Hopkins,* relations between Roosevelt and Stalin were seriously strained during the last months of the European war. Stalin's suspicion that America was plotting a deal involving a surrender of German forces in the West separate from those still fiercely fighting the Russians in the East, and his disingenuous attitude on the Polish question shocked and hurt Roosevelt. He had staked part of his place in history on the gamble that generosity and magnanimity would persuade Stalin to bring Soviet Russia back into the world community on equal and honorable terms. Who can say whether disappointment with the failure of this grand design did not hasten the President's death? And again, who can say whether, had he lived, he would not, warned by bitter experience and possessed of authority unique in world public opinion, have been in a much better position than his successor to set in motion the steps necessary to block Soviet expansion?

Warnings regarding the activities of anti-Soviet forces in

America sounded loud and shrill in the weeks following Roosevelt's death. During Harry Hopkins' final Moscow visit, Senator Pepper, Representative Coffee of Washington, and many others were quoted to the effect that American reactionaries wanted war against Russia. A little while later, Soviet journalists reported from San Francisco that the forces which Roosevelt had kept in check were regaining their influence. The pessimism aroused in the Soviet public mind by these reports was reflected in a statement of one of my Soviet friends: "Diplomacy is beginning again."

Soviet accounts of the American economic situation during the war evolved in a fashion strikingly similar to the reporting of American politics. Beginning on a large scale in 1944, in authoritative magazines such as *War and the Working Class* and *Planovoe Khozyaistvo*, indications were given that the inevitable tendencies of the American capitalist economic system held in check by the war were reasserting themselves. At first, articles on the U.S. economy were cautious and factual. Thus a review of some articles by John Dos Passos in *Harper's Magazine* on "America at War," published January, 1944, in *War and the Working Class*, confined itself to pointing out that tremendous economic and social changes had taken place in America as the result of the growth of a vast war industry. The review noted that millions of workers who had been unemployed for years had been brought into the economic process again. Millions of new workers had entered industry. New industrial centers had developed. The review stated cryptically that under American conditions all these developments had a "very peculiar character."

This article was followed in the next issue of *War and the Working Class* by a signed contribution by Professor A. Voskresenski on UNRRA in which the point was made that there was great danger of serious complications in reconverting the American economy from a war- to a peace-time basis. "The program of aid and reconstruction," said Voskresenski, "is one of the attempts of American ruling circles to avert or at least ameliorate the threat of a postwar economic crisis."

The problem of employing the industrial capacity developed in the U.S. during the war was discussed by the Soviet economist, S. Vishnev, in *Planovoe Khozyaistvo*, No. 1, 1944, in an article entitled "Technical and Economic Movements in the Industry of the United States During the War." Like most American economists at this time Vishnev believed that the postwar economy of the U.S. would face an extremely difficult problem in finding markets for capacity developed during the war. He argued that because of the reduction in labor costs which had taken place during the war, demand for labor would be much less after the war than before, if there was a return to prewar levels of production. This would result in the unemployment of millions of workers. Vishnev predicted that unemployment would become "the sharpest economic and political problem of the United States."

A good deal of attention was devoted by Soviet magazines and newspapers to various measures under discussion in the United States to deal with this threat. The trade union newspaper, *Trud*, August 30, 1944, published an article on "The Problem of Economic Demobilization in the United States," which surveyed bills before Congress dealing with reconversion problems. It took the position that progressive circles favored measures to deal with these problems which would protect the interests of the workers as far as possible. These measures were opposed by reactionary business interests more concerned with postwar profits than with popular welfare.

Soviet discussions of American economic problems pointed up the close connection between these problems and the possible line of development of American foreign policy. They maintained that America must choose between a reactionary course which would benefit only the forces of fascism and reaction, or a policy of economic collaboration with the Soviet Union. The latter would open up new markets and relieve the problem of unemployment. This concept was presented in numerous magazine articles in 1944. It first became a prominent feature of the daily press during the San Francisco Conference, when the second-ranking Soviet delegate, Dmitri Manuilski, advanced the argument that the only salvation for the American economy was economic co-operation and vast trade with the U.S.S.R.

Closely related to the general Soviet press treatment of American economic prospects was the prominence accorded to developments in the international trade union movement in 1944 and 1945. The conferences and other activities of the World Federation of Trade Unions were heavily covered. Soviet propaganda for a great world trade union movement was linked with that urging development of Soviet-American trade. Of course, the Soviet interest in the world trade union movement was more political than economic. Still Soviet propaganda sought to appeal to labor opinion in the United States by attempting to demonstrate that a pro-Soviet foreign policy would benefit labor by encouraging trade union organization interests and by assuring employment.

The foregoing analysis of Soviet opinion regarding American political and economic trends helps to explain why Moscow did not share the optimism of some American circles concerning the potentialities of a general international security organization. For if the other major members of this organization, America and Britain, were likely, as Moscow propaganda hinted even during the war, to revert to "imperialist" ways, prospects for an effective and harmonious international organization were certain to be precarious.

But the Soviet leaders could not afford to appear to be cynical or indifferent regarding international organization. Their own propaganda cast them in the role of the most sincere champions of peace and security. "One world" sentiment in America was a political factor which could not be ignored. Finally, an international security organization tailored so far as possible to Soviet specifications would be a useful instrument of Soviet policy. It would offer a highly respectable forum for promulgating and disseminating Soviet propaganda. Still more important, it could be used to prevent or hinder a renewal of the diplomatic and political isolation from which the U.S.S.R. had suffered throughout most of its history, the memory of which loomed nightmarish in Kremlin minds.

The Politburo's problem was achieving the advantages to be derived from international organization without surrendering other objectives which enjoyed even higher priority on its schedule. The latter can be summed up briefly as the expansion of Soviet offensive-defensive power and the whittling down of the power of potential enemies, a category which included all capitalist states.

Moscow's solution, somewhat oversimplified, was to talk cooperation and to act in the spirit of Communist power politics. While paying rather persuasive lip service to the principles championed by Cordell Hull, Stalin continued to act according to the strategy of Lenin. Unilateral expansion of Soviet power and the creation of a gigantic Soviet sphere of influence were accompanied by protests against Western projects for "blocs." Soviet tactics in this area were cunning but shortsighted and provincial. They were to bear bitter fruit in the postwar world.

Let us now survey Soviet wartime propaganda relating to international organization. The Soviet government was a party to the various United Nations or Anglo-American declarations regarding the desirability of setting up a general international organization after the war. It signed in January, 1942, the Declaration by United Nations. It helped to draft the declaration issued after the Moscow Conference of October, 1943, regarding the establishment of an international security organization to keep the peace after the defeat of the Axis. In general, the Soviet Union expressed solidarity with the war aims of the other allied powers.

However, Soviet adherence to these general aims and principles was cautious. It did not imply surrender of Soviet aims such as retention of the Baltic countries seized in 1940, which America did not approve.

After the Moscow and Teheran conferences, Soviet propaganda devoted increasing attention to the problems of organizing international security. At first, this subject was treated in vague general terms. Typical of such treatment was the editorial in the January 1, 1944, issue of *War and the Working Class,* which pointed out that as the end of the war approached, "problems of postwar organization" were becoming more and more urgent. The path to their solution had been mapped out at Moscow and Teheran. "This path," it went on, "leads to the establishment of a world family of democratic countries . . . prepared . . . to defend the cause of world peace and general security."

The most important and revealing of all Soviet press articles on this subject was one published by Malinin in the Leningrad literary magazine *Zvezda*, for April, 1944. This article was considered by well-informed members of the foreign colony in Moscow to have been written by a high official of the Soviet Foreign Office. It consisted in large part of a historical survey of the problem of international organization of security beginning with the Middle Ages. Most of this historical material consisted of a highly negative account of the work of the League of Nations. Malinin declared that the League had revealed its complete political incapacity, which was now obvious to everyone. After a complicated survey of the reasons advanced by many authorities as to why the League had failed, Malinin concluded that the main reason was the attitude it had taken toward the U.S.S.R. The League was "born in sin," said he.

Malinin emphasized that harmony among the great powers was essential for the success of a security organization. He set forth the main lines of what has become Soviet doctrine regarding the U.N., including the demand for a strong Security Council and the maintenance of full and unimpaired great-power sovereignty resting largely upon the veto power. Stalin, in his speech of November 6, 1944, and the Soviet delegates at the Dumbarton Oaks and San Francisco conferences presented as official policy essentially the same line as that set forth in Malinin's article.

Soviet propaganda continued throughout 1944 and indeed even after the adoption of the U.N. Charter in 1945 to emphasize the impossibility of organizing peace without great-power harmony and adequate recognition of Soviet interests; the press simultaneously furnished indications that Moscow intended to brook no interference with the developing Soviet program for Eastern Europe.

Symptomatic of this attitude was an article by Professor Boris Stein entitled "Regarding the Atlantic Charter" in *War and the Working Class* for May 1, 1944. Stein attacked American critics of Soviet policy, who, he argued, were seeking to apply the principles of a document drafted in 1941 to problems which had developed subsequently. In particular, he maintained that nothing in the Atlantic Charter or even in the Moscow Declaration of October, 1943, could be construed as conflicting with Soviet plans for the transfer of German territory to Poland.

Such articles as Stein's and the increasingly aggressive Soviet policies of 1944 which they defended, aroused fears in some American circles that Allied war aims were being jettisoned to satisfy a Soviet conception of security which seemed so demanding as to threaten the safety of other countries. For it was becoming apparent to experts in the summer and fall of 1944 that Moscow while eschewing direct attempts to incorporate alien peoples was nevertheless employing means ranging from secret police to cultural relations to secure the establishment of regimes controlled by Kremlin agents.

Moreover, beginning as early as December, 1943, when the Soviet-Czechoslovak treaty was concluded shortly before the Teheran conference, the Soviet press consistently gave a more impressive display to the growing network of treaties and other arrangements by which Russia was binding its neighbor states than to the prospective international security organization. The tendency to treat the prospects of a general international organization with reserve and to stress the value of bilateral pacts such as those concluded with Yugoslavia and Poland was particularly strong in the closing weeks of the European war. And while negotiating at San Francisco for the establishment of an international security organization ostensibly founded on the principles of the sovereign equality of nations, the Soviet government arrested in Poland sixteen representatives of the Polish government which was still recognized by the United States.

Soviet propaganda in the closing months of the war harped on two ominous themes. One demanded the "moral and political," as well as the military, destruction of Fascism. Although in principle this was acceptable to the Western democracies, the course of Soviet propaganda and policy has shown that actually it meant the establishment of Soviet satellite states. This meaning became fully apparent only after the war, but developments were already casting chill shadows before them in 1944 and 1945.

Also ominous was the demand contained in the May Day slogans published on April 28, 1945, for the further strengthening of the military and economic might of the U.S.S.R.

The promulgation of these slogans was accompanied by attacks on reactionaries in America and Europe. The Soviet press gave the impression that the microbes of Hitlerism were prevalent in both the old and the new worlds. This thesis was directed with special intensity against alleged pro-German elements in the United States and Britain.

Concurrently with emphasis upon these themes, particularly that of the moral and political defeat of Fascism, the press increasingly selected for its foreign affairs coverage material which implied or revealed differences between Allied and Soviet policies regarding the Polish, German, and other political questions. The lead editorial in *New Times,* June 1, 1945, entitled "Facing New Tasks," was symptomatic of the attitude toward the postwar world developing in high Soviet circles in the closing period of the war. The name of this militant journal was changed from *War and the Working Class* with this issue.

A new phase in history had begun, the editorial said. Fascism had been defeated but not slain. The "black forces of international reaction" which had produced Hitlerism had not lost all their strongholds. The "provocateurs of new international conflicts" were active throughout the world. The major role in working for a stable peace must be played by the U.S.S.R. and by the world working class. One of the important aspects of this editorial was that it emphasized the uniqueness and superiority of the Soviet economic and social system to that of the non-Soviet world. This theme, never abandoned entirely during the war, began in its closing months to be concretely illustrated by sharp polemical articles proclaiming the superiority of Soviet democracy to the bourgeois democracy of America and Britain.

Taken together, all of these themes indicated a tendency in Soviet propaganda, and presumably in the minds of the Soviet leaders, to revert to the prewar conception of two worlds in rivalry. At least they were significant straws in the wind indicating that the price which would have to be paid by the non-Soviet world for any sort of Soviet collaboration would be very high.

Further striking proof was furnished by Molotov's opening speech at the San Francisco Conference which evoked the shades of the Comintern in its warning that if the Conference did not reach agreement the governments concerned, except of course that of the Soviet Union, would be repudiated by their peoples. The U.S.S.R. would then find other means than the United Nations to assure the peace and security of the world. The threat implied here of returning to traditional Soviet tactics of international ideological war against the United States and Britain was to be uttered more openly in the fall of 1945. It became the embodiment of Soviet foreign policy in 1946-47.

In the preceding four chapters I have cited evidence showing how the rulers of Soviet Russia, reluctant ally of the capitalist West, clung stubbornly to fears and suspicions which Allied efforts failed to allay. By crafty dissimulation they partially concealed from an eagerly hopeful West their unwillingness to budge from their provincial but messianic dogmatism. Professed adherence to democratic war aims, sops to America's and Britain's desire for recognition of their war effort, and willingness to enter the U.N., fed Western hopes. Despite mounting anxiety, these hopes were still high in America as the war in Europe and in Asia drew to a close. They were to be dashed by the brutally aggressive course of Soviet policy and propaganda after the war. In the next chapter I shall trace briefly the highlights of the postwar Soviet reversion to a complete Leninist-Stalinist orthodoxy in thought and deed and explain why it took place.

PART THREE

Two Worlds in Rivalry

VI. Roots of Soviet Postwar Anti-Americanism

ON February 13, 1945, *Pravda's* lead editorial, entitled "The Historic Decisions of the Crimea Conference," stated that the "Crimea Conference again confirmed the fact that the union of three great powers has not only its historic yesterday and its victorious today but also its great tomorrow." On August 3, *Pravda* declared that the "successful completion of the Berlin Conference has strengthened the relations among the great powers." Following both the Crimea and Potsdam conferences nation-wide political meetings were held and it was reported that the "Soviet people unanimously approved" the conference decisions.

There is a striking contrast between the attitude toward the United States and Britain indicated by these statements and the position taken by Andrei Zhdanov, then next to Stalin the most authoritative theoretician of Bolshevism, in his address in September, 1947, at the meeting in Poland which established the Cominform. Here, two years after Potsdam, Zhdanov represented international relations as a bitter struggle between two camps. The U.S.S.R. and the "new democracies" were described as the leaders of the "anti-imperialist and anti-fascist forces." Ranged against them was the "imperialist camp" led by the United States, supported by its "satellites," Great Britain and France. According to Zhdanov the purpose of the imperialist camp was to "strengthen imperialism, to hatch a new imperialist war, and to combat socialism and democracy."

The thesis that the world is divided into two camps, one representing the rising forces of socialism and the other the decaying but aggressive forces of capitalism, has permeated all phases of Soviet propaganda and policy, both domestic and foreign, since the summer of 1947. It was formulated authoritatively, and with the utmost militancy, in Zhdanov's speech. Since then, it has been reiterated in all major official Soviet pronouncements, including the November 6 speeches of Molotov in 1947 and 1948, in Malenkov's address of November 6, 1949, and in several statements by Stalin himself. If anything, this thesis has been stated with increasing sharpness and urgency, although there have been tactical zigzags in presenting it to Soviet and world public opinion.

M. A. Suslov, in the speech delivered in his capacity as head of the Party propaganda department, on January 21, 1948, in connection with the 24th anniversary of Lenin's death, stated that "under postwar conditions the imperialists of the U.S.A. aspire to the role of world gendarme," and he also charged that "the American imperialists are clearly seeking to take the place of Fascist Germany and Japan. . . ." A year later the address for this occasion was delivered by P. N. Pospelov, the editor of *Pravda*. Like Suslov, Pospelov used somber quotations from Lenin to indicate the danger to socialist Russia and the "popular democracies" of Eastern Europe from the "imperialist beasts of prey." Marshal Vasilevski, Minister of the Armed Forces, reiterated these charges in his 1949 May Day order to Soviet troops. And Malenkov on the 32nd anniversary of the October Revolution asserted that the program of the American imperialists was more aggressive and ambitious than that of the Nazis and Japanese warlords combined.

With increasing Soviet-American tension and heightened emphasis in Soviet propaganda on the threat of American imperialism to the U.S.S.R., the Kremlin revived, although rather vaguely and cautiously, the threat of world communism. Thus Molotov in his November 6, 1947, address stated: "We are living in an age in which all roads lead to Communism." This line was emphasized in February, 1948, in numerous front page editorials and learned articles in the Soviet press celebrating the 100th anniversary of the Communist Manifesto.

The thesis of an all-out political, ideological, economic and cultural struggle between the two camps, between old and new, good and evil, the forces of the past and those of the future, has been elaborated in millions of words and communicated to the Soviet and non-Soviet public by every medium of expression, including the drama, the cinema, the other arts, and even as far as possible by the sciences. American foreign and domestic policy, institutions, and culture have been subjected to the most hostile, bitter, and contemptuous attack, the intensity of which, as Ambassador Smith pointed out in September, 1947, exceeded the fury of Soviet propaganda against Nazi Germany.

A striking recent example of this propaganda is the book by Annabelle Bucar, a former clerk in the American Embassy in Moscow, entitled *The Truth About American Diplomats.*[1] Written no doubt in part to counterbalance the series of exposés of Soviet life by Soviet defectors, the book is a virulent presentation, in the form of an alleged account of personal experiences, of the familiar Soviet charge that the American ruling classes and their official instruments are deliberately plotting the destruction of Russia in order to save decadent American imperialism.

Before proceeding to a detailed analysis and presentation of each main aspect of the Soviet anti-American propaganda campaign, it may be helpful to set forth briefly the main factors which seem to explain the shift from the coalition to the cold war.

Soviet policy and propaganda have been guided by the forces which have since 1917 shaped the attitude of the Kremlin toward the non-Soviet world. These basic factors have, however, operated under circumstances vastly changed from those of the prewar world. The reduction in the number of great powers and the acceleration as a result of World War II of revolutionary social changes have brought Russia and America face to face not only as two poles of power but as apparent champions of sharply contrasting world outlooks. These two coun-

[1] Published by *Literary Gazette,* Moscow, 1949.

tries, which before the war were in a somewhat peripheral relationship, have been plunged into a complex and difficult situation which makes each view the other as a threat to its security and even its state existence.

The American and Soviet approaches to this situation differ considerably. One reaction common to both countries has been an anxiety concerning lack of experience as a world power. This, although a minor feature, has led to mistakes on both sides and contributed to the general postwar confusion. Another and more important common denominator has been the obvious one of concern for national interests and security. But ideology, differences in historical experience, contrasting internal institutional structures, and geography have combined to make both sides analyze world politics differently. In general, the American approach has been pragmatic, tentative, even groping. It has been essentially defensive. American statesmen tended to assume that the political institutions and the norms of international politics to which they were accustomed would continue to exist indefinitely throughout the non-Soviet world. In contrast, Soviet policy has been expansionist and guided by rigid doctrines. The Kremlin continues to believe that politics both within and among nations reflects the ceaseless and relentless struggle of social forces. Its attitude is that one side or the other in this struggle must either increase its power or succumb.

The most obvious question confronting the student of postwar Soviet anti-American propaganda is whether it reflects Marxist doctrine or traditional power politics. While a good case could be made for either thesis, it seems to me that both factors have been synthesized in Soviet policy and propaganda. The main driving force behind the actions and utterances of the masters of the Kremlin is the desire to maintain and whenever practicable increase their power. But if these men are tenacious and effective power politicians they are also Marxist-Leninist politicians.

The Soviet postwar attitude toward the United States can be understood only if both its power-political and doctrinal aspects are kept in mind. Once Japan and Germany had been eliminated as great powers and Britain and France had been severely weakened, the Kremlin looked upon America as an inevitable rival and potential enemy. Of course, no matter what political institutions had existed in Russia and America the two countries would have vied for first place in a world in which such large areas were power vacuums inviting penetration by the two giants. However, it is difficult to believe that a Russia pursuing the objectives of the Tsars, for example, would so soon have found itself in so bitter a world-wide political struggle with the United States.

Long before Zhdanov's Cominform speech, quoted at the beginning of this chapter, Soviet official statements had indicated that the Kremlin continued to view the international scene through Marxist-Leninist spectacles. As early as August, 1945, Kalinin stated to a conference of Communist Party secretaries:

> But even now, after the greatest victory known to history we cannot for one minute forget the basic fact that our country remains the one socialist state in the world. You will speak frankly about this to the collective farmers. The victory achieved does not mean that all dangers to our state structure and social order have disappeared. Only the most concrete, most immediate danger, which threatened us from Hitlerite Germany, has disappeared. In order that the danger of war may really disappear for a long time, it is necessary to consolidate our victory.[2]

Molotov in his speech of November 6, 1945, stated that "as long as we live in a 'system of states' . . . our vigilance regarding possible new violators of peace . . . must not be relaxed." It is true that in this speech Molotov appealed for collaboration among the "peace-loving" powers, meaning the U.S.S.R., America, and Britain, but his reference to the "system of states" of course reminded his Soviet audience, particularly Communists both in Russia and abroad, of Lenin's famous prediction that as long as a system of states existed a series of terrible clashes was inevitable. This injunction was a typical

[2] Quoted from *Propaganda i Agitatsiya*, Leningrad, No. 18, 1945, p. 3. The speech from which this quotation is taken was also published in *Bolshevik*.

example of a common and shrewd Soviet propaganda technique; apparently harmless and noncommittal phraseology intended for the politically initiated reveals, like the visible part of an iceberg, only a fraction of the underlying meaning. Stalin's blunt restatement of the classic Leninist doctrine that capitalism leads to war in his crucial February 9, 1946, speech is too well known to require comment here. It should be pointed out, however, that this speech was the signal for the appearance throughout 1946 and 1947, and thus long before Zhdanov's Cominform address, of a succession of editorials and learned articles applying to international affairs the Leninist thesis that the whole present period of history is an era of the "general crisis of capitalism."

In terms both of power politics and of Marxist-Leninist doctrine, the international situation resulting from the destruction of German and Japanese power presented to the Soviet rulers dazzling opportunities which they felt bound to exploit. It must have seemed to them possible and perhaps probable that within a relatively short time Soviet influence would predominate throughout most of Europe and Asia. In Marxist terms, there was a "revolutionary situation" both in the war-devastated countries of Europe and in the increasingly restive semicolonial and colonial countries of Asia. Even during the war there had been straws in the wind indicating the Kremlin's awareness of the vast and increasing available opportunities for the expansion of Soviet power. A portentous indication of this was a statement in Molotov's speech in February, 1944, on the amendment to the Soviet constitution reorganizing the Commissariats of Defense and Foreign Affairs, regarding the significance of the U.S.S.R. for the "peoples of East and West." Another example of the "iceberg" technique, this statement reminds readers of Lenin of his "Better Less, But Better" essay, where he listed the proletariat of the West and the enslaved masses of the East as the "allies" and "reserves" of Soviet Russia.

The attitude taken by the British and American governments during the war, throughout most of 1945, and to a certain extent during 1946 must also have encouraged the Kremlin to believe in the possibility of a vast expansion of Soviet power. The concessions granted the U.S.S.R. particularly in the Teheran and Yalta conferences, and in some measure at Potsdam and at the Moscow Conference of December, 1945, must have indicated to the Kremlin that continued pressure, promises of collaboration, and skillful propaganda would assure them a relatively free hand for the realization of vast ambitions.

All this does not mean that the Soviet leaders approached the postwar world with rosy optimism. Neither their doctrine nor their temperament nor their experience fostered an optimistic attitude. There are abundant indications, both in the Soviet press material and public statements quoted earlier in this chapter and in the wary and suspicious behavior of Soviet leaders in international negotiations, that fear and mistrust of the capitalist "ruling classes" dominated their thinking. They certainly believed that Anglo-American capitalism, particularly what they considered to be the greatly strengthened American capitalism, would seek to maintain or expand its interests throughout the world. They were very suspicious, to mention only two examples, of alleged connections between large American corporations and German industrialists and of the increased interest of Americans in Near Eastern oil.

Above all, they viewed with deep anxiety the possibility that the entire capitalist world for the first time might be united under the "atom-dollar diplomacy" of an all-powerful Wall Street. This fear helps to explain their frantic opposition to all forms of international organization not under their control or in which they could not exercise a veto power. It impelled them to exploit short-run opportunities in the hope of bettering their position to cope with the long-run eventualities envisaged in Stalin's gloomy speech of February 9, 1946. Instead they have plunged the world into the cold war.

There were factors in the international situation, viewed in terms of Moscow's orthodox Marxist doctrine, which encouraged the Soviet leaders to believe that the Anglo-American capitalists would be greatly handicapped in resisting the expansion of Soviet power. One of these factors was the prestige of the U.S.S.R. resulting from its outstanding role in the war against Nazi Germany. Without in any way questioning the sincerity of the Soviet conviction that Soviet efforts and sacrifices had played a major role in defeating Germany and Japan, one cannot doubt that both the wartime second-front propaganda and the even more one-sided postwar Soviet presentation of respective Allied and Soviet contributions to the war were motivated by desire to exploit the prestige gained by Soviet arms. This prestige in the Kremlin's eyes was a weapon to force the American government to pursue pro-Soviet policies. It also served the purpose of concealing Soviet weakness and fostering the illusion of Russian invincibility at a time when the economy was disorganized and morale had been sapped by war-weariness and a glimpse of the Western world.

The interest displayed by the Soviets in the World Federation of Trade Unions, particularly in 1945 and 1946, reflected Soviet hope that the world labor movement would be an extremely powerful weapon of Soviet foreign policy. But the most important of all the international movements at the disposal of the Kremlin continued to be the Communist parties throughout the world. As early as April, 1945, an open indication of the Soviet Communist Party's intention to tighten discipline in the international Communist movement, a process which culminated in the formation of the Cominform, and subsequent measures, was given in Duclos' attack on "Browderism" in the French Communist theoretical organ, *Cahiers du Communisme*. The Teheran line, which had begun with the dissolution of the Comintern in 1943, allowing Communist parties a greater measure of freedom than in the prewar period, and above all permitting them to exploit for Communism the symbols of nationalism, now began, at first slowly and cautiously, to be revised.

The really decisive developments, however, in the process by which Moscow reasserted openly its domination of the world Communist movement came in the spring and summer of 1947 after the expulsion of Communists from the governments of several Western European countries. The postwar history of the world labor movement and of world communism was paralleled by developments in a whole series of Communist fronts. All of these Moscow-oriented international instruments have, at least in the Western world, if not in the Far East, proved to be wasting assets in the postwar period. This fact is one of the reasons for the closing of Communist ranks which took place in the summer and fall of 1947. The new form of "united front" tactics having at least temporarily outlived its usefulness, Moscow reverted to its traditional program of relying upon a tightly disciplined, highly indoctrinated Communist movement as, next to its own armed forces, its chief foreign policy weapon.

Another area, perhaps the most decisive of all, in which Moscow entertained high hopes for some time after the end of the war concerned the condition of the world capitalist economy. Problems of reconversion in America and Britain, particularly the expected unemployment of millions of workers, were expected to embarrass greatly the American and British governments in their struggle with the Soviet Union. Even more fundamental was the belief set forth in news dispatches, learned economic articles, and in Eugene Varga's well-known book, *Changes in the Economy of Capitalism as a Result of the Second World War*,[3] that an economic crisis of the 1921, not the 1929, variety would overtake the capitalist world within two or three years after the war's end. Varga's thesis, contained both in his book and in several important articles, particularly in his "Characteristics of the International and Foreign Policy of the Capitalist Countries During the Period of the General Crisis of Capitalism," published in *World Economics and World Politics*, June, 1946, was that the capitalist powers would probably be forced to pursue a relatively unaggressive policy toward the U.S.S.R. in the foreseeable future. This was the official Soviet line until the condemnation of Varga's book by a conference of economists in May, 1947, reported to the

[3] Moscow, 1946.

public in November, 1947, when the minutes of the conference were published as a supplement to an issue of Varga's journal.

The economists criticizing Varga accused the venerable economist of underestimating the seriousness of the "General Crisis of Capitalism" and of violating orthodox Leninism by admitting that capitalist governments could achieve some degree of economic stability and public welfare by a measure of "planning." However, if the problem of a crippling depression in the United States is viewed in the context of the general course of postwar Soviet-American relations, it becomes apparent that the Soviets must actually have been disappointed by the failure of the depression to materialize in time to permit its fullest possible political exploitation. It was not the weakness and decay of American capitalism but its surprising strength and stability which impressed them. It is very likely that Varga was condemned not for overestimating but for underestimating the strength of world, and particularly American, capitalism.

Among the benefits which the Kremlin expected to reap from postwar American economic difficulties were large credits at very low rates of interest. Stalin mentioned this possibility to the American Congressional delegations which visited Russia in the summer of 1945 and referred to it again in his answers to questions submitted by Hugh Baillie, President of the United Press, in 1946.

In another important respect, Soviet hopes appear to have been dashed. A primary objective of Soviet policy was, and still is, the military withdrawal of the United States from Europe. It appears probable that until late 1946 and perhaps even early 1947 the Soviets were confident that this objective would be realized. This aim was only the most important part of a general policy of depriving the capitalist powers of military positions which could be utilized to block Soviet expansion. The rapid demobilization of American military forces almost immediately after the end of World War II, and the "back to normalcy" attitude of American public opinion must have encouraged the Soviets in the belief that such American resistance to their expansion as they might encounter would be in the form of economic penetration rather than military force in areas in which Moscow hoped to install pro-Soviet governments. One among many indications that the Kremlin was thinking in these terms was its refusal of a treaty several times offered by Secretary of State Byrnes and by Secretary Marshall for a joint guarantee of the disarmament of Germany. Of course, the rejection of the Byrnes offer implied not merely the desire to eliminate America militarily from Germany but the even more radical Soviet desire to gain political and economic control of Germany as the key to Europe.

In general, the pattern which emerged from the winter of 1946-47 was one of Soviet expansion wherever feasible, with the Kremlin optimistic because the trump cards were in its hands. On the whole, Moscow's expectations seemed to be justified until the announcement of the Truman Doctrine in March, 1947, accompanied by a firm American stand on the German problem at the Moscow Conference in March and April of that year, soon followed by the Marshall Plan. Prior to this period, American resistance to the Soviet program had been relatively sporadic and ineffective. Moscow had retained the initiative. Nevertheless, America and Britain had clearly resisted Soviet expansion in such important areas as Iran and Turkey and had voiced displeasure about Soviet violations of the Yalta agreements in Eastern Europe. Moreover, they had forced the Soviets to make some changes in their program for the peace treaties with the former allies of Germany in Europe, which had been drafted after long wrangling in 1946 and signed in February, 1947. Finally, the United States, alarmed by the failure of the Soviets to carry out their pledges in Eastern Europe—which could be seen as early as the fall of 1944—had frustrated the Soviet attempt to install in Japan a type of control mechanism which would have permitted Russia to hamstring the American occupation authorities.

Beginning with the first serious American opposition to the Soviet program at the ill-fated London Conference of Foreign Ministers in September, 1945, Soviet propaganda had openly attacked what it referred to as "dangerous tendencies" in American policy. As this policy hardened, Moscow hurled charges that "reactionary circles" or "international reaction" were seeking to impose the will of Anglo-American capitalism on the U.S.S.R. and the "new democracies." In general, the Soviet line, until the announcement of the Greek-Turkish aid program by President Truman, was that there were two "tendencies" in international relations. One of these, represented by the Soviet Union, was held to be a continuation of the coalition policy of World War II. The other, represented by vaguely defined reactionary forces which were increasingly influential in Anglo-American policy, was the tendency toward world domination and the hatching of a new war. As we have seen, this formulation after 1947 was replaced by the theory of the two "camps," which stigmatizes the governments of America and Britain as open and fully committed agents of imperialism.

Soviet propaganda in presenting these themes has operated on two main levels, intended for two audiences. In part, its analysis of world politics has been presented in terms of Marxist-Leninist doctrine. At the same time, particularly in pre-Cominform days, Soviet propaganda has presented world affairs as a struggle between two groups of governments, one pursuing a normal, righteous, and democratic policy, the other an evil, cynical, and abnormal course.

The orthodox Marxist-Leninist line is intended for the politically initiated; that which pre-empts for Soviet purposes the symbols of Western democracy is intended to make the world believe that the Soviet Union is democratic in the sense in which this term is used in the West. It may appear superfluous to stress this point but it is actually of great importance. The Soviet leaders although intellectually committed to a doctrine of rigid determinism and ultimate cataclysmic revolution are forced to operate in an environment, even inside their own country, in which too open acknowledgment of the grim Marxist doctrine would be highly disadvantageous. Within the U.S.S.R., they simultaneously represent themselves as the agents of the "dictatorship of the proletariat" and as the elected representatives of the Soviet people, governing under the "democratic" Stalin constitution. Abroad they act simultaneously as the leaders of an international revolutionary movement and as the heads of an ostensibly normal constitutional national government pursuing a scrupulously correct course in international diplomacy. This calculated dualism is of course inherent in Leninism and is traditional in Soviet policy and propaganda. It has certainly yielded substantial political dividends. Even shrewd statesmen in Britain and America seem to have been led by the propaganda of Soviet "democracy" to offer less resistance to the Soviet program in Eastern Europe than they might have otherwise offered. It had still greater effect on public opinion in Britain and America, effect which for months after the end of World War II tended strongly to inhibit British and American leaders from admitting publicly that relations with the wartime ally were extremely bad.

Most of the foreign news carried in the Soviet press and broadcast over the Soviet radio is presented not in overt doctrinal terms but as supposedly factual accounts of relations among governments. It is made to appear that for some unaccountable reason the British and American governments are actuated by sinister motives and are continually rebuffing the sincere efforts of the Soviet government to achieve cordial good-neighborly relations. The masses, reading this selected and patterned "news," can be made to believe almost anything that the Soviet government wants them to believe about the politics of foreign countries. If news were openly editorialized, and used as illustrations for Marxist-Leninist theory, it would be less effective propaganda.

There is a very close connection between the general course of Soviet-American relations in the postwar period and the shift in emphasis in Soviet propaganda from the theme of conventional relations among the great powers to a Marxist-Leninist analysis of international relations since 1947, particularly since the beginning of the American policy of containment and rehabilitation of Europe, which has made it more and more apparent to the Soviet leaders that attempts to gain their ends by diplomatic maneuvering have produced diminishing returns.

Forced on the defensive by American policy, at least in Europe, even if only temporarily, the Soviets have more and more reverted to prewar policies of conspiracy and ideological warfare. This fact, incidentally, offers the most plausible explanation of the tendency, particularly manifest since the spring of 1949, to withdraw ranking party members from ministerial positions. It has apparently been felt that their efforts can more profitably be employed in party work, including direction of subversive activities, particularly in such areas as Southeast Asia.

This does not mean, of course, that the Soviets have lost interest in diplomatic and propaganda maneuvers in which they could profitably cast themselves in the role of peacemakers, menaced by the aggressive American imperialists. Threats and subversion having proved at least temporarily unsuccessful in Europe, the Soviets in 1948 began their "peace offensive" which has since continued and has been implemented by typically flexible Kremlin tactics.[4]

Several important aspects of the Soviet political system appear to intensify the influence of Marxist-Leninist doctrine on the outlook of the Kremlin. The existence of a totalitarian institutional pattern combined with an official creed of Marxism-Leninism tends to prevent the penetration of the Soviet official mind by ideas, facts, or insights which might alter the established pattern of thought. As far as can be determined by the most competent official or private observers, the government and party personnel responsible for informing the Soviet leaders about the politics of foreign governments and conditions in foreign countries report them in such a way as to confirm the preconceptions of their superiors, which probably in the majority of cases they share, having been subjected to the same pattern of education, training, and Draconian official discipline. Numerous Western diplomats and journalists, even during the

[4] The most comprehensive and illuminating analysis of Soviet policy and propaganda since the Truman Doctrine and the Marshall Plan forced the Kremlin on the "counter-offensive" in Europe is contained in an article in *Cahiers du Communisme*, for April, 1948, entitled "Les Fondements Théoriques de la Politique de Paix de l'Union Sovietique." This anonymous article smacks unmistakably of Moscow inspiration.

relatively friendly war period, were driven to despair by the dogmatic imperviousness of their Soviet colleagues to facts or impressions which did not conform to the Soviet propaganda line. In many instances this conformity reflects prudence at least as much as conviction, but in any case it is an integral part of the pattern of spiritual isolation in which Soviet Communists and government officials, and, incidentally, foreign Communists, have their being.

Indoctrination plus isolation helps to explain a curious phenomenon of Soviet propaganda to which one can apply the psychological term "projection." A particularly exasperating aspect of the Soviet attitude toward foreign countries and their governments is the tendency to describe policies and institutions in other countries in terms far more applicable to the Soviet leaders and their ways than to the foreign scene. The Soviet leaders project to the "ruling classes" and statesmen of foreign nations their own pattern of motivations and behavior.

Only by adopting this hypothesis can we understand fully their acceptance of beliefs about American life which hopelessly distort, though they are not entirely unrelated to, reality. The most massive of intelligence networks feeds Moscow a steady stream of impressions and stimuli. But facts are twice and thrice distorted before rebounding in the strange and wondrous shape of Tass dispatches, or *Pravda* editorials or Molotov's or Vyshinski's speeches. Distortion is guaranteed if facts are placed in the proper doctrinal framework. It is doubly guaranteed by the Soviet rulers' projection to American or other bourgeois leaders of their own political concepts in which domination rather than negotiation predominates. Reared in an atmosphere in which politics was largely conspiracy, and in which threats, shrewd bluffing, and cunning maneuver constituted the norms of political life, they interpret the actions of their opposite numbers abroad according to the same pattern. At the same time, of course, they present their own actions as the implementation of the lofty ideals appropriate to a socialist state.

Annabelle Bucar's *The Truth About American Diplomats* is a veritable compendium of Soviet projection of Kremlin motives and concepts to United States leaders. America's "ruling classes" are depicted as insecure men impelled by their anxiety to vilify the U.S.S.R. and plot its destruction. Their Politburo is Wall Street. Their agents, a small clique of officials and diplomats, conduct a foreign policy consisting of force, fraud and provocation. Their chief method of operation is espionage. Like their Soviet counterparts they pull the strings controlling public opinion.

Even minor details of the alleged American tactics described by Bucar have a pungently Soviet flavor. American personnel who make trips in the U.S.S.R. are accused of traveling solely for such sinister activities as ascertaining prices in peasant markets or observing railroad bridges. Americans are presented as working day and night to extract information from unsuspecting Soviet citizens. It is apparently inconceivable to the Soviet authorities that individual Americans might have been indulging their own private intellectual curiosity.

Now, of course, other statesmen than the men of the Kremlin tend to project their picture of their own social environment to situations where it is not applicable. Western statesmen and intellectuals who have equated their own democracy with that of the Stalin constitution have been guilty of the same error. But the Soviet leaders appear to be particularly susceptible to this tendency because of their isolation from the outside world and because of certain peculiarities of their doctrine, their personal history, and their mode of life.

Marxism-Leninism deals in broad general categories, in universals rather than particulars. It encourages its adherents to think in terms of "forces," "laws," and "classes," but not in terms of individual human beings. This kind of doctrine is most appropriate to absolute power, since it tends to justify sacrificing individuals to the group interest as interpreted by the ruler.

This highly abstract and schematic approach to politics intensifies the tendency of the Soviet rulers to project their own image to the outer world. It prevents them from exploring the minds of their foreign counterparts by the give-and-take of free discussion. Why discuss when the truth is known already, and foreign statesmen, by definition, are and must be agents of imperialism? The result is, paradoxically, that it is easy for the Soviet rulers simultaneously to condemn the enemy and still attribute to him unconsciously their own thought patterns, since, imprisoned by ideology and isolation, they cannot discover that others exist. Enclosed like the Tsars of medieval Russia within the Kremlin fortress, cut off from all normal human contact even with their own people, and working at politics twenty-four hours a day in a totalitarian system in which ruthless competition for power is unregulated by law, unmitigated by the influence of a free public opinion and unrelieved by the possibility of ever getting away from it all, these men have come to be pathologically preoccupied with their own and their regime's power and survival.

Thus the framework of Soviet institutions and the Soviet political atmosphere work to tighten the grip of Marxist-Leninist preconceptions on the Kremlin mind. The international political environment in which the Soviet state has developed has exerted a similar influence. The grim struggle of the U.S.S.R. for survival, particularly its narrow escape from destruction during World War II, has intensified the anxiety and suspicion with which the Soviet leaders approach international relations and has caused them to re-emphasize the Leninist demand for "vigilance" in dealing with the outside world. In doing so, they can appeal to centuries-old Russian memories of aggression by technologically superior foreign foes. The atomic bomb, re-emphasizing Soviet technical inferority, heightened the Kremlin's fear of America.

We must recognize that, viewed from the Kremlin, the world of capitalist states, particularly the postwar world in which there seemed a greater possibility than ever before of a united "capitalist international" opposing the U.S.S.R., looked uncertain and dangerous. But the Soviet attitude toward this world, combining bitter criticism of its unfriendliness with ceaseless and unscrupulous efforts to subvert it, has been highly inconsistent. Certainly the history of the U.S.S.R. does not indicate any tendency on the part of the Kremlin to moderate its demands in response to a relaxing of opposition to Soviet and Communist expansion. The Kremlin's emphasis on propaganda for world revolution was greater in the later 1920's, when there was no real danger of an attack on Russia by capitalist powers, than during the period of the Fascist threat in the 1930's. Moreover, never did Soviet Russia accord to any capitalist power as great a measure of co-operation as she offered to Nazi Germany during the Pact period.

It must be admitted that certain groups and individuals in public life in the West have displayed attitudes toward Russia as dogmatic and unreasonable as those of the Kremlin. Americans who belittled the efforts of the Red Army during the war or who have uttered bellicose and irresponsible threats against Russia since, have not only furnished Moscow with propaganda ammunition; they have confirmed Soviet suspicions and helped to put off still further the time of release for all of us from the prison of mutual fear. These persons, however, unlike the Politburo, do not have absolute power. They have been restrained by free discussion and the pressure of public opinion.

Therefore, while acknowledging that Soviet fear and suspicion are based partly upon a perfectly justifiable reaction to grim experiences with the capitalist world, I cannot agree with those who attribute them mainly to this factor and still less with those who justify them thereby. If there have been fears, there also have been Communist dreams of empire. Above all, there has been incapacity, induced by Marxist ideology and projection to foreigners of Soviet thought patterns, to meet the non-Soviet world halfway.

The foregoing paragraphs might give the impression that I consider the Kremlin mind incapable of rational calculation. This, of course, is not the case. The men of the Kremlin have continued in the postwar period their traditional mastery of the art of survival. Iran, Greece, Turkey, and Berlin have demonstrated the uncanny ability of Soviet leaders to press matters near but not quite to the breaking point. While this degree of Soviet rationality offers little ground for optimism, it does indicate continuance of that element of cautious realistic calculation which has distinguished Soviet from Nazi policy.

We have to consider finally one other extremely important motive for the Kremlin's anti-American propaganda, particularly that part of it which seeks to create contempt and loathing for American culture and life. This is the desire to reduce discontent among the Soviet people, particularly among intellectuals, by persuading them that Soviet culture and life are superior to the decadent, bourgeois West. This phase of Soviet policy and propaganda may well have prompted Winston Churchill's statement [5] that the Kremlin feared the friendship of the West more than its enmity.

The pursuit of this policy has required not merely depreciation of Western, especially American, civilization, but also the further reduction of the opportunities available to Soviet people for personal or other contact with American people or ideas. These opportunities were already extremely limited before the onset of the postwar Soviet paroxysm of xenophobic isolationism. This immuring of the Soviet mind was necessary for the fullest effectiveness of the postwar glorification of everything Soviet and the depreciation and vilification of everything American, including now even the area of science and technology, in which Soviet propaganda had previously acknowledged American equality or superiority.

The knowledge which Soviet people gained during and after the war of American prosperity, economic and technical strength and achievements through a variety of channels, among which the flood of American lend-lease supplies was perhaps most important, stirred inevitable unfavorable comparisons. The demoralizing effect upon many Soviet people of contact with American wares and ways was one of the strongest impressions derived from my four years in Moscow. It has been confirmed by a flood of material in the Soviet press denouncing "servility," and "kowtowing" to foreign culture, one of the main themes of the gigantic postwar Soviet cultural purge.

[5] In his speech at the mid-century Convocation of the Massachusetts Institute of Technology in March, 1949.

The wartime glimpse of the outside world aggravated what had always been a difficult problem for the Soviet rulers. In their capacity as high priests of a political religion they have for years promised their people that they were leading them to the earthly paradise of communism. A totalitarian elite by making such promises rationalizes to its own satisfaction its exercise of power. In this fact lies one of the causes of the smugly self-righteous attitude of the Kremlin, which can justify any and all means employed in pursuit of professedly noble ends.

But a social religion must ultimately be judged, if not by its priesthood, at least by its flock, in terms of fulfillment of its promises. One of the most solid facts of contemporary history is the failure of Soviet Communism to achieve its professed goal of providing the masses of the Soviet people with a rich and happy life. Even by the relatively modest standards of the Soviet people their lot has always been, still is, and will be for a long time, a hard one. Soviet propaganda, usually by implication, but sometimes openly, acknowledges that the good life is still in the rather indefinite future. It is significant that even Miss Bucar's chauvinistic book cautiously states that each Soviet citizen is assisting in creating a new era "which his children, and possibly he, will see." [6]

Soviet leaders have found it necessary to devote a great deal of effort in key postwar policy statements to explaining, minimizing or apologizing for the belt-tightening which is still the lot of so many Soviet people during the present period of "transition from socialism to communism." For example, Malenkov in his November 6, 1949, address presented as if it were an original discovery the argument that America owed its rapid economic progress under capitalism to its relative freedom from the devastating effects of wars. He went on to paint a black picture of a country with 14,000,000 unemployed suffering from worse conditions than those of the 1929-33 depression.

Malenkov's verbal and statistical sophistries can be easily refuted, though their outward plausibility may deceive the gulli-

[6] Bucar, *op. cit.*, p. 130.

ble. Even if his statistics were correct, his whole case collapses in view of the fact that the unemployed in America are materially and spiritually far better off than the semi-serfs serving as factory fodder in Soviet Russia. Arguments like Malenkov's recall to mind the statement often made by intelligent former Soviet citizens that whenever the Kremlin attributes an evil or a defect to a foreign country one can be certain it is present in aggravated form in Soviet Russia.

It would probably be difficult enough to live on slogans even if one believed that one's own country, however poor, enjoyed a better life than all others. But there is abundant evidence that many Soviet people have always suspected that life was richer, freer and more humane in Western Europe or America than in the U.S.S.R. This attitude was certainly intensified by what Soviet people learned during the war.

The Soviet leaders, with their already suspicious attitude toward America as the leading capitalist power, must have been alarmed and indignant with their people who displayed tendencies to admire Western life and culture. They were under an irresistible compulsion to eliminate what to them must have seemed a shameful and harmful attitude, and this they have done. They appealed to the national pride of the Soviet people to forsake friendship and admiration for the West. While their campaign has been in many ways crude and at times ludicrous, it has also been shrewdly calculated to appeal to the deeply rooted and partially justified feeling which has existed among the Russian people ever since they came in contact with Western peoples, that the latter were contemptuous and scornful of the Russians and did not appreciate their merits and capacities.

This campaign against Western culture is similar to but far more extreme than the measures taken often in the past by Russian rulers against foreign influences. The recurrence of this phenomenon is naturally disquieting, particularly since it is accompanied by the still more somber theme that American imperialism has replaced German Fascism as the main public enemy. However, the fact that the Kremlin feels it must resort to this tactic also permits us a measure of hope, since it indicates that now as in the past there are attributes of Western and particularly American life which have an appeal for the Russian people even if they arouse fear and aversion among their rulers.

One of the necessities of our policy toward Soviet Russia is to do everything possible to convince the peoples of the Soviet Union that the view of American institutions, life, and policy presented to them by their rulers does not correspond to reality. For, next to relative Soviet weakness vis-à-vis America, the most potent check on Soviet aggression has been and continues to be lack of enthusiasm for such a course among the Soviet people, who would suffer most by it.

VII. War and Peace

COMMUNIST leaders, beginning with Lenin, have always been almost obsessed by the problem of war and peace. Themselves the product of war and revolution, they have been imbued with the idea that conflict is the essence of human relations. Their doctrine envisages an end to this sad condition after universal establishment of the communist utopia under their auspices. But toward the world still unregenerated by the new faith theirs has been the attitude of self-proclaimed outlaws who believe that the existing state of society is one of war which will persist until it is changed by revolution and in which they can survive only by exercising a cunning and vigilance greater than that of their capitalist enemies.

All this is, of course, well known to students of Soviet communism. But it is only with this knowledge that one can understand why and how the Soviet Union conducts its "battle for peace." A rigid doctrine and a warped mentality compel the masters of the Kremlin to maintain this struggle. In its name they wage political warfare against the West. They justify their own aggression as defense and label defense against their own tactics as warmongering. Moscow is like the man who lifts the wallet from the pocket of another and shouts, "Stop, thief!" at the top of his lungs to distract attention from himself.

The war and peace theme serves many purposes of the Kremlin. It is a weapon of hope as well as of fear and terror. It is used to appeal to mankind's desire for life and happiness and to divert against Moscow's opponents and critics the righteous indignation of the masses, who are assured that the latter desire to turn them into cannon fodder. It serves to blackmail European statesmen whose efforts to strengthen the defensive capacities of their countries Moscow agents brand as provocative acts likely to arouse Russian wrath. Above all, it has been employed since the end of the war to discredit and distort American policy.

Moscow focused most of its postwar foreign affairs propaganda around the theme that American imperialism was plotting aggression. After a brief transition period necessary for canceling wartime directives and allowing memories of the coalition line to fade, America was assigned in the Soviet horror spectacle the role vacated by Nazi Germany. The foreign bogey and the spirit of evil, both necessary for Soviet tactics and both probably very real to the claustrophobic inhabitants of the Kremlin, were quickly found.

And so it is not surprising that thinly disguised indications appeared in Soviet public speeches and authoritative press articles in 1945 that the Kremlin did not share the rather optimistic expectations of British and American official and public opinion that a long period of peace would follow World War II. Some of these statements, such as Kalinin's talk to Party secretaries in August, 1945, have been referred to earlier.[1] The war theme, although still presented cautiously, became more and more prominent after the failure of the first London Conference of Foreign Ministers in the fall of 1945. Thus, for example, P. Fedoseev, then one of the leading officials of the Communist Party's propaganda department, contributed an article entitled "Marxism-Leninism Regarding the Origin and Character of Wars," to the August issues of *Bolshevik,* which by several months preceded Stalin's famous speech in which a similar theoretical analysis was presented.[2]

Fedoseev's article was really much more interesting theoretically than Stalin's speech since it not only presented in more

[1] Above, see Chapter VI, p. 107.

[2] *Bolshevik,* No. 16, pp. 31-60. This issue was released for publication on October 9, 1945. A simplified version of the same article was published in the mass magazine, *Propagandist,* No. 18, 1945.

detail the ideology of war touched upon only briefly by Stalin, but also included aspects of the subject which Stalin did not mention but which he as a good Leninist and, incidentally, as Fedoseev's ultimate superior must have approved. It began with a criticism of pacifism. Pacifism was harmful particularly because it suggested passive evasion of war and diverted the masses from active struggle against the organizers of aggressive war and against the conditions leading to war. It was a weapon of the bourgeoisie. Fedoseev emphasized the radical difference between Marxist and pacifist attitudes toward war. According to him, pacifists maintained that imperialists must be dissuaded from their crimes, but the Marxists emphasized that aggressors must be curbed and the conditions giving rise to imperialism eliminated.

Fedoseev then proceeded to a rather thinly disguised criticism of the foreign policy of Britain and other imperialist states, using many anti-British quotations from the nineteenth-century Russian publicist, Chernyshevski. In this criticism he presented virtually the same characterization of the nature of World War II as Stalin was to proclaim to the world a few months later. The Second World War had been an imperialist war for the redivision of the world in its first stage. But on June 22, 1941, it became a war of liberation. During the first stage, it was a war between those bourgeois countries which wished to seize the possessions of other bourgeois states and those non-Fascist states which already possessed extensive colonial markets and were satisfied with what they had seized long ago.

Fedoseev's analysis mentioned reactionary attempts to appease the Nazis at the expense of the Soviet Union and indicated that this was one of the causes of World War II. His article was certainly not calculated to inspire optimism, but it did not present a completely hopeless conclusion regarding the possibility of preventing future wars. Only the liquidation of "exploitation of man by man, and of nation by nation," he said, could assure the peaceful coexistence of states. But Leninism did not consider war inevitable even in the present state of affairs. War could be prevented if the "peace-loving nations" worked together, took effective measures against possible aggression and checked any subversive activities among the opponents of international collaboration. The struggle for peace implied the eradication of Fascism and its organizations and ideologies. Fedoseev took the position that the chief factor for peace in the postwar world was the Soviet Union. The stronger the Soviet state, the greater the chances of a stable and just peace. For this reason, Stalin had given the Soviet people and their armed forces the task of strengthening Soviet power in the interests of peace and against the aggressors and reactionaries.

Numerous other articles on the ideology of war, similar in tone and content to that of Fedoseev, appeared during the second half of 1945.[3] They were intended to prepare the Soviet public for a postwar continuation of the struggle between the Soviet and non-Soviet worlds. They doubtless reflected decisions and directives formulated still earlier but regarding which it was as yet expedient to remain silent.[4]

In the light of the foregoing, the furor raised in the American press by Stalin's February 9 speech and the series of similarly blunt reaffirmations of continued adherence to the Leninist doctrine on war attests to the then still poorly informed state of American opinion regarding Soviet policy. In this speech Stalin to be sure made a slight concession to the wartime coalition line by asserting, unlike Fedoseev, that World War II bore from its

[3] See for example, P. Chuvikov's article, "The Teachings of Lenin and Stalin on Just and Unjust Wars," *Bolshevik*, No. 7-8, 1945. See also *The History of Diplomacy*, Vol. 3, Moscow, 1945, blaming World War II on the policy of the Western powers. Cyril E. Black's review of *The History of Diplomacy* in *The American Slavic and East European Review*, Vol. VII, October, 1948, is a useful guide to its contents for those who do not read Russian.

[4] Interesting in this connection is Mikhail Koryakov's statement that the text of Stalin's speech to the plenary session of the Party Central Committee, in the summer of 1945, sounded like an "old victrola record": the old demarcation of "we" and "they" was again in evidence. See *I'll Never Go Back*, New York, 1948, p. 182. Testimony of reliable former Moscow hands indicates that Stalin as early as the fall of 1944 expressed to foreign diplomats the view that America and Britain were still "decadent" countries.

beginning, and not merely from the Nazi attack on Russia, an anti-Fascist liberating character. However, in explaining the origins of the Second World War, he declared that "Marxists have often stated that the capitalist system [of] world economy contains elements of general crisis and of military clashes and that in view of this fact the development of world capitalism in our time takes place not in the form of a smooth and harmonious move forward but through crisis and military catastrophes." Stalin went on to say that these cataclysms could be avoided if it were possible periodically to redivide raw materials and markets among countries in accordance with economic weight, and added, "but it is impossible to achieve this under present capitalist conditions of the development of world economy." [5]

Almost as striking as this restatement of the classical Leninist doctrine on war was Stalin's justification, in a curiously apologetic vein, of the rapid tempo of industrialization and collectivization in the U.S.S.R. on the grounds that this stern policy had been required to prepare the country for war.

It is interesting to note that Georgi Malenkov, one of Stalin's closest collaborators, placed particular emphasis in his election speech on this point. Malenkov declared that even Russia's "friends" would respect her only if she were strong. The weak, he said, are beaten.

Many other speeches delivered by the top Soviet leaders at this time were in similar vein. Kaganovich in his speech used the term "capitalist encirclement" for the first time in any major postwar official pronouncement. As befitted his role as representative of the U.S.S.R. in international diplomacy, Molotov stressed the desire of the Soviet Union for international collaboration and his country's need for peace.

It is clear from Stalin's speech, and from subsequent Soviet discussions of the problem of war which have adhered closely to the lines he laid down, that in the view of the Kremlin, there will be danger of war and of attempts to overthrow the Soviet

[5] Quoted from Russian publication of speech issued by *Moscow Worker* Publishing House, Moscow, 1946, p. 6.

system as long as capitalism exists in major foreign countries. A great mass of evidence in Soviet speeches and articles supports this statement. Moreover, the whole course of Soviet postwar domestic and foreign policy seems understandable only if we grant to the Politburo a sincere acceptance of this thesis.

Finally, the idea that the capitalist world desires the destruction of socialist Russia and will proceed toward this destruction if it dares, underlies discussion of such basic problems as the nature of the Soviet state. With regard to the problem of the continued existence of the state in the Soviet Union there have been numerous articles such as that of A. Lyapin, "Regarding the Gradual Transition from Socialism to Communism," and that of F. Oleshchuk, "Communism: the Aim of Our Struggle."[6] These reiterate the thesis that as long as the capitalist world exists, "bandit attacks" on the Soviet Union are possible. They also represent an elaboration on Stalin's rather strange theory set forth in his 1939 speech to the eighteenth Party Congress that even when "communism" has been achieved in the U.S.S.R. a state fully equipped with the apparatus of compulsion will continue to exist in the U.S.S.R. if capitalism still exists outside Russia.

The discussion in the U.S.S.R. of the capabilities and intentions of capitalist countries also revolves largely around the question of war. Both the Varga group and its now victorious critics accepted the axiom that the continued existence of capitalism threatens war against the U.S.S.R. They differed mainly in their estimate of the imminence and intensity of the war threat.

It is impossible to discuss the question of war in Soviet thinking without touching also on the problem of revolution. As "Historicus" has demonstrated in an exhaustive analysis of Stalin's works, it seems clear that Stalin has, at least since 1917, believed in the ultimate fulfillment of the Leninist idea of world revolution.[7] Beginning in the summer and fall of 1946,

[6] Both were published as periodical articles and as separate pamphlets in 1946.

[7] See Historicus, "Stalin on Revolution," *Foreign Affairs*, January, 1949.

the Soviet press published a considerable number of articles which touched, usually cautiously and indirectly, upon the relationship between revolution and socialism in the U.S.S.R. and in other countries. For example *Pravda* for October 12, 1946, carried a review by P. Yudin of Stalin's series of articles "Anarchism or Socialism?" under the title "An Outstanding Contribution to the Treasury of Marxism." Yudin directed his attention particularly to an attack on Western European socialists for their lack of revolutionary spirit. These socialists, he charged, were pursuing a policy of defending capitalism. Yudin emphasized the importance of the state both in Russia and in bourgeois countries in connection with the problem of revolution. If the "disorganized" capitalist system resisted the attack of the proletariat, this was because the capitalist order was defended by the capitalist state. Yudin asserted that in the present period the role of the bourgeois state as the servant of the capitalist monopolies manifested itself with particular force. His article raised the question of revolutionary struggle by the proletariat although only in the form of praise to Lenin and Stalin for teaching that the political struggle of proletariat revolutionary powers would lead to victory. In a lecture which he delivered at about the same time Yudin pointed out that the United States and Britain were no exception to the rule that the replacement of capitalism by socialism must take place by revolution.

Pravda, for November 4, 1946, published an article by D. Shepilov, entitled "A New Era in the History of Humanity," as part of the annual propaganda build-up for the anniversary of 1917. The October Revolution, said Shepilov, had "universal historic significance." It had begun the social transformation of the world and put an end to the "boundless domination of imperialism." The problem of socialism was now on the agenda in many countries of Europe. He quoted Lenin as follows: "Precisely when, or within what period, the proletarians of this or that nation carry the matter to a conclusion is not an essential question. What is essential is that the ice is broken, the path is open, and the direction has been indicated."

Shepilov's article set forth in condensed and sharp form the propaganda line which Zhdanov was to develop in his dreary November 6 oration two days later. According to this line, the Anglo-Saxon powers were attempting to turn the countries of Europe into appendages. As the decay of their own internal life proceeded, their attempts to poison certain strata of the Russian people with the "rotten venom of intellectual indifference, pessimism and amorality" became all the more insistent.

As indicated above, Zhdanov's speech emphasized that as a result of World War II the forces of world socialism had become stronger. In his November 6 speech, as well as in his August speech to the Leningrad writers, the opening gun in the postwar cultural purge, Zhdanov charged that the imperialist powers, feeling their position weakened because of the increased strength of the U.S.S.R. and the Communist parties, had unleashed an ideological offensive designed to sap the faith of the Soviet people in their socialist institutions.

The most militant statements regarding the world struggle of socialism and communism and implying the inevitability of world revolution have come since Zhdanov's Cominform speech and Molotov's November 6 address in 1947. In this latter speech Molotov declared:

> Today the united forces of democracy and socialism in Europe, and outside Europe, together are incomparably stronger than the opposing anti-democratic camp of imperialism.
>
> Capitalism has become a brake on human progress, and the continuation of the reckless policy of imperialism, which has already brought about two world wars, constitutes the major danger to the peace-loving nations. The Great October Socialist Revolution has opened the eyes of the nations to the fact that the age of capitalism is drawing to a close and that reliable roads have been opened to universal peace and the great progress of the nations. The feverish efforts of the imperialists, under whom the ground is giving way, will not save capitalism from its approaching doom. We are living in an age in which all roads lead to communism.

The propaganda line set forth here has been followed ever since. From time to time it is stated in a slightly more militant fashion. P. Yudin, writing in the magazine *Party Life*, February, 1948, stated in connection with the 100th anniversary of the Communist Manifesto that "by its very nature capitalism has an international character. The struggle against it can end only when capitalism has been destroyed in the entire world. The American and English imperialists by force of arms support the capitalist system wherever they can. This once again demonstrates that the working class of various countries conducting a struggle against their national bourgeoisie must always remember their international obligations also."

Yudin's statement obviously implies a connection between the "struggle" of national Communist parties and the struggle between the Soviet Union and the imperialists. This connection has been still more forcefully emphasized in articles in the Soviet press since the break between the Kremlin and Tito. A number of articles have quoted the pertinent statement of Stalin that "the international connections of the working class of the U.S.S.R. with the workers of capitalist countries, the fraternal union of the workers of the U.S.S.R. with the workers of all countries is the cornerstone of the strength and power of the Soviet republic." [8]

The article by V. Burdzhalov in the September 15, 1948, issue of *Bolshevik* bristled with phrases about "proletarian internationalism" and "world revolution." It concluded as follows: "The great historical experience of the Bolshevik Party is a guide for the activity of the Communists and working people of all countries. This is the inexhaustible source of the victories of international communism."

A great number of similar statements regarding the inevitability of the victory of world communism in its struggle against world capitalism have been published subsequently. This theme was treated with particular emphasis in connection with the 25th anniversary of Lenin's death in 1949. Pospelov,

[8] This passage from Stalin's *Voprosy Leninizma*, was quoted in an article by V. Burdzhalov entitled "On the International Significance of the Experience of the Party of the Bolsheviks," in *Bolshevik*, No. 17, September 15, 1948.

editor of *Pravda*, who delivered the major address on this occasion, expressed unusual optimism regarding the triumph of world communism. He quoted Lenin to the effect that the issue of the struggle between the two systems would be determined by the fact that Russia, India, and China constituted the overwhelming majority of mankind, and that communist victory in China indicated that this majority has matured with extraordinary speed in the struggle against capitalism. Pospelov made the arresting prediction that the twentieth century would see the complete triumph of Leninism. Still more significant is the fact that *Pravda's* editorial for January 21, 1949, quoted Stalin's famous oath to continue the work of Lenin, including a sentence pledging loyalty to the principles of the Comintern.

A little later, the magazine *Soviet Book* [9] quoted a number of statements from Stalin's works of 1926-27 to the effect that the final victory of socialism necessitated overthrowing the world bourgeoisie and that this could only be achieved by cooperation between the working class of the U.S.S.R. and the proletariat of all other countries. The article in *Soviet Book*, devoted primarily to events in China, emphasized that the experience of the U.S.S.R. could be used to advantage by the Chinese proletariat. The article made clear that this was as true today as in the period when Stalin had discussed this question during the revolution in China in 1926-27, and pointed out also that the close links between the U.S.S.R. and Communists abroad applied not only to China but to the whole world.

Two conclusions emerge from our discussion of Soviet theory on war and revolution. One is that a world movement toward communism is regarded by Moscow as inevitable and desirable. The other is that danger of war between the capitalist powers and the U.S.S.R. arises, according to Soviet theory, because the capitalists resist the progress of the world toward socialism and communism. Does this mean that in the opinion of the Kremlin war is inevitable? It is impossible, of course, to answer this question with categorical assurance. It seems to me that the

[9] February, 1949, pp. 3-14.

Politburo regards war as highly probable but not necessarily inevitable. If the forces of socialism are so strong that the imperialists are afraid to attack them, then there is a possibility that war may be avoided.

In other words, capitalism generates war and Soviet socialism generates peace. This is the theoretical basis of the whole Soviet approach to the problem of war and peace. Abundant evidence can be cited in support of this interpretation. Zhdanov, in his Cominform address and a vast volume of learned articles elaborating thereon, argues that the mobilization of the "forces of peace," of the Communist parties, and of the "progressive forces" of the world could present so mighty a front that the imperialists would not dare to go to war. Molotov in his November 6, 1947, speech expressed ironic confidence that the imperialists would not be so foolish as to hasten their own downfall by an adventurous policy. An interesting implied expression of this general thesis was contained in Molotov's reply to Ambassador Smith's note of May, 1948, regarding Soviet-American relations. Molotov rejected the American government's criticism of policy in Eastern Europe, maintaining that the social changes which had taken place in the East European countries were valuable because they rendered a new war less likely.

The problem of whether war is inevitable is only one of the baffling and difficult questions connected with the Soviet theory of war. There is an even more fundamental question. Do the Soviet leaders really believe that the United States government is pursuing a policy leading toward war? In other words, is the whole fanfare in the Soviet press and in statements by Soviet leaders about the "aggressive" American policy an expression of sincere opinion based on analysis or is it merely intended for internal consumption to lash the Russian people on to greater effort in "socialist construction"? Unfortunately, it seems to me that we must credit the Soviet leaders with a considerable measure of sincere belief in the thesis that war is likely between what they regard as antagonistic social systems. However, a distinction should probably be drawn between short-run and long-run expectations. The implications of Stalin's major speech referred to above were that there would be a period during which the Soviet Union could carry out three or more Five-Year Plans and become so strong that it could prevent or win a future war. But if Soviet leaders foresaw a considerable period of uneasy peace following World War II, why did they begin to warn their people that powerful forces in the United States and Britain, and later the governments themselves, were plotting war against them?

It is very difficult to answer this question. However, the most likely answer would seem to be as follows. Approaching the question in their doctrinaire fashion, the Soviet leaders considered it necessary to begin immediate energetic preparations for long-run contingencies. Thinking of politics as they do in military terms, they drew up plans to deal with the worst possible contingencies.[10] The pursuit of this policy had important consequences both inside and outside the Soviet Union. Inside Russia it was necessary to begin immediately after the war to remind the Soviet people that the war danger had not been eliminated by the defeat of Germany and Japan. It was also necessary to conduct the vast postwar mobilization of all spiritual and intellectual forces behind the postwar Five-Year Plans and in general to create an atmosphere of tension. These domestic policies were accompanied by a foreign policy which preached peace and collaboration but practiced expansion and consolidation of the results of expansion. Accustomed to conducting the affairs of the U.S.S.R. according to long-range plans which met with no opposition, the Soviets probably made psychological mistakes in carrying out their foreign policy planning. They forgot that their aggressive measures would arouse opposition among peoples accustomed to free discussion and possessing a free press. It seems probable that their policy aroused a degree of opposition, in America especially, which they had not expected would so soon develop.

This last factor would appear to be responsible for the almost

[10] For penetrating observations on this characteristic of Soviet policy, see Nathan Leites and David Nelson Rowe, "Choice in China," *World Politics*, April, 1949.

hysterical note which came into Soviet propaganda in the months following the organization of the Cominform. If this factor is kept in mind, the postwar Cominform thesis that the policy of the United States became exceedingly aggressive after World War II can be better understood. Gloomy as the 1946 Soviet line was, it was nevertheless calm and objective in comparison with the post-Cominform line. Incidentally, the apparent surprise in the Kremlin occasioned by the perfectly logical American reaction to the Kremlin's own policies indicates how treacherous are the occult powers of prediction which Soviet leaders claim through their mastery of Marxism-Leninism.

Thus far I have been discussing mainly the theory underlying the Soviet attitude toward the problem of a third world war. This discussion, of course, does not exhaust the subject. While operating on the basis of doctrines which prejudge the question, the Soviets at the same time proclaim in their propaganda that their opponents are so acting. It is perfectly understandable that they should do so, for if it is true, as they apparently believe, that the capitalists are eventually going to attack them, it becomes necessary to take appropriate countermeasures. It is essential not only to mobilize their own people and Communist supporters throughout the world but also to lull the suspicions of as large a portion of foreign public opinion as possible. It is desirable to prove to Soviet and world public opinion that the capitalist governments are aggressive and that the Soviet government believes in the possibility and desirability of peace and good-neighborly relations. This is the line which the Soviet leaders have been broadcasting to the world since the war.

The clearest postwar presentations of this thesis were Stalin's statements to a *Pravda* correspondent following Churchill's Fulton speech in 1946 and Vyshinski's "warmongering" speech at the United Nations General Assembly in September, 1947. But there have been many other similar statements by Stalin himself and by other Soviet leaders. It is highly significant that Stalin, although he has not made any major public speeches in the postwar period since his 1946 pre-election speech, has dealt so many times with this question of war or peace in answers to questions from Soviet or foreign newspapermen.

The line taken by Soviet leaders in these professions of peaceful intentions has been that the difference in social systems should cause no trouble in the Russian-American relations. Stalin was asked by Alexander Werth in September, 1946, whether with the further advance of the Soviet Union toward communism, the possibilities for peaceful collaboration with the outside world would not decrease. Stalin replied that he did not doubt that the chances for peaceful collaboration would not decrease but could even increase. In his interview with Harold Stassen in April, 1947, Stalin stated that there could be no doubt about the possibility of collaboration between the United States and Russia. He emphasized that if both sides desired to work together, collaboration would result. He stated that the U.S.S.R. could have collaborated with Germany but the Germans did not wish it. This was not a question of political regimes or even of social systems. After all, Stalin went on, the United States and the U.S.S.R. had collaborated during World War II although they had different social systems, but the United States and Germany, which had the same social systems, had fought each other.

What Stalin did not say was that the whole logic of Marxist-Leninist analysis of capitalism, as presented either openly or by implication in the main stream of Soviet postwar propaganda, and as taught in all Soviet educational institutions, is that by their very nature the capitalists cannot and do not wish to collaborate. The fact that he compared Nazi Germany and the United States as he did in his interview with Stassen indicates that he had in mind this crucial reservation regarding the possibility of collaboration.

Closely connected with the Soviet line regarding collaboration is the thesis of the "coexistence" of socialism and capitalism. This thesis has been set forth in such basic postwar Soviet documents as Zhdanov's and Malenkov's speeches at the founding of the Cominform as well as in the Stalin-Stassen conversation. Zhdanov in his Cominform speech said that Communists proceeded on the assumption that this coexistence would last for a long period. Of course, this is a very vague formulation. One could interpret it optimistically only if it were supported by the context of Soviet ideology and propaganda, but unfortunately this is not the case. Therefore, it must be assumed that it is part of the propaganda of deception. This still does not mean that the Kremlin disbelieves in the possibility of a considerable period of coexistence, possibly even with some sort of mutually advantageous relations between Soviet Russia and capitalist countries.

The expression of a desire for collaboration and the thesis of coexistence are the basic ingredients of the Soviet tactic of the "peace offensive." The peace offensive is neither new in Soviet policy nor is it a uniquely Soviet weapon. It was one of Hitler's favorite devices. The Soviet tactic discussed in the preceding chapter of utilizing the symbols of Western democracy and liberalism for Communist purposes logically includes the peace offensive weapon. It is probably inaccurate to apply the term "peace offensive" to such specific Soviet maneuvers as the publication of the Smith-Molotov exchange in 1948, the unsuccessful Soviet campaign during 1949 for a five-power "Peace Pact," or the series of Communist "peace" congresses held abroad. These are, rather, unusually dramatic manifestations of a general propaganda line. In making such moves, the Kremlin relies on the fact that thousands of people will read of Stalin's bids for peace while only a handful of government officials and scholars read the basic documents of Marxism-Leninism.

During 1948 and 1949 the "peace offensive" tactic was supplemented by what might be called a peace mobilization. The most conspicuous manifestations of this tactic were the "cultural" and "peace" conferences held in Wroclaw, New York, Paris, Prague, and elsewhere. Their purpose was to exploit the desire of Western intellectuals for peace and at the same time to prove to Soviet intellectuals that their "progressive" counterparts abroad supported the Soviet government's "peace" policy. While attempting to mobilize Western intellectuals against alleged warlike policies of their governments, the Soviets in the spring of 1949 simultaneously alerted foreign Communists. Leaders of the Party in many countries, including the United States, promptly stated that they would side with the U.S.S.R. in the event of war between Russia and their own countries.

In connection with the lifting of the Berlin blockade a new phase of Soviet peace strategy began. The most striking indication of this was the inclusion in the May Day slogans for 1949, repeated in those for November 6, of an appeal to the "peoples" of the United States, Great Britain and Russia to work for peace. It would appear that the Kremlin calculated on turning the Berlin defeat into a propaganda victory, for if subsequent events developed to its satisfaction, it could represent them as the result of its peace policy, but if they proceeded unsatisfactorily it could seek to prove to the American, British and Soviet publics that its peace policy was being rebuffed by the Anglo-American imperialists.

Closely connected with these propaganda tactics has been the Soviet insistence that Moscow has adhered to the Teheran, Yalta, and Potsdam decisions. This theme is used not only to exploit the universal world-wide desire for peace but also to underscore the Soviet thesis that the policy of the Western allies has changed since these decisions were taken, while that of the U.S.S.R. remains, as always, one of peace and co-operation. In presenting to its own people the thesis that Russia desires peace but her efforts are constantly being rebuffed by capitalist governments, the Soviet leadership effectively employs censorship. The Soviet people are never permitted to guess that the alleged warlike actions of foreign governments could be defensive reactions to Soviet aggression. Such Allied countermoves as the bringing of the Iranian case before the U.N. Security Council, the Berlin air-lift, or American rearmament, have been treated by the Soviet press as expressions of a hostile and provocative policy. No explanation was given to the Soviet people of Soviet demands on Iran, of the failure to carry out the provisions of the Potsdam agreement regarding German economic unity, or the whole series of Soviet actions which have alarmed the American government.

Against this background of a Soviet peace policy Moscow presents to its people and to the world a contrasting and horrifying picture of hostility, provocation, espionage, and warmongering on the part of the United States. The volume of these accusations is so staggering that they can only be suggested. A few typical examples suffice to indicate their character. A Soviet handbook on the United States, published in 1946, and very mild in tone compared to post-Cominform statements, commented on American military policy as follows:

> Appropriations for the Army and Navy constituted more than half of the entire budget and a tendency to increase them was manifested. Large armed forces were kept in being and, for the first time in the history of the U.S.A., a law on compulsory military service continued to exist. A substantial part of the war industry was also preserved. The brandishing of arms was particularly manifested in the uninterrupted production and testing of atomic bombs and in the keeping of the secret of their production. And after the termination of the war the U.S.A., striving for world domination, not only did not liquidate its military strategic bases which it had established throughout the entire world, but expanded and strengthened them more and more, even on the territory of its allies. Despite the requests of the latter, the U.S.A. did not withdraw its troops, which were present, in the summer of 1946, in 53 countries, most of them allies.[11]

Stalin's 1946 May Day order to the Red Army asserted: "We should not forget for a single minute the intrigues of international reaction, which is hatching plans for a new war." With increasing and indeed monotonous frequency the Soviet press throughout 1946 asserted that American policy was falling more and more under the control of advocates of world domination and a third world war. The November 6 slogans called upon the working people of all countries to "expose and embarrass the instigators of a new war who are sowing discord among nations and intimidate the peoples of the world with the phantom of a new war." As I pointed out in Chapter III,

[11] *Soedinennye Shtaty Ameriki*, Moscow, 1946, p. 317.

these slogans together with major policy declarations such as the annual November 6 oration, lay down the main lines of Soviet propaganda. The slogans for 1947, which have been repeated since on November 6 and May Day, were even sharper. They called upon the workers to "expose the aggressive schemes of the inflamers of a new war."

The distinction between the 1946 and subsequent slogans on the question of war is important. In 1946, and indeed until the organization of the Cominform, the imperialists were charged with utilizing the bogey of a new war in order to slow up the demobilization of armed forces in their countries, and as a weapon of international blackmail against "weak-nerved" politicians whom the Anglo-Americans were attempting to enroll in an anti-Soviet front. But since the Cominform, the governments themselves and not merely certain reactionary groups are accused of actively preparing for war. This thesis was expressed in the various documents connected with the establishment of the Cominform, and most aggressively in Vyshinski's major address to the U.N. in September, 1947.

The charges and warnings have been illustrated and made convincing to the Soviet public by a steady stream of Tass news items, reports of U.N. speeches by Soviet delegates and "international surveys" on such subjects as American overseas military bases, the unco-operative attitude of the United States toward Soviet proposals for arms reduction and prohibition of atomic weapons, the growth of militarism in the United States, and other topics concerned with American military policy and diplomacy.

Despite the melting away of American armed strength in the months following the end of the war in the Pacific, the Soviet press in the winter of 1945 and the spring of 1946 devoted extensive and disproportionate coverage to American military activity throughout most of the world. Particular attention was given to the problems of American military, naval, and air bases, and to the presence of American or British armed forces in the territory of former allied states. As early as October and November, 1945, the press treatment of American official statements or actions in the sphere of military policy was calculated to arouse uneasiness in the mind of the Soviet public. All Soviet daily papers prominently and extensively reported President Truman's Navy Day speech but omitted his assurances regarding the peaceful character of American policy, and his statement that American possession of the atomic bomb did not constitute a threat to any nation. Early in November, 1945, the press guardedly but unmistakably indicated Soviet uneasiness regarding American negotiations for air bases in Iceland, which it indicated were opposed by the Icelandic public. At the same time, it gave prominence to a House Naval Affairs Committee resolution advocating American acquisition of a number of bases in the Atlantic and the Pacific.

Thus a pattern was established which assumed sharper outline in 1946. This consisted of suggestions to the Soviet public in a steady stream of news items and signed articles that the United States was attempting to hem in the Soviet Union by a ring of bases designed as springboards for attack. This pattern has been particularly prominent since June, 1946, when the historian Eugene Tarle, in his article "Lessons of the War," traced a pre-aggression fascist pattern in American policy and voiced defiance of alleged American strivings toward a "pax americana" based on world domination. Since this time a steady stream of articles has illustrated this thesis. V. Cheprakov, in his "Military Bases of the United States of America and Great Britain,"[12] listed and described in detail American bases, both those already in existence and those which he asserted the United States planned to acquire or construct in many parts of the world. He attributed the most menacing motives to the American policy of establishing a "world system of bases," holding that it reflected imperialist and world domination tendencies. While Cheprakov's article displayed particular concern regarding American bases in the Arctic, which it characterized as occupying the fundamental position in American aviation strategy, it also discussed Atlantic, Pacific, and Near Eastern

[12] *World Economics and World Politics*, No. 10-11, 1946.

bases, going so far as to assert that the United States was seeking to transform the Pacific Ocean north of the equator into an American lake. Another aspect of the article, which is typical of Soviet discussion of this problem, was its charge that the United States was attempting to control the internal policies of the countries in which American bases were located.

Cheprakov's article is only one of hundreds or even thousands of similar items. One can pick up at random a copy of almost any Soviet newspaper published in 1946 or subsequently and find one or more items on American military bases abroad. A stereotyped charge made by the Soviet government against such neighboring states as Iran, Turkey, or Norway is that the governments of these countries are permitting their territory to be used for actual or potential bases against the U.S.S.R.

Probably one of the most effective Soviet propaganda lines designed to prove that the United States is an aggressive militaristic country has been the Soviet charge that America has blocked Soviet proposals for arms reduction. Ever since the beginning of the U.N. General Assembly the Soviet representatives have cast themselves in the role of advocates of arms reduction and have attempted to place the British and Americans in the position of obstructing disarmament. Even in the discussion leading up to the General Assembly's resolution on reduction of arms in December, 1946, the Soviets, led at the time by Molotov, attempted to make political capital out of the disarmament question rather than adopting a policy which might have led to gradual progress. It would be irrelevant to the purpose of this study to become involved in the intricacies of the disarmament problem. Suffice it to say that the Soviet policy was to demand that the United States reduce or give up entirely its one essential military advantage of superiority in highly complicated weapons, while avoiding discussion of huge masses of trained manpower, the main basis of its own military might.

In September, 1947, Vyshinski charged that the United States and Great Britain were opposed to the reduction of armaments. This was one of the main planks of his general attack on

Anglo-American policy. Then at the General Assembly session in 1948 he introduced his well-known proposal that every country reduce its arms by one-third. Had this proposal been carried out, the United States would have had about six combat divisions and the countries of Western Europe about fourteen while the Soviet Union and its Eastern European allies would have had between 150 and 200.

Considerable light is shed on the point of view from which the Kremlin approaches the question of disarmament by a statement in the official Soviet *History of Diplomacy:*

> Directly behind the tactic of masking aggression on the grounds of "self-defense" comes the concealment of aggression through the broad propagation and use of noble motives full of the "disinterested" support of this or that high ideal in the name of truth, freedom, humanity et cetera.
>
> The dissimulation of purely aggressive and predatory aims, for the sake of which wars are undertaken, is met perpetually in history. . . .
>
> From time immemorial the idea of disarmament has been one of the most favored forms of diplomatic dissimulation of the true motives and plans of those governments which have been seized by such a sudden "love of peace." This is very understandable. Any proposal for the reduction of armaments could invariably count upon broad popularity and support from public opinion. And, of course, the proposer of such a course must always have known in advance that his intentions would be divined by the partners in this diplomatic game.[13]

Another authoritative source, which like the *History of Diplomacy* is used for the education of Soviet official personnel, states: "The qualitative limitation of arms not only has nothing in common with disarmament but on the contrary permits the capitalist states to hide their unwillingness to disarm or even to limit their armaments." [14]

We have already made mention of the book by Miss Annabelle Bucar, charging that the activity of American official per-

[13] "Of the Nature of Bourgeois Diplomacy," *History of Diplomacy*, Vol. III, Moscow, 1945.

[14] *Politicheski Slovar*, Moscow, 1940, p. 473.

sonnel in the Soviet Union consisted mainly of espionage. In part, Soviet accusations of alleged American espionage have been motivated by the Kremlin's desire to divert domestic discontent against foreign scapegoats. By arousing fear of and aversion to foreign "spies" the Kremlin has sought to break down the attraction of Western culture for the Soviet people. However, the language in which these accusations are phrased indicated that their main purpose was to emphasize the alleged foreign war threat to Russia. This was indicated particularly by the tone of the articles commenting on the decree of June 10, 1947, "regarding the responsibility for disclosing state secrets and the loss of documents containing state secrets." Perhaps the most authoritative of these articles was a contribution by V. Ulrikh, the Chairman of the Supreme Military Tribunal of the U.S.S.R., in the magazine *Party Life*, for September, 1947. Ulrikh's article, "On the Vigilance of the Soviet People," asserted: "Our movement forward . . . proceeds in a struggle with the forces generated by the Capitalist world." It referred to Stalin's prewar and postwar warnings regarding the intrigues of "imperialism" looking toward a new war, and contained a lengthy account of espionage activity by capitalist states against the Soviet Union. Ulrikh declared that following World War II it was well known "even from official statements of United States political leaders that in that country a number of measures are being carried out for the strengthening and activizing of the intelligence service." He enjoined the Soviet people and officials to enforce strictly all security measures. Enemy agents, he stated, were seeking to enroll politically indifferent Soviet people in their service, and Soviet personnel working abroad were in a particularly dangerous environment.

The line taken in Ulrikh's article is typical. Throughout the postwar period, and particularly since the summer of 1947, it has been illustrated and elaborated in a myriad of ways. An interesting aspect of this theme is the charge that American research centers are engaged in anti-Soviet intelligence activity. *New Times* for September 10, 1947, published an article entitled "Total Espionage in a New Edition," which asserted that a system of total espionage had been established in postwar America, the reduction in U.S. appropriations for intelligence activity following the war having been a blind to conceal the intelligence work carried on by the "monopolies" under the guise of scholarship. The article stated further that it was "no secret" that the "veteran intelligence agent" Professor Geroid T. Robinson had been made head of the Russian Institute of Columbia University. Other organizations for preparing "special cadres" had been established by the Rockefeller and other philanthropic organizations.

Beginning in the fall of 1947 the Soviet authorities staged a series of sensational spy scares involving British or American diplomats or correspondents. These were directed at first against the British, probably because the Soviet authorities thought it would be easier to make them credible to a public traditionally suspicious of England. Among the victims of these fantastic charges have been objective correspondents and even such fellow travelers as Anna Louise Strong.

The smear campaign against foreign espionage has been extended to the Soviet-dominated countries of Eastern Europe. Alarmed by Tito's defiance, the Kremlin has sought to eliminate from the satellite Communist parties and governments all leaders who have displayed any degree of independence of Moscow control. It has supplemented police action against these individuals by propaganda accusations that they are agents of American espionage. Tito himself is now cast in the role of chief agent and spy of Wall Street.

Some other familiar features of Soviet propaganda against American "warmongering" should be at least briefly considered. One of these is the accusation that prominent American political, business, and military leaders are constantly engaged in creating a "war psychosis" by inflammatory anti-Soviet speeches and articles. Such charges were presented in their most extreme form in Vyshinski's first big speech at Lake Success in September, 1947. At about the same time of course Gorbatov published his well-known article comparing President Truman to Hitler. Although the Soviets did not succeed in securing the adoption by the United Nations of what they considered a satisfactory resolution prohibiting "war" propaganda, they made use of the resolution which was adopted in the fall of 1947 as a basis for condemnation of numerous American leaders whose statements displeased them. For the most part, this condemnation was expressed only in the form of propaganda. However, the Soviet government in some cases addressed diplomatic notes to the United States government demanding that action be taken against American warmongers. Such a note was sent by the Soviet government in 1948 with regard to a speech by General Kenny, the commander of the United States Strategic Air Force, on possible American military strategy in the event of war with the U.S.S.R.

One could compile a very long list of names of prominent Americans attacked by Soviet propaganda as warmongers. Such epithets as "cannibal" were applied to these individuals who, taken collectively, constituted in the imagination of the Kremlin a gallery of war criminals. If the Kremlin had its way, they doubtless would be treated as such.

Soviet propaganda has also devoted considerable attention to attempts to prove, by comparison of the American and Soviet national budgets, that military expenditures of the United States greatly exceeded those of the U.S.S.R. Such comparisons are fallacious for a number of reasons, the most obvious being that the U.S.S.R. budget constitutes a far larger proportion of the Soviet national income than the American budget.

The foregoing briefly illustrates some important aspects of the Kremlin's many-faceted campaign to convince the world that the United States is an armed camp against which Russia and its allies must be prepared. Everything possible has been done to keep the Soviet people alerted against this foreign threat. At the same time, the Soviet propaganda machine has sought to create the impression that if war should come the U.S.S.R. would be victorious. This has been done in a variety of ways. One was the rewriting of the history of World War II. As we have already noted, the Soviet press never gave any adequate recognition to the military role of the Western Allies.

But in the postwar period the minimization of this role has been carried to an extreme possible only in a country which in its history can relegate Trotsky—who created the Red Army—to the role of a mere foreign agent.

An unmanageable volume of evidence could be cited to show how the Kremlin sought after the war to persuade its subjects that they alone had won it. The process was a gradual one. During 1946 the press continued to admit that the Allies had rendered some assistance to the U.S.S.R., although such important official documents as Stalin's Order of the Day of May, 1946, made no mention of the role of the United States and Britain or even of the "coalition" in World War II. The only statement in this order which might even remotely be construed as recognition was a reference to the "victory of the freedom-loving peoples." Later in 1946, a new version of the official *Short Biography* of Stalin was published which stated:

> The successful carrying out of the Stalin strategic plan in 1944 had great military-political results . . . the military situation which resulted meant that the Soviet Union was in a position without the aid of the allies to occupy with its own forces all of Germany and to carry out the liberation of France. This circumstance impelled the former Prime Minister of England, Churchill, who up to that time had opposed the opening of a second front in Europe, to undertake the invasion of Western Europe.[15]

This was widely quoted in the Soviet press. I first saw a reference to it in a full-page review in *Red Star* for February 6, 1947. At about this same time, *Bolshevik* published Stalin's reply to a question regarding the military theories of Clausewitz submitted by Colonel Razin, a professor in a military academy. Stalin here emphasized in flamboyant terms the superiority of Soviet strategy in World War II to that of the Germans. He did not mention Roosevelt or Churchill, nor did he cite the role of Britain or America in the war.

[15] *Iosif Vissarionovich Stalin. Kratkaya biografiya,* Vtoroe Izdanie, Moscow, 1946.

Shortly after this, in May, 1947, V-E Day was abolished as a Soviet holiday, thus removing one more reminder of the role of the Allies in the war.

I have already indicated above that this depreciation of the Allies' war role was part of a process calculated to create a feeling of invincibility among the Soviet people. Once they had been made to forget Allied assistance, the Soviet people would remember only that the U.S.S.R. had been powerful enough to destroy single-handedly the greatest military power of all time.

The post-1947 Soviet line not merely minimized the Allied war role, but completely distorted the Allied motives for participating therein. Numerous Soviet press articles and statements in learned publications during the last three years have alleged that while the Soviet Union was fighting for democracy the United States and Britain fought to eliminate German and Japanese competition in world markets and to establish the dominant position of American capitalist monopolies. Among the best-known expressions of this view was N. Vosnesenski's book, *The War Economy of the USSR during the Fatherland War*, published in 250,000 copies in 1948.[16] Another of the numerous authoritative versions of this thesis was set forth in the 1948 edition of the *Brief Soviet Encyclopaedia.*

In many other ways Soviet propaganda has impressed upon its public the double-edged theme of the maliciousness and weakness of the Anglo-Americans during World War II. But most Soviet propaganda dealing with the general subject of war looks to the future rather than the past, and seeks to assure the best possible morale in the event of a new military conflict. Both during and since the war Soviet propaganda has refrained from disseminating information and opinions which might arouse fear of the horrors of war or suggest the possibility of defeat. It is inconceivable that there might be any printed or even open verbal expression of the anti-war attitudes and moods

[16] An English translation of this work has been published by the American Council of Learned Societies.

of disillusion so prominent in American literature following both World War I and World War II.

Even the problem of the difficulties or hardships of war veterans, including the Soviet Union's hundreds of thousands of crippled and disabled soldiers, received almost no attention in the Soviet press. It is true, of course, that a number of measures were taken to assist veterans to return to civil life and that the superiority of this Soviet treatment over the programs adopted in the Western countries was acclaimed. However, the theme was a surprisingly inconspicuous one, and disappeared from the press soon after the war. The general impression I received from reading the material on the veteran's problems in the Soviet press was that the Kremlin's attitude was unmistakably unsentimental.

All this conforms to the traditional Soviet opposition to pacifism. But silence regarding the horrors of war is only a small part of Soviet anti-pacifism. The fact is that the Kremlin does everything possible to create an atmosphere of martial glory in the U.S.S.R. There is no country in which parades, displays of armed might, martial music, and the militarization of cultural life and even of language are so highly developed. This is so obvious that it makes an overwhelming impression on any observant visitor to the U.S.S.R. This military atmosphere has not diminished in postwar Russia. Since 1948, attempts have been made to improve and intensify the military training of Soviet youth.

The Soviet press continues to glorify Soviet and Russian military traditions and to demand emphasis upon military themes in literature. *Literaturnaya Gazeta,* one of the leading Soviet literary publications, asserted on December 28, 1946: "We do not intend to abandon the war theme. We must write of war so that the generation of young people that comes after us will love arms and be ready for struggle and victory." On January 9, 1948, a *Pravda* correspondent, I. Ryabov, attacked a fable published in a Soviet children's newspaper whose moral was that bread was more important to men than gunpowder.

Ryabov asked: "Why do they write and print a story which smells of cheap pacifism?"

In addition to impressing upon the Soviet public the military might of their country, Soviet propaganda has endeavored to convince them that the "toilers" and "progressive" people of foreign lands are on their side and that the "camp of the U.S.S.R. and its friends is stronger than the imperialist camp." This theme was authoritatively expressed in Stalin's statement on the 800th anniversary of Moscow, September, 1947, when he asserted that Moscow was the symbol for the toiling people of the whole world against the domination of imperialism.

Assertions of this kind are common in the Soviet press. An amusing example is the statement in a Soviet economic journal on the 10th anniversary of the publication of the short course on the history of the Communist Party. The journal categorically insists that this anniversary is observed by the "toilers of the whole world." [17]

This general propaganda line has been applied, but with considerable caution, to the United States. The peoples of Italy, France, England, and America are said to be strong in their sympathy for the Soviet Union and are anxious for peace, but they are led by unscrupulous reactionaries, imperialists, and warmongers. The Soviet press describes the American people as imprisoned by the deceitful propaganda of their bourgeois masters, with a class-conscious fraction of the masses struggling to escape. At times in the postwar period the Soviet press has published material which would make Soviet readers believe that the majority of the American people are opposed to their government's world domination policy and favor the U.S.S.R. An indirect expression of this view was contained in *Pravda*, February 6, 1949, in the form of a quotation from the British Communist, Palme Dutt, in the London *Worker* to the effect that the overwhelming majority of Americans opposed their government's foreign policy of "threats of resorting to war."

From time to time, particularly in the fall of 1947, the Soviet

[17] *Voprosy Ekonomiki*, No. 8, 1948, p. 66.

press has published "lists of letters from Americans" received by Soviet correspondents in the United States or sent direct to Moscow. *Pravda* on October 1, 1947, published a dispatch by Boris Izakov and Yuri Zhukov quoting letters attacking American "warmongers" and praising Vyshinski's speeches. According to Izakov and Zhukov, these letters expressed "the genuine voice of the America of simple people and not the America of trusts, dollar diplomacy, and propagandists of the delirious idea of world domination." Occasionally *New Times* publishes a letter from a Mr. Perkins of Boston with appropriate comments.

In these and other ways the Kremlin strengthens its psychological war potential while sapping that of other countries. It wages what in many ways amounts to war in the name of peace. We can probably expect no let-up in this trying and disturbing campaign until and unless the Soviet rulers free themselves from the obsessions which stimulate it. But we can hope by study of the tactics and ideas analyzed in this chapter to immunize ourselves against their effects. Much progress has been made in this direction since the end of World War II and, with increasing understanding of the Soviet mentality, still more will be made in the future.

VIII. The Kremlin and the Atom

SOVIET policy and propaganda regarding atomic energy reflect the basic Soviet thesis that postwar international relations have been essentially a struggle between American imperialism and Soviet socialism. The speeches of Soviet statesmen, such as Molotov or Vyshinski, and a stream of press and radio comment have denounced American atomic policy as militaristic. America has been accused of pursuing "atomic diplomacy" to further her imperialist aspirations for world domination. The Soviet line, especially since President Truman's statement that an atomic explosion had occurred in Russia, has stressed the failure of "atomic diplomacy." Moscow has contended that the atomic bomb though highly destructive cannot decide a war, and that progressive forces are so strong that "international reaction" dare not unleash an atomic war against Soviet Russia. Since Mr. Truman's announcement, Soviet leaders, particularly Malenkov in his November 6, 1949, speech, have sought to exploit Western fear of a two-way atomic war, which Moscow warns would bring death to the capitalist system and misery to the American people.

With the allegedly reactionary and inhuman American atomic policy the Soviets have contrasted their own professedly noble and progressive approach. They have maintained that only Soviet policy offers a solution to the problem of preventing the use of atomic weapons. And only in a planned socialist economy like that of the U.S.S.R. can the vast potentialities of atomic energy for human welfare be realized.

This propaganda line may well reflect a Soviet estimate of

the military and economic consequences of atomic energy which might be summed up as follows: short-run menace and embarrassment; long-run gain to the U.S.S.R. In the period following Hiroshima, the A-bomb added to the military power of the capitalist opponent. It also created psychological embarrassment for the Kremlin in respect to both foreign and Soviet public opinion. For it led to a serious depreciation of one of Moscow's major political assets, the impression of overwhelming Russian power built up by Red Army performance during World War II and by Soviet propaganda.

But these and other negative consequences of atomic energy as viewed from the Kremlin are perhaps more than balanced by long-run calculations, based partly on ideological considerations and partly on analysis of long-term trends which may seem to be altering in favor of the U.S.S.R. its relative power position vis-à-vis the United States. It is at least possible, and I think probable, that the Soviet leaders are genuinely convinced that the Soviet economic system is better adapted to the utilization of atomic energy for generating power, for example, than is American capitalism. Even if this is not assumed, the Soviet leaders might well calculate that in the long run the Soviet Union will benefit relatively more than the U.S. from the industrial utilization of atomic energy. Since Russian economy is less developed than the American, there are more compelling incentives for atomic industrialization and a greater relative over-all possibility of expansion. Add to these factors such others as the growing Soviet demographic advantage over the United States, and the likelihood of optimism about the relative long-run Soviet position in the atomic age becomes greater.

Add too the Soviet calculation regarding social-economic "contradictions" in the capitalist world, and it becomes clear that the Kremlin might well reason that atomic energy, even as a military factor, may be an American asset of diminishing value. For if it be true that anti-capitalist, pro-Soviet forces will inevitably increase in power in Europe, Asia, and America, these forces may be counted on to work at least to prevent the use of American atomic power against Russia, and at best eventually to bring about a situation leading to establishment of a pro-Soviet government in the U.S. Included in this calculation has doubtless been realization of the difficulty of launching a "preventive" war under the American form of government.

Another factor which should be mentioned in this connection is the relative cheapness of human life in Soviet Russian military-political calculations. That this is a deeply rooted aspect of official Soviet thinking is scarcely a matter of argument. If this factor be combined with the confidence based on an expanding population and the feeling, springing from Marxist doctrine, that "history is on our side," it might well make an atomic arms race or even, perhaps, an atomic war seem less frightful than it does to informed Americans.

At the very least, the combination of all these factors might encourage the Soviet leadership to believe that once Russia possessed atomic bombs in sufficient quantities to threaten real retaliation, American fear of an atomic war would be so much greater than Russian fear that the same sort of tacit agreement might be reached on non-use of this weapon as prevailed with respect to poison gas during World War II.

If this analysis of Soviet views is correct, and I think that the available evidence offers some basis for thinking so, then not only the Soviet propaganda line regarding atomic energy but also Soviet policy in the U.N. negotiations on atomic energy control become at least in some degree understandable. For such an analysis as I have sketched would lead logically to the sort of policy the Soviets have pursued.

The Kremlin's atomic policy has been twofold. First, the Kremlin simultaneously sought to solve what it obviously hoped would be the short-run problems of the period when America had a monopoly of atomic weapons and to press forward with the development of its own atomic facilities, both military and nonmilitary. With its usual facility for turning real liabilities into at least apparent propaganda assets, it exploited America's unwillingness to surrender a trump card of its power position by accusing the U.S. of "atomic diplomacy" and opposition to disarmament. This argument has probably had considerable influence on Western public opinion, especially among intellectuals, though its value has diminished.

Second, the Kremlin has struggled with the problem of dealing with the proposals offered by the United States for the international control of atomic energy. If we take seriously the Soviet leaders' adherence to Marxism-Leninism and take into account such factors as their fear of the effects of contact with foreigners on the Soviet people, it is not difficult to understand why the American proposals for international control should have seemed sinister to the Kremlin. For they would have opened up the U.S.S.R. to foreign inspection, would have led to increased contact between Soviet and foreign scientists and technicians, and according to Soviet propaganda, would have led to the creation of an American-dominated international atomic trust with incalculable power over the economies of all countries.

The Soviet answer to the American control proposals has been to stall and obstruct in the United Nations and to do everything possible to prevent their serious consideration, while at the same time attempting to throw the onus of blocking progress toward international control on the Americans.

This is an attempt to explain the Soviet attitude, not to justify it. I share the view of most American atomic scientists that the Soviet attitude toward our control proposals has been unenlightened. However, one must recognize that viewed from the situation in which the Politburo found itself, and considered in the light of the Kremlin's warped and anxious attitude toward the West, its policy and expressed attitudes toward atomic energy control have a certain consistency.

I wish to emphasize the tentativeness of these hypotheses. There is probably no subject regarding which the Soviets have been "cagier" than atomic energy. While references to it have been frequent, and concern with it has been great, it has at the same time been treated with a caution which should serve as a warning against categorical judgments by the foreign student. Much of what the Soviets have said about it seems to me intelligible in the light of the hypothesis stated above, but there is sufficient obscurity and confusion in the pattern of Soviet reactions to suggest that in large measure the Kremlin has been groping uncertainly and uneasily toward an atomic policy.

The first Soviet reaction to Hiroshima might be characterized as one of stunned near silence. Two days after the Hiroshima raid the Soviet newspapers published a brief Tass dispatch summarizing an American military communiqué on the raid. The Nagasaki raid was not reported in a news dispatch but was referred to for the first time in an article in *New Times* for September 1, which presented the first Soviet editorial reaction to the atomic bomb in the indirect and cautious form of a roundup of foreign press comment. Any suggestion that this new weapon might have played a part in forcing the Japanese surrender was deleted by Soviet censors from the reports of foreign correspondents in Moscow.

It should be pointed out, however, that apparently by one of those rare errors sometimes committed by the Soviet censorship, the first Tass dispatch reporting the use of the bomb included a statement that it was equal in explosive power to 20,000 tons of TNT. Probably as a result of this slip, gossip regarding the fearsome power of the bomb swept Moscow.

The *New Times* article, written by M. Rubinstein, who has since contributed frequently to the Soviet press on this subject, contained or suggested most of the main lines of Soviet propaganda on atomic energy which have been disseminated in the post-Hiroshima period. It minimized the military significance, contesting the view that Japan's surrender had resulted from the bomb, but at the same time pointed out that it was a weapon which could inflict great destruction on civilians. It introduced the concept of "atomic diplomacy" although without using that expression. Rubinstein indicated that imperialists who had not heeded the lesson of Hitler's failure wished to keep the atomic bomb an American secret weapon for use in a future war. He said that progressive circles in America realized that the development of atomic energy made still more urgent the problem of assuring world security. These circles favored the establishment of a "genuine international collaboration" in the domain of science and realized it was more than ever incumbent that the United Nations prevent war. Finally, Rubinstein set the tone of future Soviet comment on the technical-economic significance of atomic energy, noting that it was "one of the greatest discoveries of modern science and technology which may have incalculable effects on every sphere of human life."

In his November 6 speech two months later, Molotov made two significant references to atomic energy. In the section of his speech dealing with foreign affairs he attacked foreign imperialists allegedly advocating an arms race. He declared that in this connection it was necessary to speak of "the discovery of atomic energy and of the atomic bomb the use of which in the war with Japan demonstrated its enormous destructive force." He went on to say that atomic energy had not been tested as a means of aggression or safeguarding peace and that there could be no technical secrets of great significance which could remain in one country or one narrow group of countries. Consequently, this discovery must not be allowed to encourage a foreign policy of force.

In the section of his speech dealing with Soviet domestic problems Molotov referred to the modern period of highly developed technology "in which the utilization of atomic energy has already become possible" and he made his well-known promise that "we shall have atomic energy and much else." The concern of the Soviet elite with this question was indicated by the fact that the Soviet press, in reporting Molotov's speech, stated that the above remarks were greeted by "stormy, strong prolonged applause."

A few weeks after Molotov's speech I happened to be present at a Soviet gathering, one feature of which was a sort of political vaudeville performance of a type quite common in Russia. The master of ceremonies at this performance stated that as Molotov had promised that the U.S.S.R. would have atomic energy, this meant that they must have it already. Subsequently, I heard of numerous similar statements conveyed by the same type of media. They seem to indicate a determined effort on the part of the Soviet government to neutralize any damaging effects on popular morale or reflections on the prestige of the Soviet leadership caused by stories regarding the bomb or the subject of atomic energy in general.

Perhaps the most important aspect of Soviet opinion regarding atomic energy is the Kremlin's estimate of its military significance. This is at the same time the most difficult factor in Soviet opinion to evaluate. For reasons of foreign and domestic politics, the most obvious one being the fact that atomic weapons were first perfected by the leading capitalist power, Soviet leadership at least until recently was under constraint to play down their military significance. As far as can be learned from Soviet published materials, Soviet opinion does genuinely attribute to the atomic bomb considerably less military significance than the majority of qualified opinion in the United States or Britain.

A typical expression of Soviet opinion on the subject was contained in an article by Rubinstein in *New Times*.[1] The article was entitled "The Atomic Age as American Scientists Picture It." Reviewing the American symposium entitled "One World or None," the title of which Rubinstein declared was rather startling, he criticized what he considered an overestimation of the military power of the bomb. He declared that American scientists in their anxiety to secure effective international control of atomic energy were holding up a "bogey." They were falling into "adventurist," blitzkrieg military doctrines.

One of the most systematic brief Soviet treatments of atomic energy is an article entitled "Atomic Energy and Prospects for Its Use," published in the mass circulation *Agitator's Notebook*.[2] It belittled the military value of the atomic bomb, asserting that it had played no special role in the recent war and that the havoc which it caused in Japan could have been achieved more cheaply by other means. It maintained that atomic bombs could be produced in small quantities only and could not be applied against large armies or well-dispersed industries. It

[1] No. 12, 1946.

[2] *Bloknot Agitatora*, No. 15, May 31, 1946.

contended, moreover, that the bomb could not replace other military weapons.

Soviet press coverage of the Bikini atomic tests in the spring and summer of 1946 also conformed to the tendency to minimize the bomb's military significance. The tests received very modest coverage in the Soviet press, which adopted a tone of mixed amusement and depreciation. Typical of this was an article by the well-known Soviet correspondent Boris Izakov in *Pravda* for July 3, 1946. Izakov wrote "as might have been expected they showed the atomic weapon as a tremendous destructive force but still the results of the tests proved more modest than the American press had predicted." In his account, Izakov went out of his way to describe the fine, frisky condition of the goats and other animals which had participated in the tests. He also poked fun at the "atomic mania" in the U.S., where, he said, atomic cocktails and atomic blondes were the rage.

A far more authoritative indication of the rather low Soviet estimate of the bomb's military significance came from Stalin himself. In September, 1946, Alexander Werth asked him whether monopoly possession of the bomb by America was a principal threat to peace. Stalin replied:

> I do not believe the atomic bomb to be as serious a force as certain politicians are inclined to regard it. Atomic bombs are intended for intimidating weak nerves, but they cannot decide the outcome of war, since atomic bombs are by no means sufficient for this purpose. Certainly monopoly possession of the secret of the atomic bomb does create a threat, but at least two remedies exist against it:
> (a) Monopoly possession of the atomic bomb cannot last long.
> (b) Use of the atomic bomb will be prohibited.

Molotov echoed this statement later in the disarmament discussion in the U.N. when he said on November 28, 1946:

> It is well known that many articles have recently been written just to create a panic about atomic bombs, although no one has yet proved, and no one can prove, that atomic bombs can play a decisive part in the course of a war.

These quotations and references are typical of Soviet opinion publicly expressed throughout the postwar period. A similar point of view has been voiced in the well-known book by the British physicist, Blackett, entitled *Fear, War and the Bomb.*[3] It is impossible to know whether this line of argument corresponds to the real beliefs of the Soviet leaders. My impression is that while they underestimate the military significance of atomic energy, at least if one accepts as a correct evaluation the viewpoint of American experts in this field, they do not do so to the degree indicated by the propaganda line. After all, the Soviets have received from Bikini, as well as from their official personnel in Japan, eyewitness reports of atomic bomb effects. This fact, combined with the frequent statements of Soviet leaders that the bomb has tremendous destructive potentialities for use against civilian populations, indicates that it is certainly not taken lightly by the Kremlin.

On the other hand, there is substantial reason to believe that it is difficult for the Soviet leaders to realize the full military significance of atomic weapons. The nature of their military experience and their military establishment, in which masses of infantry and artillery have dominated, and apparently so continue, probably causes them to underestimate both long-range bombing and atomic weapons. It might also be argued that the refusal of the U.S.S.R. to adopt a constructive attitude toward international control of atomic energy is a clear indication of Soviet underestimation of its destructive import. This might be argued even if one recognized the validity of the Soviet contention that the American control proposals would constitute an undesirable infringement on Russian national sovereignty. For if Soviet leaders were convinced that such regulation was the price of survival they might perhaps accept it.

More light may be shed on this aspect of the question by the discussion later in this chapter of Soviet criticism of the alleged American use of atomic energy as an instrument for world domination, but I should like to point out here that even the

[3] This book was first published in England under the title *Military and Political Consequences of Atomic Energy.*

overwhelming destructiveness of the atomic bomb need not necessarily seem to the Kremlin a sufficient reason for accepting effective international control if the United States can be prevented from using this weapon.

Additional observations regarding the psychological problems confronting the Soviet leaders as a result of the development of the atomic bomb may be of interest. These are closely connected with the problem of Moscow's estimate of Soviet military potential. As I indicated in the preceding chapter, it is contrary to Soviet practice to permit the dissemination of facts or ideas which would be detrimental to morale. This consideration alone undoubtedly explains a great deal of the Soviet depreciation of the atom bomb. The Soviet people have not been subjected to the somber reflections induced in many Americans by the writings of John Hersey, David Bradley and many others on the catastrophic consequences of atomic warfare. Nevertheless, there are indications both in Soviet published material and in the observations of foreigners who have been in the Soviet Union that the bomb created widespread fear and produced other psychological phenomena viewed with concern by the Kremlin.

Alexander Werth wrote in *International Affairs* in 1946:

> . . . And then came the atomic bomb. I was in Moscow at the time, and the effect was overwhelming. In the press there was only a brief summary of President Truman's first statement on the Hiroshima raid; and nothing else. The news of the second bomb on Nagasaki was not even published. I asked the editor of one important paper why, and he said: "Because our people are much too upset by the whole damned thing." And another Russian said to me in a tone of genuine melancholy: "Our people really thought that this war would be our last war with the Capitalist world; but now we wonder." Soon afterwards, I went to Berlin, and there, one evening, in a Russian officers' mess I fell into conversation with a young Russian captain who was very drunk. But I remember his remark: "With these atomic bombs, very few people will be left alive after the next war, but," he added, with maudlin tearfulness, "the work of Lenin and Stalin cannot die, and the last people in the world

will be Communists." Which, of course, was not a political, but an alcoholic reaction.

A few chance conversations which I had with Soviet people in the weeks and months following the first scanty reports which reached the U.S.S.R. regarding the atomic bomb left me with a rather similar impression. It seemed to have aroused intense and even obsessive curiosity. A Soviet bookseller remarked to me early in September, 1945, that the Americans had something very interesting, "the atomic bomb," but that very little had been written about it in the Soviet Union. Another Soviet person in praising the magazine, *Amerika*, said that reading it helped one to understand how the Americans had succeeded in inventing atomic bombs. An employee of a foreign embassy remarked that Soviet people now thought that the Americans could conquer the world.

Three other remarks on atomic bombs which I heard from members of the Soviet "intelligentsia" were in a somewhat different vein. A rising young Soviet diplomat shortly after November 6, 1945, remarked at a party that gold had lost its value and uranium was now more important. He said that the Soviet Union had more uranium than any other country. An admiral with whom I exchanged a few cautious words on a trip to Vladivostok remarked that it would be a fine thing if science were employed for human welfare rather than such purposes as the production of atomic bombs. On this same trip a Soviet engineer predicted a new catastrophe within no more than ten years after World War II. Among other things he referred to the possibility of the use of atomic bombs in a new war. When I jokingly remarked that a South Sea island would then be a good place to go, he said that eastern Siberia would be even better. A Soviet educator talking to a foreign diplomat on a journey early in 1946 said that the atomic bomb had been a great boon to Soviet scientists as it had caused the government to raise their salaries.

The press and official statements also indicated concern regarding the effects produced on the Soviet public mind by the atomic bomb. Molotov's promise that the U.S.S.R. would have atomic energy probably falls into this category. His statement in his November 6, 1947, speech that the atomic bomb no longer was a "secret" was doubtless part of a policy attempting to reassure the Soviet people regarding Russian possession of this awesome force. Beginning in the fall of 1945, a series of Stalin prizes were awarded to Soviet scientists for work in atomic physics. These awards have doubtless been calculated both to stimulate atomic research and to create an impression of active work in progress in this field. Still more significant is the fact that the Five-Year Plan for Soviet science published early in 1946 placed primary emphasis in the field of physical science on atomic energy, radio location, and jet propulsion.[4] It should also be recalled that an important feature of Stalin's key February 9, 1946, speech was his injunction to Soviet scientists to overtake and surpass the scientists of foreign countries. It is obvious that the development of atomic energy was one of the factors impelling Stalin to issue this call.

An interesting statement—and the only one of its kind I have discovered—was published in the magazine *Za Oboronu* (*For Defense*) in 1948:

> The . . . appearance of the atomic weapon and the practical utilization of rocket propulsion in aviation and artillery confront local anti-aircraft defense workers with new tasks. It is now necessary to emphasize more than ever the observance of anti-aircraft defense requirements in planning and building cities.[5]

I am inclined also to think that the desire to counteract some of the adverse effects of the leadership of America in developing this greatest of technical marvels has been one of the factors behind the frantic postwar Soviet propaganda campaign to establish the "priority" and superiority of Russian and Soviet science and technology.

[4] For a brief summary account of the plan see Soviet Embassy *Information Bulletin*, April 20, 1946. Detailed information is contained in several issues of *Vestnik akademii nauk*, for that year.

[5] See issue No. 2, February, 1948.

Let us turn now from speculation on the Soviet estimate of the military menace of atomic war, and psychological problems related thereto, to Soviet criticism of U.S. atomic policy. This can, in a very general way, be categorized under the rubrics of "atomic diplomacy," American atomic non-disarmament and, finally, attempts at atomic monopoly by the U.S. through our atomic energy control plan. All three of these points are inextricably interrelated, and I shall treat each separately only for clarity of exposition.

The accusation of "atomic diplomacy" is vague and most difficult to evaluate. It is hard to know whether this charge is merely one facet of the over-all postwar Soviet anti-American propaganda stemming mainly from general ideological considerations, or whether it has a degree of autonomy. To pose this question is in a sense to ask the unanswerable question whether atomic energy has been a decisive factor in Soviet policy. I shall have more to say about this presently, and will indicate here only that my answer is largely negative. It seems to me that there is no main feature of postwar Soviet policy or propaganda which cannot be explained by factors which would have been in operation if the power of the atom had not been unleashed. But, as we shall see later, the atomic problem did heighten postwar anxiety, and did cause changes in each super-power's estimate of its rival's power position.

As indicated before I am inclined to regard the "atomic diplomacy" line as a reflection of the postwar Soviet thesis that there have been "two tendencies" in international affairs—the Soviet and the American. The Soviet press began as early as September, 1945, to suggest that American "reactionaries" counted on using the threat of atomic attack as a political pressure weapon against Russia. In that month, in addition to the Rubinstein article mentioned earlier, there appeared an "international survey" in *Pravda* on September 9, attacking the New York *Times* for allegedly regarding the A-bomb as the "apotheosis" of American civilization. A few days later, on September 14, *Pravda* again criticized the *Times*, now for allegedly proposing the use of the "secret of the production of the atomic bomb" in settling international questions, and quoted Walter Lippmann to the effect that to follow such counsels would lead to uniting the world against America.

But it was not until after the failure of the London Conference in October and the subsequent general deterioration of Soviet-American relations, that accusations of "atomic diplomacy" or "atomic imperialism" became intense and bitter. A notable example of this tying-in of the atomic problem with the general course of Soviet-American relations was an article by A. Sokolov in *New Times*, November 15, 1945, entitled "International Collaboration and Its Foes." The gist of Sokolov's article was that influential imperialist groups in the U.S. and Britain, believing that the development of the atomic bomb had made the Soviet Union a secondary power, were advocating a policy of employing the atomic threat to dominate Europe, to bring about the isolation of the Soviet Union, and finally to provoke war against her.

Since the appearance of Sokolov's article, accusations of this nature have been such a constant phenomenon in the Soviet press and in public lectures and official statements that merely to sample them would require reams of paper. I shall cite here only one additional example from a lecture delivered in Moscow on December 11, 1946, by the well-known Soviet commentator, I. Ermashev, on "Atomic Diplomacy and International Collaboration." Ermashev stated that:

> international relations have recently assumed outstanding significance primarily because of the creation of the atomic weapon. The great question today is whether peace will be firm and lasting or whether it will be chaotic and brief.
>
> "Atomic diplomacy" is the name given to the foreign policy of the imperialist countries in the postwar period. . . . What is "atomic diplomacy"? It is a course of governmental activity pursued by the reactionary forces of the U.S.A. and Britain to seek to impose their will on other countries and ultimately to achieve world domination. It is directly contradictory to the principle of equal rights of people. It is a weapon of international reaction aiming at

ever new conquests. But the atomic bugbear, according to Stalin, is designed merely to frighten the weak-nerved.

The "atomic psychosis" continues and is manifested most strongly in the U.S.A. Certain "atomic maniacs" believe that by the atomic weapon the U.S.A. will guarantee peace to the world. Professor Urey, for example, states that the U.S.A. may be compelled to apply the atomic weapon to insure peace. . . . It is evident that the Anglo-Saxon ideology of world domination on one hand and blackmail on the other are characteristic of "atomic diplomacy." . . . The world will not permit domination by one power or by a group of powers. The reactionaries in America and Britain have calculated their forces but they cannot terrify the world. Lippmann has stated that the atomic bomb must not be used as a weapon but as an instrument for the political education of mankind. However, the Soviet people will not be intimidated. The policy of blackmail characterizing "atomic diplomacy" is doomed to failure. It is noteworthy that many American intellectuals condemn this policy, as likewise do the simple people throughout the world.

Turning now to the Soviet criticism of America's refusal of atomic disarmament, we find ourselves dealing with a much clearer, more definite line than the vague accusation of "atomic diplomacy." The Soviet position regarding this point is so well known that we need merely to refresh briefly the reader's memory. Since June, 1946, the U.S.S.R. representatives in the U.N. have pressed for the adoption of a convention which would prohibit use, possession or manufacture of atomic weapons, or the facilities for their production. Gromyko, Vyshinski, Molotov, and Malik, have presented this demand with remarkable but typical Soviet persistence. Malik proposed in February, 1949, that the U.N. Atomic Energy Commission submit to the Security Council by June 1, 1949, a draft convention on the prohibition of the atomic weapon as well as a draft convention on atomic energy control, both conventions to be concluded and to go into effect simultaneously. Until September, 1948, the Soviets had taken the position that the convention on prohibition must take effect before a control arrangement could be worked out. In November, 1949, Vyshinski restated this before the U.N.

Special Political Committee, declaring, *inter alia,* that despite its possession of the atomic weapon the U.S.S.R. would continue to insist on the prohibition of its use.[6]

As is well known, the Soviets have sought to link their demand for atomic disarmament with proposals for reduction of so-called "conventional" armaments. Since the fall session of the U.N. General Assembly of 1948 they have presented these demands in one package comprising a proposal for a simultaneous one-third reduction of conventional armaments and a convention on prohibition of atomic weapons.

With each presentation from 1947 through 1949, the Soviets accused the U.S. of sabotaging the resolution of the U.N. General Assembly of January 24, 1946, on "Establishing a Commission to Examine Problems which arise in connection with the Discovery of Atomic Energy," and of December 14, 1946, "On Principles Determining the Universal Regulation and Reduction of Armaments."

The United States' position has been that atomic disarmament is so vital and difficult a problem that it must be considered as a separate question and that effective international control over the manufacture of atomic weapons must be established before America could be expected to surrender its atomic bombs and the secrets of their manufacture. True to their habit of attributing to an opponent their own practices and tactics, the Soviets have accused the U.S. of blocking "control" over atomic weapons, and have published numerous articles under such titles as, "Why Is There Still No Control over Atomic Energy?" In a typical article published in *Pravda* for August 22, 1947, the well-known Soviet commentator, A. Marinin, charged, *inter alia,* that "the cause of atomic energy control has bogged down precisely because such a 'solution' of the atomic problem corresponds to the intentions of the U.S."

Thus the campaign against American refusal to surrender one of its trump cards of military strength—an action of a kind to which the U.S.S.R. has, needless to say, never resorted—has

[6] For Vyshinski's concluding speech, see *Pravda,* November 17, 1949.

been linked in Soviet propaganda with the problem of control over atomic weapons. The absurdity of the Soviet argument that America is blocking "control" of atomic energy has been amply exposed by American representatives in the U.N. Little argument has been needed to prove the American contention. It was necessary only to point out that although detailed discussion of the control problem began in the U.N. in June, 1946, it was not until June 11, 1947, that the Soviets, through Gromyko, actually proposed a "plan" providing for a very limited system of international inspection to supplement their proposals for a convention on prohibition of atomic weapons. This proposal and the unsubstantial additions thereto subsequently made by the Soviets were inadequate.

There is no need to give here details of the American argument demonstrating the inadequacy of the Soviet "control" proposals. Their essence has been that a system of continuous, unhindered inspection by a genuine international body and the establishment of an international organization to direct the various processes connected with the extraction of uranium and other ores and the manufacturing process involved in production of atomic energy, were minimum essentials of any system to which the term "control" could be accurately, realistically, or honestly applied.

The Soviet accusations that America, not Russia, has been blocking atomic energy control in the postwar period have been fallacious and disingenuous in the extreme. In my opinion, they have been aspects of a tactic of stalling and maneuvering designed to make the best of what the Soviets hoped was a short or at most a "middle-run" situation characterized by their disadvantageous position in the atomic energy field.

To obtain the fullest possible understanding of this point it is necessary to examine Soviet criticism of the American atomic energy control proposals. This will, I think, clarify why, from the point of view from which the Kremlin has always regarded international relations, the American plan for atomic energy control was bound to be—as Gromyko pronounced it from the very beginning of discussion in June, 1946—"totally unacceptable." To say this, is not to accept the validity of the Soviet criticisms. Whatever integrity they have comes from assumptions regarding American intentions which seem to make sense only within the framework of Leninism. This fact, however, does not absolve us from the necessity, if we would understand Soviet policy, of attempting to "put ourselves in Stalin's place."

Soviet criticism of the "Baruch plan" has followed two main lines. The first and most fundamental, but the least valid from any but a narrowly Soviet nationalist point of view, is that the plan would confer unfair military and economic advantages upon the U.S. It would do so by the very fact of the establishment of an international control body. It would also—and here I think a slightly better case can be made for the Soviets—be detrimental to Soviet interests because of the series of stages provided in the plan before the U.S. would surrender its bombs and secrets to the international control agency. Another and far more justifiable Soviet objection is to the provision of the Baruch plan requiring abolition of the veto in respect to the control of atomic energy. At the very least, it seems to me, this provision of the American plan conferred a propaganda advantage upon the Soviets.

Let us briefly examine Soviet arguments regarding these points.

The essence of the Soviet argument against the setting up of the Atomic Development Authority envisaged in our plan was set forth in a *Pravda* editorial of June 24, 1946. This took the line that the American plan was designed to assure a U.S. monopoly of atomic energy for an indefinite period. The U.S., asserted *Pravda*, evidently intended to define "at its own pleasure" the preliminary stages before the plan would become fully effective. The editorial raised the question why other countries should trust America when she did not trust even her "partners." It went on to quote an American senator as allegedly saying that the Baruch plan would make it certain that the U.S. would never have to disclose the secrets of production of the A-bomb. "Such an interpretation of the Baruch plan evidently corresponds to the facts," it added dryly.

This editorial raised by implication a Soviet objection to the Baruch plan which was frankly dealt with in a series of articles in *New Times* during 1946 and 1947, and which has bulked large in Soviet propaganda on the subject ever since. The objection was that the American plan would lead to the establishment of an international atomic energy trust by which "Wall Street" would exert economic and political domination of the world. A typical example of this argument was an article by Rubinstein in *New Times*, No. 14, 1946, entitled "Monopoly Trusts Control Atomic Energy." Rubinstein asserted that the proposed Atomic Development Authority would be "a sort of international cartel," sole owner of all uranium, thorium, etc., throughout the world, which would serve as the instrument of monopolists seeking to establish a world government of monopoly trusts. That he had in mind the possible danger of this "world government" interfering with the internal economic development of the U.S.S.R. was indicated by the fact that he stressed that the Soviet "proposals" left the organization of the utilization of atomic energy for "peaceful" purposes to individual states, and that he also emphasized the advantages of the Soviet system over capitalism in utilization of atomic energy for power production, etc. Numerous similar articles have appeared in the Soviet press.

The Soviet objections to the American proposal for abolition of the veto right in this question furnished a convenient propaganda weapon for the Soviet contention that these proposals were designed to bring about "Wall Street" domination of the world. Ever since the introduction of the American plan into international negotiation the Soviet contention has been that the attempt to eliminate the veto was designed to destroy the U.N. and convert it into an instrument of American imperialism. There can be little doubt that a situation in which, by a simple majority, the U.S. and like-minded states could demand the imposition of sanctions against the Soviet Union for violation of obligations in respect to atomic energy control would afford genuine grounds for alarm to the Kremlin. In view of this and related facts, it seems clear that it was probably a serious mistake in policy and certainly in propaganda tactics for the U.S. to include in its atomic energy control proposal the abolition of the veto. Such a view was held, it is known, by a number of competent Americans concerned with the working out of the American proposals in 1946.[7]

It has been noted at several points in this chapter that the Kremlin may likely consider that in the long run the U.S.S.R. will be the principal beneficiary of the use of atomic energy, largely because it stands to gain more than "capitalist" America by the production of atomic power. This view is implicit in much of the Soviet criticism of the American proposals for atomic energy control. It must, however, be said that this point is more frequently put in negative than in positive form by the Soviet press. One frequently reads statements to the effect that atomic energy, if used as a source of power, would lead, under capitalism, to calamitous unemployment and economic chaos. A characteristic expression of this line of thought was Rubinstein's statement that atomic energy brilliantly confirmed Marx's prediction that under capitalism productive forces become "destructive forces."[8] For this and related reasons, so runs the Soviet argument, only the U.S.S.R. can look forward with confidence to the atomic age.

A well-known statement by Vyshinski in his November 10, 1949, speech to the U.N. General Assembly's Special Political Committee represents the most extravagant expression of this line. According to the verbatim record made by the U.N., Vyshinski said that Soviet Russia was already utilizing atomic energy to raze mountains and irrigate deserts. *Pravda* in its version of the speech reduced this boast to an expression of a desire to use atomic energy for the performance of such tasks. Vyshinski emphasized Soviet use of atomic energy for national

[7] See for example the New York *Herald Tribune* for March 28, 1948 (p. 12), revealing that Chester Barnard and David Lilienthal had unsuccessfully "pleaded" with Mr. Baruch not to include abolition of the veto in the American plan.

[8] *New Times*, No. 12, 1946.

welfare and charged that the U.S. was hindering its application "for peaceful purposes." [9]

No doubt in part this line of argument is sour grapes. Doubtless also it is partly intended for foreign and domestic propaganda consumption as part of the process of ideological mobilization of both foreign and Soviet intellectuals against the evils and defects of capitalism, which is so basic a feature of Soviet policy.

There is, however, considerable evidence, both in the Soviet press and in statements by Soviet representatives at U.N. meetings, indicating that this is not by any means pure propaganda but at least in part rational calculation. The leading Soviet authority on atomic questions, Rubinstein, in a number of articles has described the splendid prospects in the U.S.S.R. for the utilization of atomic energy as a power source.[10]

One of the most striking indications I have seen of hopeful Soviet expectations regarding exploitation of atomic energy was an article in *Young Bolshevik* (*Molodoi Bolshevik*), No. 3-4, 1946, by the leading Soviet philosopher T. Stepanyan. Stepanyan stated:

> It may also be assumed that the development of science, particularly the impending release of atomic energy . . . will lead to a technical revolution unparalleled in history, which will mark an important leap in technical progress. Such leaps and bounds will be integral elements in the gradual general process of transmission from socialism to communism.

When the U.N. records were opened in September, 1948, they disclosed that Dr. Dmitri Skobeltsyn, a "leading Soviet atomic scientist," had predicted that "atomic energy might permeate the various national economies in, say, ten years," a view far more optimistic than that of most Western scientists.[11]

[9] See the New York *Times* for November 30, 1949, and *Pravda* for November 17, 1949.

[10] See for one example his article, "The Development of Soviet Science and Technics in the New Five Year Plan," *Propagandist*, No. 9, 1946.

[11] See Peter Kihss in New York *Herald Tribune*, September 20, 1948.

It seems to me that such evidence ties in logically to support my thesis that atomic energy is in Soviet eyes a temporary liability but, given the inevitably favorable course of social development and a shrewd policy, a future plus factor for the U.S.S.R.

In setting forth this hypothesis, I wish, however, to offer certain reservations. It is possible that the Soviet leaders may not be as optimistic about the possibility of successfully utilizing atomic energy as they would have us believe. Thus far Soviet record in technological progress has not been brilliant even if the Kremlin's achievements have been considerable. Moreover —and here I am on such highly speculative ground that I shall confine myself to merely raising a question—will not the possible social effects of the raising of the standard of living incident to successful atomic industrialization be disturbing in Soviet Russia? What new elements in the elite might appear? What new demands and discontents might develop?

But all that is far away. In the meantime, what generalizations can be drawn about the effect of atomic energy upon Soviet attitudes and policies in the postwar period and for the foreseeable future? I would offer the following tentative conclusions. The introduction of the atomic variable into the Soviet-American political equation has produced no fundamental measurable result. It has probably acted as a deterrent on Soviet expansion, but this effect may have been partly balanced by spurring the Soviets to a more aggressive ideological policy. In a sense, it is true that from the Kremlin's point of view the Cominform is the counterweight to American atomic superiority, though the fact that it was the European Recovery Program and not the atomic bomb which elicited the Cominform seems to indicate the relative unimportance of the atomic question in Kremlin calculations.

The only moral which it is possible to draw from the evidence seems to be that ideologies and institutional patterns and not weapons, no matter how destructive, are the decisive factors in international affairs. Therefore, if there is a solution to the awesome problems posed by atomic energy, it will be shaped gradually out of whatever structure the statesmen and peoples of the world may be able to build. Pending that, the only available practicable policy for the United States would appear to be to maintain a power position which it would be irrational for the Kremlin to attempt to disturb but which would not create such anxiety in the Politburo as to cause it to lash out in a war of desperation. In the meantime, it would seem desirable to adopt an attitude of invincible, creative patience in the pursuit of all possible agreements with the U.S.S.R. which do not entail danger to American security, in all fields including that of atomic energy control.

IX. The Foreign Policy of "Imperialism"

AMERICAN officials responsible for the conduct of foreign relations believe that one of their major tasks is to extend the area of voluntary co-operation among nations. They sometimes refer to the Department of State as the Department of Peace.

Naturally, the official Soviet view of American foreign policy and its architects differs from that of most Americans as night does from day. Moscow stops at nothing in its efforts to incite hostility, fear, and suspicion of American policy and its executors. The tactics of Vyshinski and other Soviet representatives might have excited the admiration of Goebbels. The Soviet press has even gone so far as to pin the label of "warmonger" on such a sincere and patient worker for international amity as Cordell Hull, whom, when it suited the Kremlin's purposes, Soviet propagandists praised for his efforts to strengthen Soviet-American ties.[1]

Soviet slander and political rowdyism serve the purpose of supporting the major Soviet thesis that America, and not the surging, expanding international Communist movement and its Soviet managers, is aggressive.

Let us now survey the main lines of Soviet propaganda regarding U.S. foreign policy.

This propaganda has interpreted the American foreign policy of defense against Moscow's power drive as a program of isolating and encircling the U.S.S.R. The American effort to re-establish a balance of power in Eurasia has been distorted into

[1] See for example the scathing review of Mr. Hull's *Memoirs* by B. Rodor in *Voprosy storii* (*Problems of History*), Nov. 1, 1949.

a plan for the enslavement of the countries lying between America and Russia and for their conversion into instruments of Wall Street. According to the Soviet press and radio, the "American party" in France, Italy, Germany, or Japan acts as the agent of the United States in pursuit of nefarious designs intended to subject their people to American domination and to keep reactionary classes and regimes in power. America is represented as utilizing in pursuit of these aims a wide range of tactics in which fraudulent promises and threats of force predominate.

The above line is presented within the framework of the accusations discussed in preceding chapters that American imperialism desires to destroy the U.S.S.R. and the countries of "popular democracy" in Eastern Europe by war. It is in fact the logical application of this basic theme to American foreign relations. Like the over-all concept which it illustrates, it conforms also to the Marxist-Leninist doctrine which serves as the basic integrating principle of Soviet propaganda. It should also be emphasized that the Soviet version of American foreign policy, though logical in terms of Marxist-Leninist dogma, is just as devoid of respect for truth as the general Soviet line regarding American "imperialism" and "warmongering." It totally ignores and suppresses the fact that the American policies which it condemns, such as those embodied in the E.R.P., the North Atlantic Pact, and the arms-aid agreements, were defensive reactions to Soviet policies. These programs have been presented by Moscow as flowing inevitably from the predatory nature of American capitalism. Again, with typical Soviet inconsistency, these policies allegedly determined by the "laws" of capitalism are attributed to the lust for power and wealth of a little group of all-powerful Wall Street magnates. And, of course, in the interest of effectiveness of presentation, the Soviet propaganda regarding the role of the United States in Europe, in Asia, in Africa, and the Americas, deletes facts which would cast doubt on the accuracy of its interpretation. The Soviet people always hear only one side of the story.

In the press coverage of U.N., meetings of foreign ministers, and other international gatherings, this principle is exemplified by simultaneous publication of full texts of Soviet representatives' speeches and one or two paragraph summaries of those of American spokesmen. The only notable exception to this rule, worth mentioning because of its rarity, was publication of one of Mr. Byrnes' speeches by the Soviet newspapers during the Paris Peace Conference in 1946, after Byrnes had dared the Soviet government to publish his speech as well as Molotov's on the same subject.

This one-sided presentation is calculated to prevent public discussion and the creation of a critical, informed opinion regarding international affairs in Russia and other Communist-dominated countries. Moreover, applied as it is to all news about foreign affairs, it tends to make non-Soviet or anti-Soviet opinion seem like a thin weak voice in comparison with the thunder issuing from the Kremlin and echoed throughout the world by a mighty chorus of popular assent. Like the propaganda themes to be discussed presently, this slanting and distortion foster the purpose of Soviet propaganda regarding American foreign policy, which is to persuade the Soviet people, and the other peoples of the world, that both right and might are on the Soviet side. Presentation and content alike are intended to demonstrate that the wicked plans of Wall Street to organize the world against Russia are doomed to fail, and that it is capitalist America, rather than mighty socialist Russia which will be isolated and encircled by the forces of progress.

To achieve this objective the Soviet propagandists manipulate the symbols of "democracy," "sovereignty," "socialism" and others calculated to mobilize Soviet and non-Soviet opinion. Simultaneously, while attempting to rally, inspire, unite and expand their own forces, the Kremlin's propagandists work tirelessly to discourage, deceive, lull and divide their democratic opponents. In particular, they do everything in their power to sow discord between America and Britain.

Beginning in 1945 or even earlier, but set forth most bluntly in Zhdanov's "Founders' Day" Cominform address, the official

Soviet explanation of the driving forces behind American foreign policy has been roughly as follows: Enriched by the war and strengthened far beyond its rivals, Britain and France, not to mention Germany and Japan, American capitalism became after World War II more aggressive and expansionist than it had been before the war. It abandoned its prewar isolationist foreign policy and switched to a drive for world domination. Its grandiose aspirations have been motivated by a combination of factors including a desire to utilize excess production capacity accumulated during World War II, lust for super-profits, and hatred and fear of the increased power and prestige of the "socialist" camp headed by Russia.

Let us glance very briefly at pre-Cominform manifestations of this line of Soviet economic-political analysis. Eugene Varga's study, *Changes in the Economy of Capitalism as a Result of the Second World War*,[2] authoritative in the U.S.S.R. until its condemnation by a conference of economists in May, 1947, emphasized that one of the consequences of the war would be increased sharpness of competition for foreign markets.

Varga's cautious indirect formulations regarding intensification of competition for markets take on added meaning when they are viewed in the light of Stalin's famous February 9, 1946, speech, where he reaffirmed Lenin's thesis that competition for markets and raw materials under capitalism leads to war.

As Soviet-American relations became more and more tense in 1946, increasingly sharp and explicit formulations and explanations of American policy appeared in Soviet literature. For example, a Soviet handbook on the United States published in the fall of 1946, to which reference has been made earlier, stated: "Interfering with the economic disarmament of aggressors . . . the reactionary groups attempted to preserve im-

[2] *Izmeneniya v Ekonomike Kapitalizma v Itoge Vtoroi Mirovoi Voiny* (*Changes in the Economy of Capitalism as a Result of the Second World War*), Moscow, 1946. See especially pp. 7, 12, 170, 319. See also my article "The Varga Discussion and Its Significance" in the *American Slavic Review* for October, 1948.

perialist forces . . . to assure the intensification of their economic expansion and political penetration."[3]

Following Zhdanov's speeches in the fall of 1946 calling upon Soviet intellectuals to undertake a "counter-offensive" against capitalist propaganda, articles such as that of the well-known propagandist, D. Shepilov, in *Pravda* for November 4, entitled "A New Era in the History of Humanity," became typical. In this article Shepilov alleged that the program of depriving European countries of their independence and turning them into appendages of the Anglo-Saxon powers was "the real policy of Anglo-Saxon democracy."

Finally, in his Cominform speech, Zhdanov established the line which has been used ever since when he declared:

> Whereas before World War II the more influential reactionary circles of American imperialism had adhered to an isolationist policy and had refrained from active interference in the affairs of Europe and Asia, in the new, postwar conditions the Wall Street bosses adopted a new policy. They advanced a program of utilizing America's military and economic might not only to retain and consolidate the positions won abroad during the war, but to expand them and to replace Germany, Japan and Italy in the world market. The sharp decline of the economic power of the other capitalist states makes it possible to speculate on their postwar economic difficulties, and, in particular, on the postwar economic difficulties of Great Britain, which make it easier to bring these countries under American control. The United States proclaimed a new, frankly predatory and expansionist course.[4]

Since the delivery of Zhdanov's speech, American foreign policy has been interpreted, with increasing frequency and intensity, as in large part an attempt to solve by foreign economic and political expansion internal problems engendered by the contradictions inherent in American capitalism. At the same time, paradoxically, the thesis has often been repeated that

[3] *Soedinennye Shtaty Ameriki* (*The United States of America*), 2nd ed., Moscow, 1946, p. 318.

[4] Quoted from English edition of Zhdanov's speech published by Foreign Languages Publishing House, Moscow, 1947, pp. 12-13.

United States capital has been inspired to expand in order to exploit the opportunities created by World War II.

So much for the Soviet explanation of the "driving forces" of American diplomacy. Let us now survey the major themes of Moscow's propaganda campaign to discredit American policy.

Postwar Soviet propaganda criticism of American foreign policy, as indicated above, has followed two main lines. First, it has accused the United States of an aggressive policy of military blocs and alliances. Second, it has charged that the United States seeks not only to convert foreign countries into instruments of American military policies but also to deprive them of their internal economic, political and cultural independence, and in fact to convert them into "colonies" of Wall Street. It has maintained that the United States was supporting reactionary and Fascist forces all over the world and preventing the free expression of the will of the people in countries in which American influence was strong.

Soviet propaganda in support of the first of these contentions has taken many different forms and has been applied to most of the major foreign policy measures of the American government. The Soviet press and radio have attacked as part of a policy of hostile military encirclement American attempts to strengthen the defensive power of Turkey or Greece, all measures designed to facilitate military co-operation between the United States and Britain or Canada, as well as the American economic policies embodied in the European Recovery Program. In general, it may be said that wherever there have been American troops or bases, the use of American military equipment or instruction of local police forces by American military or even non-military technical experts, as in Iran, Moscow has raised a furor and sought to prove its thesis that America is organizing the encirclement of Russia.

As early as the fall of 1945, the Soviet press abounded in material mostly lifted from the foreign press suggesting that the United States was seeking to turn Japan into a buffer state and a military base directed against the U.S.S.R. The presence of small American armed forces in China furnished the grounds for charges that America was seeking to turn this enormous country into a United States military base. Constant denunciation of the presence of British military forces in Greece was maintained during 1945 and 1946. Frequent suggestions that the British or Americans were maintaining Nazi-German military formations in their zones in Germany appeared in the fall of 1945 and during 1946.

While voicing criticism of the alleged extension of American and British military power, the Soviet press during 1945 and 1946 carried out its own program of military-political expansion in Eastern Europe under the guise of a spontaneous movement in the countries of Eastern Europe toward "democracy" and co-operation with their great Eastern neighbor.

As Anglo-American co-operation developed and became increasingly close in 1945 and the early months of 1946, the Soviet press charged with increasing frequency that America and Britain were forming a two-power military "bloc" seeking to impose its will on the rest of the world. Such charges were buttressed by references to the continued existence of joint Anglo-American military staff organizations. Molotov in a statement regarding the Paris Peace Conference published in Soviet newspapers for May 27, 1946, charged that the American "peace offensive" expressed itself "in the desire to impose the will of two governments on the government of a third state." He stated also that "the world press is full of reports to the effect that certain circles in the United States, having formed a bloc with their friends in Great Britain, are seeking to establish naval and air bases in all parts of the globe." He went on to charge that as a result of Anglo-American policy, advocates of a new world imperialist domination by one state had acquired great weight in a number of countries.

Beginning in June, 1946, there began a violent propaganda offensive against the United States, in which at first primary emphasis was placed on American policy with regard to China and Latin America. The United States was accused of seeking to organize both Latin America and China as American military preserves. At the same time Professor Tarle, one of the most effective Soviet publicists, published the article to which I referred in Chapter VII, "Lessons of the War," which traced an aggressive "pre-Fascist" pattern in United States domestic and foreign policy and voiced Soviet defiance of alleged American strivings for world domination. From this time on, the Soviet press and propaganda line regarding the United States has been a continuous tirade of violent denunciation.

Let us now turn to Soviet treatment of the Truman Doctrine. This doctrine, which has had tremendous significance in postwar international affairs, was the opening move of effective American resistance to Soviet expansionist pressure. Prior to its announcement, American resistance had been sporadic and ineffective. As the *Economist* pointed out on May 7, 1949, "The tide of Stalinist expansion was at its height, and Europe was asking whether America would step in firmly where Britain was obviously faltering under a burden too great for it." Greece, together with Turkey, constituted an important objective in the grandiose Soviet program of expansion. The two countries had been under relentless Soviet political and propaganda pressure since 1944. Failing to fulfill what appeared to be an agreement for a Soviet-British division of influence in the Balkans resulting from the Churchill-Stalin meeting of October, 1944, the Soviets had launched a typical campaign of Communist-led political penetration and subversion.

Soviet pressure on Turkey began on a great scale in 1945. It was applied by methods of psychological warfare, diplomatic maneuvers, including unsuccessful attempts to secure from Britain and America a free hand in this area, and military pressure which placed upon Turkey a grave economic burden. The Western powers had already made it clear in 1946 that they would not be indifferent to Russia's attempt to force Turkey to grant the U.S.S.R. the military bases which it desired on Turkish soil. However, it was feared in the spring of 1947 that Turkey's position, and with it that of the Anglo-Americans in the eastern Mediterranean and indeed throughout the Middle East, would be imperiled by a Communist overrunning of Greece.

Against this background, the anger and frustration reflected in the Soviet press reaction to the Greek-Turkish aid program of the United States is understandable. This Soviet reaction was expressed in front page editorials in *Pravda* and in *Izvestiya* on March 15, 1947, three days after President Truman's message to Congress outlining the Greek-Turkish aid program, in extensive quotations from statements by Henry Wallace and other critics of the program, and in numerous editorials. The lead article in *New Times*, March 21, perhaps best summed up the Soviet line. It stated:

> The direct purpose of the measures outlined in President Truman's message is to secure for the United States definite strategical positions in the Mediterranean and the Middle East. But the more general purport of the message is that it constitutes a frank proclamation of power politics in international affairs.

New Times stated further that this course had been more and more gaining the upper hand in American foreign policy since the death of President Roosevelt. Greece and Turkey were only steppingstones in American expansion. The real meaning of President Truman's message was the open proclamation of America's claims to hegemony over the whole world.

The reaction of the Soviet press to the Truman Doctrine exemplified the characteristic Soviet tactic of presenting American defensive measures as aggressive and expansionist. Nothing was said about the possible effect on American or British security of Soviet pressure designed to undermine Greece and Turkey. Since the proclamation of the Truman Doctrine Soviet propaganda and political pressure has been maintained against the Greek and Turkish governments and the American aid policy. An exceedingly trying war of nerves has been waged, in which promises and threats have been alternately or simultaneously employed as circumstances dictated. Against Greece and American policy in Greece, such measures as the formation of the Greek rebel government and its various peace proposals were employed. The Soviet government has assisted the Greek rebel government in the U.N. Its peace proposal of the spring of 1949 was calculated to assure the Greek Communists a foothold in whatever new government might be set up in Greece as a result of possible adoption by the United States of Soviet proposals. The United States wisely spurned the Kremlin's bait. With regard to Turkey, denunciation and vilification, coupled with military maneuvers on the Russian-Turkish frontier, have been prominent in one of the most important Soviet political and propaganda drives of the postwar period.

While American measures to defend the Anglo-American position in the eastern Mediterranean bulked large in Soviet propaganda, they soon yielded in prominence to the furious barrage of hostile attacks which greeted the next great step of American foreign policy, the European Recovery Program. Against the Marshall Plan the Kremlin and its agents throughout the world mounted the most gigantic propaganda and agitation campaign in history. This attack was not only directed against the plan's alleged threat to peace, but also against its alleged designs against the independence of Europe. Repeatedly the Soviet press has called it "the American plan for the enslavement of Europe." This and other aspects of Soviet propaganda against E.R.P., designed to appeal to national patriotism and to anti-capitalist sentiment in Europe, as well as to corresponding sentiments among the Soviet public, will be discussed presently. Here we are concerned with those criticisms of E.R.P. which proclaim it a program for establishing an American military instrument in Western Europe, designed for use against Soviet Russia.

Molotov in his statement of June 2, 1947, rejecting the British and French proposals regarding the organization of American aid to Europe, hinted cautiously but unmistakably that the Soviet government would brand these proposals as a plan for establishment of an anti-Soviet bloc. He declared that the Franco-British proposals could "split Europe into two groups of states." The Anglo-French proposals regarding Germany's position in the program would bring about utilization of German resources not for reparations to the deserving countries of Eastern Europe but "for other aims." That he had in mind the possibility of inclusion of Germany in an American bloc was indicated further by his criticism of the policy of "federalization of Germany" and "the line toward the increasing separation of Western German territory from the remainder of Germany" which he said was proceeding steadily.

During the summer of 1947, the Soviet press charged with increasing frequency and urgency that the Marshall Plan was a continuation, skillfully disguised, of the Truman Doctrine and that its aim was the organization of a Western bloc directed against the Soviet Union. A typical expression of this thesis was contained in a brochure by one of the leading Soviet political commentators, K. Hofman, asserting that

> the basic political aim of the Marshall Plan is the organization under American guidance of a "Western bloc" directed against the Soviet Union. It is proposed to include Western Germany in this bloc. The economic foundation of the bloc should be the revived industrial, and therefore, military, potential of Germany. The plans for restoration of the Ruhr are the first step in this direction.[5]

Similar characterizations of the alleged aggressive military purposes of E.R.P. were given by Zhdanov in his Cominform speech in the fall of 1947, and by Molotov in his November 6, 1947, address. The emphasis on the role of Germany in Soviet criticism of the E.R.P. is but one of many indications of the crucial role assigned to Germany in Soviet political calculations.

Soviet propaganda regarding American policy and Germany is one of the main instruments of Soviet determination to gain control of all Germany. But it is disguised as resistance to alleged American attempts to revive Germany as an aggressive military power for use against the U.S.S.R. On the one hand, the Soviets have constantly charged the United States and Britain with failure to carry out the Potsdam Agreements regarding denazification and the demilitarization of Germany. On the other hand, they have appealed consistently to German nationalism by proclaiming themselves the champions of German

[5] K. Hofman, "Chto Neset Plan Marshalla Evrope" ("What the Marshall Plan is Bringing to Europe"), stenographic report of lecture delivered September 1, 1947, Moscow, 1947, p. 9.

unity. They have emphasized this theme more stridently than ever since setting up the puppet German Democratic Republic. Their policy pursues the twofold aim of cultivating German sentiments and attitudes favoring the establishment of a pro-Soviet government for all Germany, and of exploiting fear of revival of German militarism to create opposition to the American plan for the rehabilitation of Western Europe.

A conspicuous manifestation of the unscrupulousness and disingenuousness of Soviet propaganda regarding Germany developed late in 1949. On September 18, the Soviet Military Administration charged that the police forces and "other military formations" of Western Germany totaled 470,000 men. In late 1949 and early 1950 the charge that the Western powers were reconstituting a powerful German army became one of the most prominent Moscow propaganda themes. At the same time the Kremlin unleashed a vicious campaign to incite German hatred of the West and to terrify pro-Western Germans, in which Malenkov's advice that Germans should take their political fate into their own hands, and Eisler's threat to "break the necks" of anti-Soviet Germans, figured prominently.

While pursuing its "peace and unity campaign" in Germany, and charging the West with reviving German military power, Moscow was obviously intensifying the two-faced campaign referred to above designed to make Germans instruments of its ambitions and to confuse and scare Western Europeans with the bogey of German militarism. The available evidence indicated that behind the smokescreen of anti-Western accusations the Kremlin was stepping up its schedule for the development of para-military forces in the Soviet-controlled part of Germany.

Soviet propaganda is, of course, supplemented by action. One may often gauge the importance of an issue in the eyes of the Kremlin by observing the nature of the demonstrations staged by the Kremlin and its Communist agents to dramatize the propaganda issues. This observation applies with equal force to the Soviet opposition to E.R.P. in general and to Anglo-American policy respecting Germany in particular. Gigantic demonstrations designed to terrorize the Western peoples and their governments have been staged against both. The Soviets, through the agency of the Cominform, consolidated the ranks of international Communism for the struggle against E.R.P. and sought to wreck it through a series of strikes in Western Europe. In the case of Germany, they resorted to the Berlin blockade. These measures were designed to exploit the world-wide fear of war and hope for peace upon which the Kremlin has played ruthlessly throughout the postwar period.

Every measure was accompanied by an enormous volume of propaganda designed to mobilize all possible opposition to American policy and to dishearten and discourage anti-Soviet forces. In this connection, it should be emphasized again that the Kremlin is acutely aware of the importance of creating the impression of the success and invincibility of its cause. Thus, the attacks on the E.R.P. have consistently stressed not only its sinister character but also the inevitability of its failure. The same observation applies to the airlift and other Allied measures designed to counter the Soviet-imposed Berlin blockade. But despite these skillfully orchestrated Soviet propaganda and pressure policies, American policy in 1947 and 1948 not only proceeded with E.R.P. but passed to a new stage in its over-all program of containment and rehabilitation.

In 1948 and 1949 an unprecedented development took place in American foreign policy. The U.S. decided in addition to its domestic rearmament to aid the rearmament of Western Europe and to enter into a defensive military alliance, the North Atlantic Treaty. The tone and intensity of Soviet propaganda against this treaty are typified by an official statement of the ministry of foreign affairs of the U.S.S.R., which occupied two full pages, or almost half of the entire space in all Soviet newspapers for January 29, 1949. This statement was divided into three sections headed respectively, "The Western Union, Weapon of the Aggressive Anglo-American Bloc in Europe"; "The North Atlantic Pact and the Anglo-American Plan of World Domination"; and "The North Atlantic Alliance, A Mine Under the U.N." These reviewed and excoriated the whole series of measures, including the Brussels Pact of March,

1948, the Rio Agreement of 1948, and other defense measures, entered into by the United States or other Western European or Western Hemisphere countries. This Soviet foreign office communiqué set the main line for a campaign against the North Atlantic Treaty which exceeded if possible the urgency and intensity of Soviet propaganda against E.R.P.

This campaign was waged by press and radio, by statements of foreign Communists to the effect that the Communist parties of their countries would fight on the side of the U.S.S.R. in the event of war, by the Soviet representatives at U.N. meetings, and in every other available medium. Its major theme has been that the North Atlantic Treaty is the chief instrument of an Anglo-American drive for world domination. The Pact has been declared a symbol of revived Fascist aggression, an excuse for military provocation on the part of the United States and an hysterical attempt of American capitalism to solve domestic problems such as unemployment by an armament race in preparation for a catastrophic war.

These and other propaganda themes all grouped around the general thesis that the North Atlantic Treaty is another evidence of the attempt of the United States to organize as much of the world as possible in military encirclement of the U.S.S.R., were of course supplemented by the stepped-up pace of the Soviet peace offensive of 1949, in which the most striking development was the inclusion in the May Day and November 6 slogans of an appeal to the people of the United States, Britain, and Russia to struggle for peace. They were summed up and emphasized in Malenkov's charge on November 6, 1949, that the program of American "imperialism" was more grandiose than that of Japan and Fascist Germany combined.

The foregoing survey of Soviet propaganda regarding American foreign policy indicates that the Soviet Union seeks to persuade world public opinion, including Soviet opinion, that American imperialism wishes to convert the peoples of the world into cannon fodder. But, as noted earlier, this appeal to the elemental instinct of self-preservation is supplemented by other propaganda lines designed to appeal to national pride and other deep-rooted political sentiments. Soviet propaganda in pursuit of this latter objective has attacked many aspects of American foreign policy, particularly E.R.P. and American policy in the U.N., as a threat to the national sovereignty and the political and economic independence of the peoples of the world. Let us examine this line as applied to E.R.P.

Molotov in his July 2, 1947, statement criticized the Anglo-French proposals for organizing American economic aid to Europe as "a form of international co-operation, which is founded on the dominant position of one or several strong powers in relation to other countries which have fallen into the situation of states deprived of independence and are in a subordinate position." Molotov motivated this accusation primarily by reference to the "Anglo-American proposal for establishing an organization to co-ordinate the economy of European states," which later developed into the organization of the sixteen nations which joined the Marshall Plan. This line set by Molotov became a regular refrain in Soviet press comment on the E.R.P. It has been repeated often and in many languages and media. Of course, it takes on many aspects. Sometimes alleged American pressure to hinder the industrialization of Western European countries is stressed. At other times, Soviet propaganda alleges that American capital is using the E.R.P. for dumping at high prices poor quality American goods in European markets. Sometimes the emphasis on the loss of European independence is political, and at other times economic. The official declaration of Soviet trade unions regarding the Marshall Plan published in the Soviet newspapers February 28, 1948, summed up the whole issue as follows: "Thus the Marshall Plan leads in fact to the liquidation of the national sovereignty of the Western European countries, as it seriously hinders the national industrial development of these countries."

Articles in the Soviet press under such titles as "The Americanization of Belgium" or "The Marshallization of Britain" portray Western European countries as colonies of the United States. Such articles are designed to appeal not merely to the working classes of these lands, but to all classes, which Soviet propaganda hopes to unite against alleged American interference in the internal affairs of their countries.

Soviet propaganda regarding the respective role of the United States and the U.S.S.R. in U.N. matters strikes the same lofty note of defense of the independence and sovereignty of nations against the rapacious expansionism of Wall Street. It has the same objective. The Soviets accuse the United States of by-passing the U.N. in its E.R.P. proposals and program. A typical example of this charge was contained in Vyshinski's speech of September 18, 1947, at the U.N. General Assembly, where he asserted that the "so-called Truman Doctrine and Marshall Plan" were striking examples of violation of U.N. organizational principles. Reference has been made in the preceding chapter to Soviet charges that American atomic energy proposals are directed against the basic U.N. principle of unanimity. A similar line has been taken by Soviet and satellite representatives in the U.N. toward all American proposals for strengthening the U.N. organization and for reducing the obstructionism injected into the U.N. activities by excessive Soviet use of the veto power.

American initiative in bringing about the creation of the "Little Assembly," and subsequent American support for its activity, was bitterly condemned by the Soviet representative and by Soviet propaganda. To put it briefly, the Soviet position is that the United States has sought to turn the U.N. into an annex of the State Department. All of this fits into the over-all Soviet thesis that the United States seeks world domination and rides roughshod over the sovereign rights of nations. Needless to say, no argument could come with less consistency from the representatives of a power whose rulers work ceaselessly to establish the universal dominion of a single political party and political creed.

Another important thesis in Soviet denunciation is that the United States supports reactionary, anti-popular forces. The Soviet definition of such forces is extremely broad, and embraces in effect all elements that oppose Soviet policy. Thus not only the Franco government in Spain, or the "Monarcho-Fascist" government of Greece, but the Labor government of

Britain and the Liberal or Socialist regimes of many Western European countries are attacked as American lackeys. The National government of China and the various regimes which have governed Japan since the end of the war have regularly been similarly characterized as lackeys or puppets of American imperialism. A massive and never-ending stream of news and editorial items drives home this general thesis in Soviet domestic and foreign propaganda. If one were to believe this propaganda, he would be forced to the conclusion that the United States practices the same methods of political and police control as does the U.S.S.R.

A well-known Soviet commentator, M. Marinin, summing up in *Pravda,* April 27, 1948, the results of the Italian elections, described them as the outcome of an "international conspiracy against the Italian people" which employed threats and deception to bring about a "doubtful majority." The Communist parties everywhere are portrayed in the Soviet press as the sole representative of the peoples leading the struggle against domination by the reactionary agents of the United States. Typical of this line was a statement in the Central Committee magazine, *Party Life,* for May, 1947, which asserted that "the reactionary circles of France, in cahoots with the imperialists of America and England, see in the French Communist Party the main force blocking the establishment in their country of the unlimited domination of the financial-industrial trusts and monopolies." [6] With tireless repetition the Soviet press records the various activities of the United States and "the American Party" in the political life of the countries of Europe and Asia. Everywhere rages the duel between the popular forces of progress and the agents of reaction.

The Soviet press seizes eagerly upon such colorful events as the libel suit brought by Victor Kravchenko against the Communist newspaper *Les Lettres Françaises* in the spring of 1949. According to *Pravda* and other Soviet newspapers, Krav-

[6] Quoted in the article by S. Nikandrova entitled "The Communist Party of France in the Struggle for the Democratization of the Country," p. 53.

chenko's suit was a scheme concocted by the American intelligence service. The whole affair, according to *Pravda*, "exposed the unbelievable crudity of the methods utilized by the State Department, and the complete immorality of the Parisian lackeys of Wall Street."

This line is applied not only in France or other Western European countries, but also in Germany, Japan, Iran, Turkey—in fact wherever the Kremlin has not established domination and where substantial American influence exists. The theme is calculated to appeal to working class and socialist resentment against local and American capitalism. In many countries of Asia and Africa it seeks also to appeal to the pervasive anti-Western attitudes.

Tito's refusal to submit to Kremlin domination gave rise in the summer of 1948 to a new and increasingly strident version of the Soviet accusation of American encroachments against the sovereignty of other peoples. With genuine alarm Moscow pondered the possible consequences of the first defiance of its authority by a Communist state. It launched a vicious war of nerves against Tito and instituted in 1949 and 1950 the purges of "Titoists" in its still subservient satellites, which intensified the already developing police terror throughout the Soviet orbit.

As the ideological justification of its campaign to crush all manifestations of independence among the Eastern European Communists the Kremlin could think of nothing better than to denounce Tito, Kostov, and other Communist veterans as agents of the American intelligence services seeking to restore capitalism in their countries and to hand them over to foreign imperialist domination. This line regarding "Titoism" was set forth authoritatively and comprehensively in the Cominform communiqué of November 29, 1949, the first official Communist document to acknowledge the danger of the international extension of this heresy. An indirect but provocative indication of the Kremlin's concern regarding Tito was the total omission of his name or that of his country from Malenkov's otherwise gloating enumeration of the buffer countries ringing the U.S.S.R., which he listed to support his thesis that Soviet frontiers had become more impregnable than ever.

As will be pointed out in detail in the next chapter, the Soviet account of American interference in the internal affairs of foreign countries is supplemented by vilification and depreciation of American life and culture. Just as in the Soviet discussion of the general problem of war and peace the Kremlin's accusations of sinister malevolence in American policy are accompanied by assurances to Communist forces and their agents throughout the world that American policy is doomed to defeat and the future belongs to the Communists.

Except for the spreading acceptance since late 1949 of the fact that the U.S.S.R. possesses atomic weapons, recent events in China have furnished the most impressive evidence that Moscow's boasts are not entirely unfounded. Malenkov, in his November 6, 1949, address, hailed the Chinese Communist victory as a great triumph of Marxist principles. *Pravda* editor, P. N. Pospelov, in his speech on the 26th anniversary of Lenin's death, January 21, 1950, delivered in the presence of top Chinese Communist leaders, laid even greater stress on the significance of Chinese developments. He devoted to them most of the foreign affairs section of his speech. Soviet propaganda, probably in order to lull Western alarm at these cataclysmic events and to counter charges of Red imperialism, emphasized their contribution to the defensive strength of the Soviet Union even more than their role in furthering Communist dreams of empire.

Moscow's presentation of the Chinese revolution was curiously egocentric in tone. Pains were taken to make it clear that the people of China should be grateful to Leninist-Stalinist leadership for liberation from Western imperialism. Doubtless this attitude reflected Muscovite imperiousness, but at the same time it may have indicated anxiety lest the Chinese leaders should eventually alter their exclusively Soviet orientation.

Moscow's propaganda regarding China has been less flamboyant than might have been expected. But it should be noted that it was accompanied by increasingly frequent repetition of Stalin's statement that armed struggle was the key to the liberation of colonial countries. This and other evidence indicated the Politburo's confidence that still further fruit was ripe for Moscow's picking in the East.

Numerous theoretical arguments are advanced in support of the professedly optimistic outlook of the Kremlin. Essentially, they can all be reduced to the familiar fundamental Marxist-Leninist theory of the fatal "contradictions" inherent in capitalism. Among the most important of these contradictions are the irreconcilable antagonism between the United States and Britain, and between the Anglo-American bloc and Western Europe, or between the colonial and semi-colonial countries of Asia, Africa, or South America and American imperialism. Now each one of these "contradictions" is utilized by Soviet propaganda and policy in various ways, which are themselves often contradictory.

Thus for example, the Soviet line seeks to unite the people of Europe behind Soviet leadership by charging that Britain and America have formed a bloc against them. At the same time, it does everything possible to inflame mutual resentment between Britain and America by telling the British that they have become a colony of Wall Street. For American consumption it manufactures charges against British imperialism and colonialism. In similar fashion, the bogey of German militarism and the memory of wrongs committed by the Germans in the last war are exploited to line up Western European and Eastern European peoples behind Soviet policy, while the Soviets simultaneously seek German support by recalling the suffering inflicted on them by Anglo-American bombing.

These international contradictions are supplemented in Soviet propaganda by calling attention to social contradictions within each nation, such as the well-known struggle between the proletariat and the bourgeoisie. Soviet propaganda reminds one, in fact, of a juggler with a dazzling bag of tricks. Is it not possible that too much cleverness will in the end be self-defeating?

The answer to this question can be furnished in the long-run only by the organizing capacity, the vigilance and self-discipline of the Western world. It will depend in particular upon the internal soundness of American democracy. As we shall point out in the next chapter, the Kremlin hopes fervently that the American giant has feet of clay.

X. The Postwar American Domestic Scene

LIKE its interpretation of American foreign policy, Moscow's picture of life in America exemplifies basic tenets of Soviet Marxism and aims at both Soviet and foreign propaganda targets. The Kremlin's version of American institutions and culture is a multi-purpose political weapon. It seeks to assure the Soviet elite of ultimate victory over American "bourgeois" democracy. It consoles the Soviet masses by trying to demonstrate to them that the lot of their brothers in even the greatest and richest capitalist country is far worse than their own. It seeks to persuade the peoples of Europe and Asia that America is the heart of a dying world from which can emanate no hope or promise for the future and to which it is futile and dangerous to turn. Finally, to all in America who will listen, it sets forth as the model for the future the Soviet way of life, which Moscow professes to believe will some day be installed in America as well as the rest of the world.

It is logical in terms of Marxism-Leninism and faithful to the spirit and emphasis of Soviet propaganda to discuss the Kremlin's presentation of the American scene under four main rubrics. A mighty stream of communications conveying each of these four basic themes has radiated from Moscow throughout the postwar period. The first deals with the fatal ills of the American capitalist economic system. The second describes the social problems of the United States in somber colors. The third draws the inevitable political conclusion from these economic and social fundamentals. Finally, to use a classic Marxist term, the cultural and spiritual "super-structure" of American capitalism is presented as a complex of devices by which the ruling class poisons and perverts the mind of the masses.

Soviet propaganda regarding the American economy, although bewilderingly multi-faceted in presentation and crushing in volume is nauseatingly repetitious in pattern. In the postwar period it has consisted first, of a dogmatic reaffirmation of the decades-old Leninist thesis regarding the general crisis of capitalism and second, of the reporting of American economic developments in this context. The faint glimmerings of a critical re-examination of economic doctrines on the basis of facts acquired during the wartime collaboration between the Soviet Union and its capitalist allies have been ruthlessly suppressed by the heavy hand of orthodoxy. As is well known, this development on what the Soviets call the "economic front" has been but one phase of a paroxysm of ideological rededication.

The reaffirmation of orthodoxy in the field of economic doctrine may be illustrated by analysis of the discussion of the well-known work of the venerable Soviet economist, Eugene Varga, *Changes in the Economy of Capitalism as a Result of the Second World War*. As is usually the case in major Soviet ideological operations, numerous premonitory signals of the coming storm were flashed for months before Varga's work was denounced as heretical and its author discredited. In July, 1945, the authoritative Central Committee Theoretical Journal, *Bolshevik*, in an article by G. Aleksandrov, then head of the administration for propaganda and agitation of the Central Committee of the Communist Party, entitled "On Certain Tasks of the Social Sciences under Contemporary Conditions," emphasized that "an important task of our economists is the study and explanation of the superiority of the socialist system of economy." Aleksandrov enjoined Soviet economists to pursue a "vigilant study" of developments in the capitalist world. He flayed a hapless Soviet economist named Sazonov who had been so rash as to maintain that economic laws prevailing in the U.S.S.R. were similar to those obtaining in capitalist countries. Sazonov was also accused of the perhaps even more serious heresy of advocating freedom of trade on the basis of a free market in the U.S.S.R. It is interesting to note that Sazonov had committed these heresies in a doctoral dissertation published in 1943. As is so often the case in Soviet Russia, intellectual work which had been approved earlier was condemned when the general party line had changed.

A similar fate overtook the well-known Soviet legal scholar, Kechekyan, for publishing an article in which he maintained that the essence of social relations in bourgeois society consisted not in exploitation, but in "non-interference" by the state in the economic sphere. His article had been published in the leading Soviet legal journal, *Sovetskoe Gosudarstvo i Pravo*, as a discussion piece. However, the authoritative Central Committee newspaper, *Kultura i Zhizn* (*Culture and Life*), in its issue of July 20, 1946, declared that since the views expressed by Kechekyan had been anti-Marxist they were not a fit subject for discussion.

On October 30, 1946, *Culture and Life* published an article sharply criticizing the theoretical "backwardness" of the Institute of World Economy and World Politics, headed by Varga. It urged Varga's Institute to "concentrate its attention on a deeper theoretical analysis of problems of the present stage of imperialism and the general crisis of capitalism." One other of the many significant straws in the wind preceding the all-out Soviet ideological campaign against America was a book printed by the publishing house of the higher party school attached to the Central Committee of the All-Union Communist Party entitled *On the Five-Year Plan of Restoring and Developing the National Economy of the U.S.S.R.; Materials for Lecturers and Propagandists.*[1] This book proclaimed bluntly that "the struggle to solve the basic economic tasks of the Soviet Union proceeds and will proceed under conditions of further development of competition in the world arena of the socialist and capitalist economic systems." [2] This work contained numerous assertions to the effect that the Soviet Union had been winning

[1] Moscow, no date, but judging by internal evidence published probably in the spring or summer of 1946.

[2] *Ibid.*, p. 3.

this competition in the inter-war period and that it was going to defeat its capitalist rivals in the postwar period. Already, the Soviet Union had a new intensive upsurge of its economy, while the United States was returning to its prewar situation of chronic unemployment.

In May, 1947, a conference of Soviet economists was called to discuss Varga's book, which until then was presumably authoritative, and indubitably the most scholarly and comprehensive presentation of the official Soviet line regarding the economic situation of the capitalist countries, including and emphasizing the United States. It should be noted here that Varga's book was only one, although certainly the boldest, most comprehensive, and most important of an ambitious series of scholarly works on the economy of the United States and other capitalist countries projected during the war and already approved for publication by the end of 1945.[3] Not only Varga and his books, but the other works in this series were subjected to scathing attacks. The same development took place, as we have seen, in literature, philosophy, and other fields of intellectual activity. In general, one can say that almost all scholarly works produced in 1945 and 1946 have been condemned. This ideological heresy hunt has led not only to a lowering of intellectual tone in the Soviet learned journals and to an accompanying rise in the level of invective in academic periodicals, but, and this is far more tragic, it has led to the snuffing out of promising tendencies toward ideological rapprochement between the U.S.S.R. and the capitalist world.

Although Varga's bold attempt to sum up the effects of World War II on the capitalist economy seemed to me, when I first read it, an orthodox Marxist-Leninist work presenting in fact a harsh and excessively pessimistic analysis of the capitalist democratic world, it appears in retrospect that this work was indeed, at least in some degree, "reformist" and "revisionist" as its critics declared. True, Varga affirmed that after some ten years the final changes in capitalism caused by the war

[3] For a list of these works and their authors, see *Mirovoe Khozyaistvo i Mirovaya Politika,* No. 12, 1945.

would manifest themselves in the United States, Canada, and a few other countries retaining some degree of economic health after the war. These final changes would be expressed "in the sharpening of the fundamental contradiction of the capitalist system, that is the contradiction between socialist production and private appropriation" and above all in the sharpening of the "problem of realization, or in other words the problem of the market." [4] Moreover, preceding this final slump into the "general crisis of capitalism," Varga foresaw, some two to three years after the end of the war, a "crisis of overproduction" in the United States similar to the depression of 1921, from which, however, he did not expect as complete a recovery as in the 1921-29 period. He painted in black colors the chronic and hopeless ills from which American capitalism suffers, and held out no hope that any of the various expedients proposed by American economists could bring about a genuine cure for these ailments.

However, while Varga had painted a gloomy picture indeed, he had introduced qualifications constituting a certain softening of the orthodox line regarding the contradictions of capitalism. His worst offense from the theoretical point of view was his thesis that during the war the capitalist governments had introduced a measure of planning in their national economies. He explicitly stated that these wartime measures in Britain, America, and Germany were not planning in the Soviet sense, and he made it clear in the course of his argument that even this degree of planning could not be achieved in peacetime in the capitalist countries. But he departed somewhat from the uncompromisingly bleak traditional Soviet attitude toward the possibility that capitalist regimes might achieve some degree of economic stability and social welfare.

In the first place, and most important, he interpreted planning in the capitalist countries during the war as planning by the state in the interest of the bourgeoisie as a whole. According to Varga, the state had forced the various capitalist monop-

[4] Varga, *Changes in the Economy of Capitalism as a Result of the Second World War*, Moscow, 1946, p. 12.

olies to conform to a general program conceived in the interest of capitalists as a whole, but taking into account to a certain degree also the interests of such groups as the farmers. This line, according to Varga's critics, contradicted the position of Lenin, according to whom the state was merely the tool of the big monopolies.

Secondly, although Varga credited capitalism with little ability to continue even the wartime degree of planning in the national economy, he did, partly explicitly, but to a greater extent implicitly, admit that in such countries as the United States or Britain a measure of planning was characteristic of the postwar capitalist economy.

"The economic role of the state," he said, "as we pointed out above, is diminishing since the end of the war, but all the same it continues to remain significantly greater than was the case before the war." [5] He stated further that while scientific societies for planning had been formed during the war in the United States and Britain, following the war the question of planning receded into the background. Still, he wrote, "it will again become actual in two or three years when a regular crisis of overproduction develops." [6]

Perhaps even worse was his implied admission that the postwar American standard of living could be maintained at a higher level than before the war. This admission crept in when he emphasized the great increase in American productive capacity resulting from the war. It was indicated by such statements as the following: "In any case it is clear that it would be a mistake to unqualifiedly regard the expansion of basic capital which took place in the U.S.A. during the war as an increase of the national wealth on the same scale for the postwar period." [7]

Probably far more serious, however, from the Kremlin's point of view were the implicit and explicit political conclusions, particularly concerning the relations of America and Europe and America and the Soviet Union, which Varga drew from

[5] *Ibid.*, p. 33.
[6] *Ibid.*, p. 50.
[7] *Ibid.*, p. 84.

his basic economic premises. He saw a great and useful role for American credits in the postwar rehabilitation of Europe.[8] He predicted hopefully that the attitudes of the capitalist countries toward the Soviet Union would not be the same as in the prewar period, and that the reactionary forces would not "lightly decide upon armed conflict."[9] He took what was later denounced as a reformist attitude toward colonial problems, maintaining, among other things, that the position of India vis-à-vis Great Britain had greatly improved. Finally, to mention only one other of the errors charged against him, he characterized the economies of the "new democracies" of Eastern Europe as "state capitalism" and he assigned to them a minor role in the world economic situation.

All these and other heresies of Varga's book and his numerous periodical articles were excoriated in the economists' conference of May, 1947, the stenographic report of which was published in a 64-page supplement to *World Economics and World Politics* for November, 1947. Probably because of his failure to see the handwriting on the wall and his stubbornness in refusing to recant, Varga lost his position as the leading Soviet economist. His institute was abolished.

The new dean of Soviet economics, K. V. Ostrovityanov, who had already in May, 1947, been made chairman of the economists' conference, and had in the fall of that year become head of the Academy of Science's Institute of Economics, the supreme body in the field, conducted in October, 1948, a sort of inquest on Varga's views.[10] Finally, in the spring of 1949 in a letter of recantation, Varga, who had proved more courageous or at least more stubborn than almost any other victim of the postwar ideological reconversion, acknowledged the correctness of the criticism directed against him.

What was the tenor of this criticism? What were the motives underlying the anti-Varga campaign?

[8] *Ibid.*, p. 268.

[9] *Ibid.*, p. 319.

[10] See Nos. 8 and 9, 1948, of the journal *Voprosy Ekonomiki* (*Problems of Economics*), for a stenographic report of this conference.

Since the discussion in the U.S.S.R. regarding Varga's views has been rather widely publicized, it is appropriate to deal briefly with the first of these questions.[11]

The flavor and essential content of the criticism of Varga are well represented in the following key quotations from the October, 1948, discussion of his book, taken from the opening and concluding remarks of chairman Ostrovityanov. In his opening remarks, in referring to the works of Varga and his former colleagues in the old Institute of World Economics, Ostrovityanov stated:

> Criticism has disclosed in these books a system of mistakes of a reformist character. These mistakes consist in ignoring and distorting the Leninist-Stalinist theory of imperialism and the general crisis of capitalism, in glossing over the class contradictions of present day capitalism, in ignoring the struggle of the two systems, in unmarxist claims regarding the decisive role of the bourgeois state in the development of the economy and the possibility of planning in the capitalist countries . . . in an uncritical attitude and kowtowing toward bourgeois science and technology.[12]

In his closing remarks, Ostrovityanov again roughly handled Varga's reformist views. It is interesting to note that in addition to repeating the standard accusations against the old man, Ostrovityanov also repeated the criticism, uttered by some of the speakers, of Varga's failure to recognize the possibility, nay, probability, of an "armed clash" (*sic*) "among imperialist countries" in view of "the aspiration of American imperialism for world domination and the enslavement of Western Europe."

However, the essence of Ostrovityanov's renewed attack was contained in his statements that: "Comrade Varga stubbornly persists in denying his crude errors of principle. . . ." And "Comrade Varga had not grasped the elementary fundamentals of the Bolshevik Party principle in science. . . ." Again Varga was accused of "reformism," and what seem to me at least in-

[11] See my article, "The Varga Discussion and Its Significance," *American Slavic Review*, October, 1948.

[12] *Voprosy Ekonomiki*, No. 8, 1948, p. 71.

sulting and threatening insinuations against his sincerity and loyalty were freely uttered.

What is the explanation of this extraordinary inquisition? In view of the secrecy shrouding Soviet affairs, any answer must be highly speculative. However, my guess is indicated by what I have written elsewhere: "Varga's gloomy picture of world capitalism, produced in response to the demands of 1945 and 1946, but carrying traces also of the line of the period of the 'Anglo-Soviet-American coalition,' . . . became obsolete. It was considered necessary to depict world capitalism as still more decadent and basically weak, but also as more evil and aggressive than Varga and his colleagues had portrayed it."[13]

I am, of course, acutely aware that this formulation leaves many questions unanswered. Was Varga attacked for overestimating or for underestimating the strength of the capitalist enemy? Was the attack on him part of an ideological preparation for possible war? Or did it fit into the design, which I have attributed to the Soviet leaders, of insulating the Soviet people, particularly intellectuals, against the demoralizing facts about life in the United States? To these and similar questions, no dogmatic answer is possible. Probably the safest rule is to assume that the Soviet leaders are guided by a combination of ideology and expediency, of aggressiveness and defensiveness, and that the relative weight of these elements in the equation shifts with changing circumstances.

In both the "pre-Varga" and "post-Varga" period of Soviet economic theory concerning the present status of capitalism, abundant evidence indicates the crucial importance in Soviet political calculations of the anticipated—and as one of the speakers in the May, 1947, Economists' Conference put it, "longed for" —collapse of capitalism. As the London *Economist* cleverly said on May 17, 1947, Soviet policy could be summed up as "waiting for the slump." One could fill reams of paper with quotations from the Soviet press regarding the coming depression in America. As I have noted earlier, news items regarding difficulties connected with reconversion in America be-

[13] "The Varga Discussion and Its Significance," *loc. cit.*, p. 233.

came frequent in the Soviet press as early as the spring of 1945. In the summer and fall of 1945, these became staple fare. A typical example, the prominent roundup in *Pravda,* August 15, 1945, entitled "On the Economic Position of the U.S.," recorded a reduction in steel production, and hammered the thesis that American production was based on war orders and would drop severely.

After the reconversion period was over, a running fire of items reported the disastrous effects of inflation in the United States but at the same time continued predicting a depression. With inflation-ridden and depression-threatened America, the Soviet newspapers and radio contrasted the U.S.S.R. with its steady "upsurge" in the national planned economy. A *Pravda* editorial, January 16, 1946, stated that "while in capitalist countries the return to peacetime development is being marked by a growth of unemployment and in some cases serious economic crises, the victorious end of the war is heralding a new rise in Soviet national economy."

Naturally enough, much attention has been devoted in the postwar Soviet press to strikes and unemployment in America. An analysis of the news items appearing in the eight leading Soviet daily newspapers during January, 1946, showed that about half of the space devoted to the United States domestic scene related to strikes and unemployment. Alexander Dallin in a study of the American news in *Pravda* for the year 1946 found that industrial strikes, unemployment, inflation, and the inevitability of an economic crisis made up one of the four main news themes.[14]

And of course not only the daily or even the periodical press as represented by *World Economics and World Politics* or *New Times*, has dealt with America's postwar economy and the coming crisis. Several of Stalin's postwar utterances, which have been mentioned previously, touched directly or indirectly on the "crisis" of American capitalism and explained the alleged slowness of demobilization and the creation of a war scare in

[14] "America Through Soviet Eyes," *Public Opinion Quarterly*, Spring, 1947, pp. 26-39.

capitalist countries as a capitalist desire to avert unemployment by inflated war production and armament.

A curious and little-known account of a conversation between Stalin and Leo Krzycki, President of the American-Slav Congress, on January 3, 1946, which, if accurate, is highly significant, was published in the *Advance* for March 15, 1946. According to Krzycki, Stalin asked about the American economic situation and again and again sought the answer to the question whether America would be able to give jobs to all who sought them. Krzycki states that he told Stalin that he foresaw a permanent army of unemployed in America because of the lack of a planned economy. Stalin, according to Krzycki, countered by saying that Soviet Russia could use many thousands of qualified mechanics and added that the Soviet Union was ready to guarantee to any American mechanic willing to go to Russia the highest possible American standard of living.

In his important conversation with Stassen in April, 1947, Stalin again hammered the theme of an approaching economic crisis in America.

Molotov, too, has dealt with America's real and anticipated economic problems in many of his important postwar speeches and statements. At the Paris Conference of three foreign ministers on June 28, 1947, he said: "It is well known that the U.S.A., in its turn, is also interested in utilizing its credit possibilities to expand its foreign markets, particularly in connection with the approaching crisis."[15] In his November 6, 1947, speech Molotov stated: "If among the ruling circles of the United States of America internal affairs did not arouse great worry, particularly in connection with the approaching economic crisis, there would not be such an abundance of economic projects for the expansion of the United States of America . . ."[16] Since these speeches, statements that capitalism is dying and that we are living in the "age of Communism" have been frequent in the Soviet press.

[15] V. M. Molotov, *Voprosy Vneshnei Politiki,* Moscow, 1948, p. 467.
[16] *Ibid.,* p. 495.

Molotov in his November 6, 1948, speech referred to the "obsolescent capitalist system, with its private ownership and anarchy of production and the social and political antagonism and crises which rend it." Capitalist countries are doomed, he said, to "periodic shocks and revolutionary upheavals."

With the increase in unemployment in the United States in the early months of 1949 the Soviet press stepped up its news coverage of American economic conditions. Items appeared frequently under such headings as "The sharpening of the economic situation in the United States." *New Times* for June 15, 1949, suggested that millions of unemployed American and Western Europeans could be put to work for orders for the Soviet Union and Eastern European countries. This editorial was only one of many items which related the question of the supposedly deepening economic crisis in the United States to one of the Soviet Union major foreign policies, namely, the apparent desire to increase East-West trade, on Soviet terms. This campaign had been proceeding in the U.N. economic commission for Europe since the summer of 1948 and had been publicized in many ways, including statements by the Soviet ambassador to the United States and Soviet representatives in U.N. General Assembly meetings. The prominence of this theme of East-West trade, which apparently was one of the Soviet concerns in connection with the Paris Conference of Foreign Ministers in June, 1949, is indicated by the fact that, according to Joseph B. Phillips, writing in *Newsweek* for June 20, 1949, *Pravda* or *Izvestiya* on five of the seven days of the week ending June 4 carried news stories on this subject.

Thus 1949 found Soviet propaganda regarding the American economic situation reverting to the thesis of the beneficial effects for American labor and industry of trade with Russia and the "new democracies." This theme was set against the background of doctrinaire Marxist-Leninist predictions of the catastrophic consequences for America of a new economic crisis. These and other propaganda sub-themes connected with the U.S. economy are perfectly consistent with the Soviet analysis of the nature of American capitalism and the Kremlin's foreign policy deductions based thereon. For the U.S.S.R. seeks persistently and consistently to extract for itself the maximum gains from the contradictions of American capitalism. It no doubt looks forward to the expected crisis of the American economy with relish and foreboding. The crisis according to the Marxist analysis is expected to weaken the enemies of the U.S.S.R. and at the same time make them more desperate, like a crazed victim of a fatal malady. The American masses and intellectuals are expected to become increasingly susceptible to the appeal of the Moscow propaganda line.

Soviet propaganda regarding social conditions in the United States is a logical corollary to the Kremlin's above diagnosis of the maladies of American capitalism. Moscow's distorted interpretation is presented in a vast stream of slanted newspaper and magazine items, with which the student must piece the picture together for himself. Sociological studies of foreign countries or of the U.S.S.R. itself are not produced in Russia. There has been no postwar study of capitalist society or culture comparable to the now discredited Varga series on the capitalist economy. It is obviously dangerous to produce comprehensive analytical studies. Moreover, the peculiar pragmatism of the Politburo which demands operationally useful propaganda products from intellectual workers in all fields requires Soviet social scientists to produce only those studies having political propaganda value either in terms of basic Marxist-Leninist doctrines or the current propaganda lines. Despite all this, it is not too difficult—in fact it is all too easy—to set forth the main lines of the Soviet picture of American society.

This is a uniformly somber and negative picture of disintegration and decadence, of irreconcilable class conflicts, of deprivation of and discrimination against the toilers, and of parasitic privileges for the ruling class maintained by force and fraud. Soviet comment on American social problems constantly hammers the thesis that these problems will become ever more acute and will remain incurable until the capitalist system is overthrown.

A very large part of the Soviet propaganda material dealing

with American social problems consists of statements or alleged factual accounts of the pathetic lot of various social groups in the United States. The *Agitator's Notebook* (*Bloknot Agitatora*), for January, 1949, quoted an agitator's speech to factory workers as follows:

> Not long ago I read several articles on the life of American workers. Gloomy pictures of capitalist realities appear before one's eyes. Unemployment is increasing constantly in the U.S.A. Wages are being cut and prices are rising and the standard of living of the toilers is deteriorating. It is a calamity if a worker becomes ill. He loses all possibility of receiving any means of existence, for there is no social insurance in the United States.[17]

This *Notebook* was published in an edition of 171,000 copies, for distribution among professional Communist Party agitators.

Another issue of the same publication [18] contained an item entitled "How the Workers Live in the U.S.A.," in which a Bronx truckdriver describes the unbearable hardships of the life of a worker in the United States. His wife states that obtaining food and clothing for her family is an almost impossible task. Both of these items were somewhat inconsistent, as they harped simultaneously on the evils of inflation and deflation. They are typical of a vast mass of material published in the Soviet press, the thesis of which is that although dreadful poverty prevailed among American workers before the Second World War, this poverty since the war has become still worse. The American worker is pictured as undernourished when employed and subjected to humiliation and degradation when unemployed.

The Soviet armed service radio broadcast on July 14, 1948, that the American worker's wages did not suffice for the purchase of an overcoat once in six years. On December 3, 1947, the trade union newspaper *Trud* published a dispatch entitled "In New York" by its correspondent Lapitski, containing the statement that more than one-third of Americans live in con-

[17] *Bloknot Agitatora*, No. 2, January, 1949, p. 13.
[18] *Ibid.*, No. 33, 1948.

demned houses. Lapitski's article gave the impression that the majority of the inhabitants of New York City live in frightful slums. In this connection, it may be recalled that Stalin in September, 1947, on the occasion of the 800th anniversary celebration of the founding of Moscow, contrasted the absence of slums in the Soviet capital with the existence of slums in capitalist countries, which doomed the majority of the toiling masses to slow death. The ridiculousness of Stalin's statement is obvious to all who have seen Moscow, which by New York or Chicago standards consists of a few islands of relative splendor such as the Kremlin, a city within a city, set in an ocean of slums.

The plight of American miners and farmers is painted in as black colors as that of factory workers and city dwellers. The magazine *Slavyane* (*Slavs*), September, 1948, alleged that the average American mining family hardly had a toothbrush to its name. It described as typical a mining family which possessed four beds for ten members of the family, no running water, and one towel. With regard to the plight of American farmers the Moscow radio on the eve of Thanksgiving, in 1948, broadcast a grim picture of the life of these American peasants, the majority of whom did not have enough food to live on. This was also true, according to the Soviet radio, of the majority of the American people in general.

The first issue of the economic journal *Voprosy Ekonomiki* (*Problems of Economics*) carried a review by M. Pevzner of Cary McWilliams' book *Ill Fares the Land*. Pevzner referred to the miserable plight of "millions" of "superfluous tramps" on American farms. He stressed the unusual misery of the "toiling masses of the village in the present period of the general crisis of capitalism." He criticized McWilliams for creating the impression that the plight of the American farmers, particularly migratory agricultural laborers, could be relieved by reforms without violent revolution. He quoted Molotov to the effect that capitalism had become a "brake on progress."

Lest it be supposed that Soviet comment and reporting on the situation of the masses in the United States is confined to impressionistic accounts which might leave the impression in the mind of Soviet readers that they deal with special cases, it should be emphasized that at least since the formation of the Cominform in the fall of 1947 the Soviet press has again and again stated that the vast majority of American families cannot make ends meet. An early example of this was an article entitled "The Unvarnished Truth Regarding America," published in *Trud*, October 19, 1947. It quoted *Pravda* correspondent Yuri Zhukov's "American Notes" to the effect that even in 1944 seventy per cent of American families could not meet their living expenses. It took the usual Soviet line that the situation of the mass of Americans had since then grown worse. Throughout 1948 and 1949 this sort of statement was repeated hundreds of times in the press and over the Soviet radio.

In the interests of complete accuracy it should here be pointed out that earlier, in 1945 and 1946, a somewhat less distorted, although not basically different picture of the life and living standard of the American masses had been presented. The series of articles published in the summer of 1946 by the noted Soviet journalist and novelist, Ilya Ehrenburg, describing his impressions of America derived from a trip in the spring of that year, gave the impression, at least to shrewd Soviet readers who are adept at reading between the lines, that the American standard of living was relatively high. Ehrenburg gave the impression that Americans could afford to be very wasteful. He stated that Americans like only new clothes, and that they hardly finished furnishing one apartment before they start looking for another. An American, he said, never has clothes made to order, for in any shop he can find a cheap well-made suit.[19] To be sure, Ehrenburg's articles were on the whole contemptuous of American culture and devoted much attention to many negative aspects of American social life such as racial discrimination. However, their generally favorable tone was so striking as to inspire much rather surprised comment among Soviet people, some of which came to my own attention while I was in Moscow.

[19] A translation of the above articles by Ehrenburg was published in *Harper's Magazine* for 1946.

Ehrenburg's articles were somewhat similar in tone to a very interesting lecture on the United States which I heard the leading Soviet geographer, N. N. Baranski, give in Moscow on July 17, 1945. Baranski presented what seemed to me at that time the prevailing impression of America among Soviet intellectuals. Except for perfunctory remarks characterizing the U.S. as "a mighty and noble ally," most of Baranski's material fitted into the then current Soviet thesis that while the United States offered much that was worthy of emulation in technical fields, its social system, that of a capitalist country which had entered the imperialist stage of development about 1900, was characterized by many evils. I found particularly interesting in Baranski's lecture his thesis that capitalist machine civilization had molded the psychology of the American people. Even farmers in America were capitalists on a small scale, and no such love of the land existed among Americans as could be found in Europe. The Baranski-Ehrenburg line of 1945 and 1946 represented a continuation of the sort of attitude toward the United States set forth in the famous book *One Story America*, to which I referred in the first chapter of this study. It certainly was not flattering. But compared with the postwar "cultural purge" and post-Cominform line their views were models of objectivity.

Let us now return to the main stream of postwar Soviet comment on American social problems. As is well known, one of the chief targets of Soviet propaganda has always been the evils of racialism in the United States. A great volume of virulent propaganda regarding the situation of Negroes in America has been appearing in the Soviet press since 1945. Like the general anti-American line, the attitude on this question has grown sharper since 1946. Items which appeared on racial questions in 1945 and 1946 were unfair, one-sided, and created the impression of discrimination without presenting positive facts regarding Negroes and other minorities in America. Those which have been published in 1947, 1948, and 1949 have been not only unfair but lurid and fantastic. The tone of Soviet comment on the Negro question in the United States in the past two years is represented by an article by David Zaslavski in *Pravda*, December 8, 1948, entitled "The America of Lincoln Before the Court of Lynch." Zaslavski took the case of a lynched American Negro named Mallard as the text for his excoriation of American racialism and the American system in general. "If Lincoln had fallen into the hands of Lynch," Zaslavski said, "he would have been hanged, beaten, and burned alive. The morality of Lynch is the morality of the real rulers of America." A fine example of the way in which Soviet propagandists utilize isolated facts to draw general conclusions which may be employed in their ruthless ideological war against American democracy is afforded by the following quotation from the Zaslavski article: "You say that in the United States there exists freedom of the person? Answer: 'Mallard.' You say that in the United States there exists culture and law? Answer: 'Mallard.' You say that in the United States there exists freedom of the press? Answer: 'Mallard.'"

The Soviet propaganda machine grasps eagerly at all examples of discriminations against Negroes and utilizes them in this manner. Extreme prominence was given in the Soviet press to American newspaper articles suggesting that Mr. Ralph Bunche declined an appointment as Assistant Secretary of State because of discrimination against Negroes in the city of Washington. The Soviet youth newspaper *Komsomol Pravda* gave much publicity in 1949 to a series of articles by Paul Robeson entitled "Two Worlds."

It should also be mentioned that Soviet propaganda devotes a great deal of attention to the plight, both past and present, of the American Indian. Nor does it neglect real or fancied discrimination against Jews, Armenians, Chinese and other peoples. Even the relatively mild Ehrenburg articles referred to above charged that the United States had created a "racial hierarchy" in which the aristocracy were the English, Scotch and Irish, followed by the Scandinavians and Germans, the French and Slavs, the Italians, the Jews, the Chinese, and lower still the Puerto Ricans, and finally at the bottom of the scale, the Negroes.

Another favorite thesis of Soviet propaganda is the alleged extreme discrimination against women in the United States. This is a constant refrain given special emphasis every year in connection with International Women's Day, which is celebrated in the U.S.S.R. on March 8. A resolution of the Central Committee of the Communist Party on International Women's Day published in *Pravda*, March 6, 1948, contained the characteristic assertion that "in the bourgeois world working women continue to remain the most oppressed of all the oppressed strata of society." *Komsomol Pravda* for October 25, 1947, contained an item typical of Soviet propaganda treatment of this subject. It referred to an earlier article published on December 27, 1945, written by one of the top officials of the Communist youth league, Olga Mishakova, asserting that as a result of loss of wartime employment American women were being forced to return to the hardships of housework and that many of them had been forced to engage in prostitution in order to make a living.

Much more could be said about the position of labor, the farmers, women, youth and other groups in American society, but these quotations are sufficient to indicate the flavor of Soviet propaganda treatment of American minority problems. With the sad plight of the American majority Soviet propaganda contrasts the privileged position of the capitalist ruling classes. It stresses the division of America into exploiters and exploited. The resumption of this line in the postwar period received cautious but authoritative expression in the press campaign of the summer and fall of 1945 on the theme of "Soviet democracy" versus "bourgeois democracy," about which I shall have more to say presently. Thus Molotov in his speech of November 6, 1945, referred to "genuine people's democracy, which we have not known in past times and which cannot exist in any state divided into the classes of oppressors and oppressed." A typical expression of this thesis in somewhat different terms was contained in an article by D. Shepilov in *Pravda*, November 4, 1946, making the statement that "the exploiting classes constituting 7.9 per cent of the population hold in obedience the remaining 120 millions of the population."

Such general statements are accompanied frequently by assertions that while the poor have grown poorer in postwar America, the rich have been growing much richer because of enormous profits. Finally, these economic-sociological theses are backed up by descriptions by Soviet journalists of life in New York or Washington which create the impression that these cities consist of a few palaces of the rich and a mass of miserable hovels of the poor. One Soviet journalist published an article in *New Times,* December 24, 1947, entitled "A Trip to Washington," in which he began by referring to the flop-houses of the Bowery discharging their contents, as if this were a typical New York scene. The contrast between rulers and ruled, between rich and poor, was summed up in an article by the well-known Soviet commentator Marinin in *Pravda,* April 28, 1947, as follows: "The present-day bourgeois systems in England and the U.S.A. are like pyramids, the foundations of which are poverty and deprivation, while the heights are adorned with diamonds and gold."

Against this background of inequality, injustice and discrimination the Soviet press paints a depressing picture of the resulting struggle for existence and its accompanying vice and crime. It contrasts Communist morality with bourgeois morality on the basis of the familiar Marxist thesis that morality is the expression of class interests. The purpose of morals under capitalism is to safeguard private property. The purpose of Communist morality is to strengthen socialism. According to the Soviets, bourgeois society is founded upon the principle of plunder or be plundered. As capitalism has developed, the gulf between ideals of freedom and equality and the reality of exploitation and oppression has widened.

An unusually systematic presentation of the contrast between morality and behavior patterns in the U.S.S.R. and in capitalist countries such as the U.S. was contained in an article by V. Kolbanovski in *Bolshevik* for August, 1946. Kolbanovski saw in capitalist morality selfishness, indifference to human suffering, and a wolfish struggle for existence. He contrasted with this a picture of morality and conduct in socialist society based upon solidarity, fraternal mutual aid, and unity of purpose. Socialized joy in work and universal devotion to basic moral principles were contrasted with selfish capitalist individualism and hopelessness about the future.

Such articles are typical. They attack the evils which, although existing in capitalist society, are also in full flower in the U.S.S.R. They contrast the real evils of capitalism with the imaginary virtues of Soviet Communism. These general criticisms of the morality of American capitalist society are of course supplemented by appropriate items regarding vice, crime, juvenile delinquency, and many other negative aspects of American life.

The Soviet propaganda treatment of postwar American politics conforms to and reflects Moscow's interpretation of American society. American political institutions and the political struggle waged within the limits which they set are said to be determined by class relationships. The Soviet account of the postwar American political scene has dealt extensively with the general concept of the inferiority of bourgeois democracy to Soviet democracy, referred to earlier, and with the particular course of political events since the death of President Roosevelt. The general line has been that since Roosevelt's death reactionary and even fascist forces have played an increasingly powerful role in American politics, both domestic and foreign.

Soviet criticism of American bourgeois democracy follows well-known conventional Leninist lines. It is, however, important to emphasize the enormous volume of material devoted by the Soviet press and on the Soviet radio to this question. Literally millions of words were poured out by the Soviet press in connection with the elections to the U.S.S.R. Supreme Soviet in 1946 and 1950, and the republic and local Soviet elections of 1947 and 1948, regarding the superior merits of Soviet political institutions. Similar material was produced in staggering abundance for the election of judges to the "people's courts" which took place in 1948. Ironically enough, these were the first elections of the lower Soviet judiciary, although the Stalin constitution of 1936 prescribed the election of judges and Soviet statesmen and propagandists had frequently and unfavorably contrasted the appointment of judges in capitalist Britain, for example, to the election of the judiciary in the U.S.S.R. prescribed by the Stalin constitution.

The propaganda regarding democracy has followed Lenin's line that proletarian democracy is a million times more democratic than bourgeois democracy. It maintains that only in the U.S.S.R. have class antagonisms been eliminated, and that only where the people own the means of production can there be true democracy. It contrasts this happy situation with the dictatorship of the bourgeoisie in capitalist countries like America. According to this Soviet propaganda, American democracy is merely "formal" democracy. Since the bourgeoisie control the means of production, they have the real power, including political power. Moreover, according to the Soviet line, even formal political rights are limited in America. Discrimination against Negroes and devices like the poll tax exclude considerable segments of the population from enjoying even the limited political rights available under American democracy. In the field of civil liberties, in which actually the Soviet Union has the worst record of any modern state, the Soviet propagandists maintain that Soviet citizens are better off than those of America. They harp constantly on the police terror under which Americans are said to live.

But let us now turn to the postwar Soviet line regarding the course of postwar American politics. This line, staying always within the framework sketched above, maintains that the major American political parties are instruments of Wall Street. The Kremlin must have faced some embarrassment in reintroducing this traditional Soviet view of American politics. For, after all, during the war Stalin himself had favorably contrasted Anglo-Saxon democracy with German fascism. It is true, of course, that he had expressed, even then, certain reservations regarding British and American democracy. The death of President Roosevelt must have been a stroke of luck for the Soviet propagandists. It enabled them to suggest that with this great progressive figure removed, American capitalist politics moved naturally to the right. That this hypothesis is correct is suggested by the astute way in which Soviet propaganda handled Roosevelt's death. It treated it as "a great divide" in American history. Roosevelt was acclaimed as a world "town crier" of democracy and international collaboration, two concepts which had been intertwined in both wartime and postwar Soviet propaganda. At the same time, it was suggested that the future would show whether or not Roosevelt's successor would continue his policy.

As is well known, the postwar Soviet line has been that President Truman rejected the Roosevelt policy. This is tersely summarized in the following quotation from a Soviet handbook:

> Under the pressure and in the interests of monopoly groups, the composition of the government was changed; ministers of the Roosevelt cabinet were gradually replaced by conservative figures. Reactionary forces took measures against the vital interests and democratic achievements of the working class. . . .[20]

There were further charges that not only the wealthy but the military were taking over the American government. The Soviet press pounded away at the theme that the appointment of General Marshall as Secretary of State, of General Smith as Ambassador to Moscow, and similar postwar developments, indicated that a coalition of the military and Wall Street was directing the postwar policies of the U.S. The new forces in charge of American politics have throughout the postwar period been accused of basing their policy on repression and terror against labor and progressive elements. Such charges have been accompanied by allegations that the American ruling classes, intoxicated by "atomic diplomacy" and a new Anglo-Saxon version of Hitler's philosophy of a master race, have been seeking to transform the United States into the base for a policy

[20] *Soedinennye Shtaty Ameriki* (*The United States of America*), second edition, Moscow, 1946, p. 311.

of world domination. Such charges became especially sharp following Winston Churchill's famous Fulton speech.

Against this background the Soviet press has portrayed the heroic struggle of the American working class and progressive intelligentsia, led by the American Communist Party. Of course, with changing circumstances in the postwar period the definition of progressive has tended to change. More and more it has narrowed down to Communists and outright fellow travelers, as the popularity of pro-Soviet forces and movements in the United States has tended to decline. One theme has, however, remained relatively constant. This is that the American working class and progressive intellectuals are actually or potentially pro-Soviet. The Soviet press has constantly assured its readers that the real America is on the side of the Soviet Union and the forces of peace and progress.

In order to demonstrate the correctness of this thesis it has had to exaggerate grossly the importance in American politics not only of the Communist Party, but also of Henry Wallace and his political movement. In the 1948 election campaign far more space was given to Wallace and his party than to the Republicans and Democrats combined. The flavor of the Soviet pro-Wallace publicity is illustrated by an article published by the well-known Soviet journalist, Yuri Zhukov, in *Pravda*, February 2, 1948. Here Zhukov cited as typical of the average American a Wyoming cowboy who appeared at the U.N. General Assembly meeting in order to get acquainted with the Soviet representative. In the same article, Zhukov referred to Mr. Wallace's "peasant hands" and "face of a scholar." He stated that one and one-half million CIO members were supporting Wallace's movement. This, of course, was a larger number than Wallace's vote in the election.

During the election campaign, the Soviet press emphasized that there was no essential difference between the Democrats and Republicans. In Soviet propaganda Dewey and Truman were "two sides of the same coin." The Democrats were said to be just as "tightly bound to the chariot of Wall Street monopolies" as the Republicans. Apparently expecting the defeat of

Truman, Moscow was prepared to exploit it as the defeat of a warmonger. Less than a week before the election Stalin himself told a *Pravda* interviewer on October 28, that just as "Churchill, the chief war instigator, had already succeeded in depriving himself of the confidence of his nation" so "the same fate awaits all other warmongers." Following the election, after a few days of stunned confusion, Soviet propaganda turned a flip-flop. In his November 6, 1948, speech Molotov explained that the defeat of the Republicans had meant the defeat of the "openly reactionary and most aggressive" forces. Mr. Truman was for some time cast by Soviet propaganda in the role of beneficiary of the American people's desire for a continuation of the Roosevelt policies. The small size of the Wallace vote and the defeat of Dewey, who the Soviets obviously expected would win, dictated this new line. For only by such a line could something be salvaged of the Soviet thesis that the mass of the American people favors a pro-Soviet American foreign policy.

It should not be supposed that Soviet propaganda entirely ignores the indifference or hostility of the majority of the American people to Communism and to the political institutions and principles embodied in the Soviet system. These attitudes are explained in various ways. True to the Leninist line, the Soviet press and propagandists emphasize that the mass of the American people are dupes of a cunning and corrupt press, controlled by a small group of Wall Street magnates which distracts their attention from the realities of the class struggle and the desirability of a progressive movement which would culminate in a revolution. Not only the press but all the agencies for molding opinion and in general the entire fabric of intellectual, cultural and educational life in the United States comes under relentless and virulent Soviet attack.

Beginning with discussion of freedom of the press in late 1944 and early 1945, a determined effort has been made by Moscow propagandists to demonstrate the corruption, venality and viciousness of the American press. The volume of material devoted to this question is enormous. All of the stock allegations regarding the domination by big capitalist interests, by advertisers, etc., over both the news and editorial content of the American press have been refurbished and re-emphasized. The importance of this campaign may perhaps be best illustrated by mentioning the fact that the first of the series of anti-American plays, Constantine Simonov's "The Russian Question," was devoted to this problem. This play dealt with the sad fate of an American journalist whose conscience would not permit him to carry out the orders of his chief, the press magnate, MacPherson, to go to the U.S.S.R. for the purpose of gathering material to illustrate a pre-arranged thesis. This thesis was that Russia desired and was fomenting war against the United States. Simonov's play furnished a convenient vehicle not only for the arraignment of the American press and American business but also for depiction of the harrowing fate awaiting an honest intellectual in America. It has been followed by a long series of similar productions.[21]

Perhaps I should emphasize here that Simonov's now famous play was not the first of the recent Soviet attacks on the American press, even in fictional form. The play by Korneichuk, "The Mission of Mr. Perkins to the Land of the Bolsheviks," to which I have referred in a previous chapter, cast a sensationalistic American journalist in the role of villain. Another forerunner of the Simonov attack, though not in fictional form, was contained in an article by the well-known Soviet writer Kozhevnikov in *Pravda* for October 8, 1945. This article, entitled "This is Stronger Than Anything Else," described his encounter with an American journalist of Slavic descent in Belgrade in the course of which the American portrayed United States journalism, and culture and life in general, as a grim, dark struggle in which only the corrupt and dishonest could survive. Like Simonov's hero, Kozhevnikov's American journalist had been deserted by his wife because he could not make

[21] "The Russian Question" was first published in the December, 1946, issue of the literary magazine *Zvezda*. Beginning in March, 1947, it played in some 500 theaters in the U.S.S.R., and probably enjoyed the largest circulation of any play in history.

enough money to support her in the style she fancied for herself.

It is not surprising that the Soviets should lay such great stress on the depreciation of American journalism. As good propagandists, they realize only too well the importance of the press and other media for influencing public opinion. They are fond of quoting statements by Lenin and Stalin regarding the role of the press as a "collective organizer" and "collective agitator." But the attitude which they take toward the American press is paralleled, as I have pointed out previously, by their attitude toward all other American intellectual and cultural media and pursuits.

Ever since the newspaper *Kultura i Zhizn* (*Culture and Life*) began publication in June, 1946, and since Zhdanov inaugurated the "cultural purges" in the fall of that year, all phases of American culture, ranging from philosophy through the social sciences, the natural sciences, the fine arts, and even including sports, have been subjected to attack. As with criticism of American social and political systems, the attack on American culture was accompanied by mounting praise for Soviet culture and the "Soviet man," its most important product. This all-out campaign had already been foreshadowed even during the war, with the appearance in September, 1944, of two articles by a well-known Soviet writer, Sobolev, denouncing the false glitter of bourgeois civilization which had proved dangerously seductive to Russian troops in Rumania.[22] Perhaps because this and other relatively mild warnings proved ineffective, the vast ideological housecleaning inaugurated by Zhdanov in the fall of 1946 was undertaken.

The postwar Soviet attitude toward American bourgeois philosophy has been set forth in a massive array of full-dress articles, two of the most important being "Contemporary Bourgeois Philosophy in the U.S.," by M. Dynnik in *Bolshevik* for

[22] For other background, see my articles in the January, 1948, *Foreign Affairs* and the May, 1949, *Annals of the American Academy*, entitled respectively "What Russians Think of Americans" and "The Soviet Union between War and Cold War."

March 15, 1947, and G. Aleksandrov's article in the July 15 issue of the same magazine, devoted to a vicious attack on John Dewey. Dynnik referred to American philosophers as "the chief bulwark of international philosophic reaction." And he stated that American philosophy "comes into ever closer accord with the reactionary policies of American imperialism." Aleksandrov accused the veteran independent liberal Dewey of being a "typical merchant" peddling the intellectual wares of a decaying bourgeois society.

Particular attention has been devoted by Soviet propaganda to attacking the social sciences in America. An article in *Pravda*, July 25, 1948, by Minister of Higher Education Kaftanov asserted that "the bourgeoisie is utilizing science, particularly social science, to confuse the mind of the workers. . . ." The first issue of *Bolshevik* for 1947 contained an eight-page article on American sociology by N. Baskin which began by quoting Lenin to the effect that "in general . . . economists and professors are nothing but the learned clerks of the capitalists. . . ." Another example of the same type of article, the flavor of which is suggested by its title, was that of L. Alter in *Planovoe Khozyaistvo* (*Planned Economy*), Number 5, 1947, entitled "Theoretical Armorbearers of American Imperialism," in which a vicious attack was made on American economists. Anyone who familiarizes himself with the content of these and many similar articles in the Soviet press and learned journals cannot but agree to extend to the whole field of intellectual activity the remark made by Sidney Hook in the November, 1947, issue of the *Modern Review* that "philosophy in the Soviet Union is a matter for the police."

American literature and art are as roughly handled by the Soviet officials responsible for molding public opinion as philosophy and social science. Even during the war, as I pointed out in Chapter IV, there was criticism of American war literature. This was intensified in the postwar period in a steady stream of vitriolic critical articles. Typical of these was an attack on Ernie Pyle by R. Orlova in the literary magazine *Znamya*. According to Orlova, Pyle belonged to the majority of American war writers and reporters who under Wall Street's "instructions" played down the political significance of the war. Pyle's picture of the American soldier was that of the mercenary who can be made to turn his bayonet against anyone, since he does not care whom he fights. Orlova attacked Pyle's and other American accounts of the war for this lack of "heroism." In part, this reaction probably reflects the inability of Russians to understand the American and British habit of matter-of-factness regarding matters about which Russians use highly emotional language. At the same time it expresses the postwar Soviet attitude of fear and suspicion of American cultural influence. Pyle was quite popular among Soviet readers. At about the same time as this criticism was published I met, while traveling, an intelligent young Soviet tourist guide who was reading his book, *This is Your War*, in English, apparently in blissful ignorance that it had been denounced as harmful and subversive.

Before the all-out anti-American campaign began in late 1946, American literature, at least its accusatory and critical segment typified by Dreiser, Upton Sinclair, Hemingway, Erskine Caldwell and many others, had been one of the few aspects of American culture the merits of which even such leading Soviet publicists as Zaslavski and Ehrenburg were not afraid to acknowledge, both in private to other Soviet intellectuals and in public print. Ehrenburg, in his articles on America following his trip to this country in 1946, indicated that while American newspapers obviously were intended for morons, American literature was the best in the world. A relatively objective *History of American Literature* was published in 1946 by the State Literary Publishing House. Of course the material on American literature in this period placed it within a dogmatic Soviet Marxist framework. But it was not couched only in a tone of abuse.

Now all this has changed. Denunciation of American writing and writers has embraced even the formerly much praised and translated Upton Sinclair who has been called a phony radical and an agent of the bourgeoisie. John Steinbeck, whose articles in the New York *Herald Tribune* following his Russian summer trip in 1947 displeased the Soviet authorities, has been likened to a hyena. The Communist writer Howard Fast is today outstanding among a dwindling handful of American party-liners who still enjoy the Kremlin's favor.

The nature of the Soviet cold war line regarding American literature may be illustrated by quotations from a public lecture given in Moscow in April, 1947, by M. Mendelson. It should be emphasized, however, that this lecture was mild in tone. Later attacks have been far sharper.

"A general summary of the development of American literature in the forties can bring no satisfaction to Americans," Mendelson said. He quoted Howard Fast to the effect that in America one evil leads to another, shame is piled upon shame, but all this is met by silence from literary people. What "dry terror" asks Fast, has "paralyzed the pens?" He went on to say that although "the forties brought a sharp drop in the American literary pulse," there was hope for the future. "Progressive American writers," he concluded, "look to the achievements of Soviet literature in order to raise their criticism of bourgeois reality to a new and higher level . . ."

Typical of the Soviet attitude toward American motion pictures was a slashing article by the famous and now deceased director Serge Eisenstein, in *Culture and Life* for July 31, 1947, entitled "Dealers in Spiritual Poison." Eisenstein had studied American cinema techniques in Hollywood before the war and used them extensively in his work. During the war he frequently came to the American Embassy to see showings of the latest U.S. films. He liked Americans and saw as much of them as he dared. It is almost certain that his attack on American movies was written with tongue in cheek. Like Pudovkin and other Soviet cinema leaders he had been subjected to the humiliation of public recantation for ideological sins—in his case for a film on Ivan the Terrible which was condemned for portraying this favorite of Stalin as a "degenerate" and his dread body guard as similar to the Ku Klux Klan.

In his *Culture and Life* article Eisenstein attacked American films such as *Going My Way* and *Anna and the King of Siam* for presenting the poison of political indifference and class harmony in a sugar coating of patriotism, sentimentality and humor. His analysis followed the well-known Marxist line that bourgeois culture is opium for the masses, but it was presented with considerable skill.

Distortion of this sort has been characteristic of the postwar Soviet approach to all aspects of the American scene. The interpretation of almost every conceivable topic, from anthropology to atomic physics, has been increasingly dominated by the interests of the Kremlin's anti-American campaign. Now, of course, no honest American can deny the truth of many of the Soviet charges against American life. But to present them, unrelieved by counter arguments or qualifications, as the whole truth about America can only lead to the kind of misunderstanding which has throughout history produced tragic consequences. At the very least, it renders communication and cultural interchange increasingly difficult and militates against the sense of identity among peoples the fostering of which should be a prime goal of statesmanship.

The spectacle is a sorry one. Some consolation can be derived from the fact that it reflects Soviet weakness in the current competition of civilizations. The Soviet rulers are stuck with a story in which they only half believe but to which they are committed. No doubt they are sincere in much of their criticism of capitalism. But data regarding life in America and Russia and the desperate vehemence of Soviet depreciation suggest that a worm of doubt gnaws at Kremlin faith. I am certain that this is still more true of the subjects of this vast experiment, the Russian people.

XI. The Russian People: the Kremlin's Achilles' Heel

ONE of the most significant problems of Soviet-American relations is the degree of success achieved by the Soviet propaganda machine in convincing the people of the U.S.S.R. that America is their enemy. Can the Kremlin make them believe that the American way of life, far from offering anything worthy of their emulation, is the embodiment of corruption and evil? I shall examine this question on the basis of my four years of personal experience in the U.S.S.R., supplemented by the exchange of impressions and opinions with many other persons resident in Russia during and since the war, and by such hints as can be gained from the Soviet press regarding the image of America in the minds of Soviet people.

This problem involves the attitudes of Soviet people not only toward the United States and the Western world in general, but also toward their own government and social and political system. This is so because in the totalitarian Soviet system dissent from or lack of enthusiasm for the official ideology tends, in the absence of domestic ideological competition, to focus on non-Soviet symbols, if knowledge of another way of life or system of thought becomes available. This line of reasoning must not be stretched too far. It would probably be a mistake to assume that a negative attitude toward their own system always leads them to a positive attitude toward America. Many factors, such as the extreme isolation of the Soviet people from information regarding the United States and the outside world in general, militate against a transference of ideological allegiance from Soviet Marxism-Leninism to any other system of ideas. Some of these I shall discuss presently.

Let us now turn to an appraisal of Soviet popular opinion of America, as distinguished from the official one. At the outset, it must be strongly emphasized that the student of this question, no matter how careful his work, must inevitably operate in an exasperatingly speculative realm. It is extremely doubtful whether anything comparable to what we in America know as public opinion exists in the U.S.S.R. To a very large degree opinion is manufactured by the government. That this is not entirely so, however, is suggested by the material presented in this chapter. If the nature of public opinion in the U.S.S.R. is wholly unlike that in America, the task of measuring it is even more elusive. Probably even the Soviet government, despite its all-penetrating party and police information services, is incapable of conceiving of or carrying out scientific public opinion research as it has been developed in recent years in the United States. Whether or not this is the case, it is certainly true that it is extremely difficult to make a scientific survey of Soviet opinion outside the U.S.S.R. The inaccessibility of adequate samples to the foreign observer because of restrictions on contacts between Soviet citizens and foreigners, as well as the ideological conditioning of Soviet people, are among the obvious reasons why this is so. Despite these and other obstacles, it seems to me that on the basis of contacts of competent foreign observers with Soviet or former Soviet citizens, as well as study of the Soviet press, some valuable tentative conclusions regarding Soviet popular attitudes toward the United States may be reached. These conclusions furnish the basis for hope that the attitudes of the Soviet people towards the United States may be regarded as a potential asset which can be exploited by an enlightened and intelligent American policy toward the U.S.S.R.

My own knowledge, in so far as it is based on personal experience of Soviet opinion, embraces the period from late 1942 to the end of March, 1947. In other words, it antedates the most tense period of the Soviet-American cold war. Although there is some reason to believe that the pattern of attitudes has not changed as much as might be supposed, and has perhaps not changed essentially at all, it would certainly be idle to exclude the possibility that the Kremlin's "hate America" campaign has enjoyed some success since I left the U.S.S.R.

I am perforce using the term popular opinion in a rather loose sense. It is my impression that the Soviet population can be divided roughly into three main groups: the man in the street, the intelligentsia, or skill group, and the elite. My own experience indicated that the masses were the most susceptible to foreign influence—provided of course that they came in contact with them—of any major group in the Soviet population. As might have been expected, those citizens who stood highest on the Soviet pyramid of power and privilege, were most heavily indoctrinated with Soviet Marxism-Leninism, and most completely identified themselves with the regime, were least likely to be pro-American. Political indoctrination and rank in the Soviet hierarchy were inversely proportionate to what from the point of view of the Kremlin could be considered as ideological infection.

The intelligentsia was, and I am certain still is, in a special, complex intermediate category. Foreigners who were in the U.S.S.R. while I was there and whose work or activities brought them into contact with Soviet intellectuals found them in many cases to be the friendliest and most receptive to foreign ideas of any group. Foreign officials, newspaper correspondents, and members of various scientific or technical missions visiting the Soviet Union found that in large measure they and their Soviet colleagues could speak a common language so long as the Russians acted as professional men rather than politicians. Soviet scientific and particularly medical personnel, scholars, writers, artists, librarians, and educators were surprisingly friendly and co-operative. Within the limits imposed by the system of controls, which were strict during the coalition period, Soviet professional people did everything possible to co-operate with and expand the area of contact with their foreign counterparts. Certainly their behavior and attitudes contrasted sharply with that of party workers and bureaucrats, not to mention the officials of the secret police. This is not to say that party members were uniformly hostile to foreigners. On the contrary, foreigners who worked in Moscow and other parts of the U.S.S.R. in the period prior to the cooling of relations among the wartime allies, found many party members who were friendly, and who wished to establish close personal relations with foreigners. But on the whole, party members and professional party officials, or to use a Soviet term those drawn from the "cadres" of the Soviet regime, were either coldly aloof, disdainful or hostile.

This breakdown of attitude patterns and social groups, rough as it is, helps us to understand why in the past three or four years Soviet intellectuals have been under such heavy ideological pressure to eliminate from their thinking all traces of "subservience to bourgeois culture" or "cosmopolitanism." It also helps to explain the anti-Semitic tinge of the campaign, for the Jewish members of the Soviet intelligentsia are even more inclined than their non-Jewish colleagues to sympathetic interest in cultural internationalism. Doubtless the Kremlin's fear of Zionism also played a part in its denunciation of "passportless tramps."

It should not be assumed, however, that the attitude of Soviet intellectuals, even during the war, was one of uncritical admiration toward the United States. On the contrary, many, perhaps the majority of Soviet intellectuals had negative attitudes of one sort or another. In part, these seemed to me to be derived from Marxist ideology. To an even greater degree they seemed to reflect the approach toward American civilization which has been traditional among European intellectuals, particularly continentals. I was often told by Soviet intellectuals that while the common man admired America, the intellectuals had far greater respect for the culture of Britain or France than for that of the United States, which they considered crude and standardized. But despite these qualifications, it was apparent that many Soviet intellectuals were capable of a considerable degree of objectivity in appraising American culture and civilization.

Intellectuals, at least during the war, were permitted a little more freedom of contact with foreigners than were party and government officials. However, the contacts were almost entirely official or semi-official. Only a very small number of Soviet intellectuals, and these on the whole not of the highest rank or distinction, were permitted to enjoy any sort of normal social relations with foreigners. I coined the term "official hosts" for this little group of professional people and artists. Some of my British friends call them "tame Russians." Even members of this small and, during the war and postwar period, favored group, many of whose members have since disappeared, would usually visit foreigners' places of residence only if the latter had the rare good fortune to live in apartment houses inhabited mostly by Soviet citizens, rather than the foreign embassy buildings where the majority of foreigners lived.

The ordinary, non-intellectual Soviet citizen differed in two important ways from either the officials or the intellectuals in his attitudes toward foreigners. He was less afraid to associate with them. And if he did establish acquaintance with foreigners, particularly Americans, he was much more likely to display an uncritical attitude of admiration for things foreign. Of course even the humblest Soviet worker or clerk ran some risk in associating even during the friendliest period of the wartime alliance, extending roughly from the Teheran Conference of December, 1943, to the end of the war in Europe. However, during this period, and provided the Soviet citizen who became acquainted with a foreigner did nothing conspicuously disgraceful to the Soviet regime, such as excessive and habitual drinking in the company of foreigners, or conspicuous display of gifts received from them, the risk was probably not very great. This was particularly true in such areas as Murmansk or Archangel, the American air bases in the Ukraine, or the other points where relatively large numbers of Americans came into contact under the favorable circumstances accompanying the handing over of vast American supplies to the Soviet authorities.

Even in Moscow, with its heavy concentration of party members and police, it was relatively easy for a foreigner who spoke Russian tolerably well to make the acquaintance of Soviet people and to maintain acquaintance with them for months. One might, for example, meet a Soviet factory or office worker on one of the suburban trains, or in a park or theater and establish a close friendship. Almost invariably, if the foreigner in these relationships showed a reasonable degree of friendliness, sincerity and sympathy, it was reciprocated with almost pathetic eagerness on the Soviet side. Indeed, it was my impression that ordinary Soviet people were frequently so impressed and affected by these contacts with foreigners that it would be no exaggeration to say that they had a psychologically disintegrating effect on them.

What did Soviet people admire in America and Americans? Perhaps the most obvious fact was that there seemed to be a certain affinity and sympathy between Americans and Russians as people. Despite the great differences of historical background, the two peoples share certain personal traits and attitudes. Both Russians and Americans tend to be rather breezy and informal in comparison with Western Europeans, particularly the British. Often, however, an awkward ceremoniousness renders normal business or social relations difficult. Unfortunately what seems to be the natural directness and simplicity of the Russians is often overlaid, especially among officials, by a wary and cunning suspiciousness, the product of the bitter struggle for survival under the Soviet regime. This quality, however, as far as I was able to observe, was much less developed among rank-and-file Soviet people. And under favorable conditions, almost all Russians seemed to be able to shed it and to find much common ground with Americans. I often heard Russians say: "Americans are simple people." This appeared to be high praise. The word simple (*prostoi*) means in Russian unaffected, sincere. Most Russians whom I knew or about whom I heard seemed to like Americans' directness.

They were also favorably impressed by American lack of pretense and what they considered the "democratic" American manner. Twice during my stay in the U.S.S.R. one American diplomat astonished and pleased employees of the American Embassy by occasionally taking the wheel of an embassy truck. The Soviet employees pointed out that physical and manual labor were separated by such a wide gap in the U.S.S.R. that no Soviet official would do such a thing. This gap between the educated man and the "simple" person was also observed by some of the American engineers stationed in the U.S.S.R. while I was there.

Russians liked Americans also because they were, as they said, "polite" and "cultured" people. American politeness was particularly admired by Soviet women. I have talked with a number of Americans who were stationed during the war at the American bases in the Ukraine, or who served in our short-lived weather mission in the Soviet Far East in the summer and fall of 1945, and with Americans who came in contact with Soviet people in many other parts of the U.S.S.R. In many cases they reported that Russian women who have known foreigners stated that they had been so impressed by their politeness and courtesy that after knowing them they did not wish to associate with anyone but foreigners. These observations tally with statements that I heard myself from Soviet people, both men and women. A young Soviet woman who had worked for a time on the dining car of a Soviet railway line connecting the U.S.S.R. and one of the contiguous countries told me that it was very difficult to reconcile herself to Soviet life after contact with the "polite" and "cultured" foreigners whom she had met. A moderately high party functionary told an American friend that it was terribly difficult for him to live in the U.S.S.R. after his experience in Poland.

At first when I heard such statements they puzzled me. Later, however, I came to believe what Russians meant by American or European "politeness" was a degree of respect for human beings as individuals which did not exist in their own society. At the same time, the word "culture" as used by Soviets meant good manners, courtesy and poise. Thus, in Soviet terminology, a person is "cultured" if he does not push or shout in a crowded subway train or theater entrance. Respect for personal property was also included in this conception. In this connection, an incident in my trip in the spring of 1946 to Vladivostok is worth noting. I got off the train at Novosibirsk with a middle-aged woman official of a Soviet government department. As we were leaving the train, she warned me not to leave any of my possessions in the train, adding: "You are not in America, you know."

To the American traits admired by the Soviets one must add efficiency and punctuality. Americans obviously enjoyed a reputation as hard, efficient workers. This aspect of the Soviet popular image of the Americans owed much to official Soviet propaganda which had for years praised this American characteristic. I think that it also reflected the favorable impression made by American engineers and technicians, who played such a large role in assisting the Soviet government during the earlier phases of its planned industrialization program.

Now, of course, the positive attitudes of Russians toward Americans were stimulated during the war. After all, capitalist America had come to the aid of socialist Russia against another capitalist power. Despite the minimizing of American military and material aid by the Soviet propaganda machine and the covert efforts by party agitators to depreciate its significance, it made a great impression. After all, tangible evidence of American aid was omnipresent. In all parts of the Soviet Union in which I lived or traveled, I saw American foodstuffs, clothing, and other products on sale in government stores, on the black market, or in use in Soviet homes. I was told by Soviet friends that American food and American clothing were much more important to the armed forces than to the civilian population. Russians often told Americans they would have starved without lend-lease food. Both lend-lease and UNRRA supplies bulked large in the popular consciousness.

American aid during World War II reinforced in the Soviet popular mind the impression of America as a friend in need which had been established by the A.R.A. during the famine that followed the First World War. I saw many striking evidences of the widespread distribution of American products in Russia. For example, fifty-nine of the sixty trucks which participated in the May Day parade at Vladivostok in 1946 were American. Much American equipment was also used in the May Day parades in Moscow in 1945 and 1946. In 1947, however, use of American equipment in such demonstrations was conspicuously discontinued. On my Vladivostok trip in 1946, I was impressed by the enormous quantity of American lend-lease equipment which choked the railroad stations, warehouses and sidings along the way. I also observed a great number of American locomotives and railway cars on this trip.

Considerable evidence came to the attention of foreigners indicating the gratitude of the Soviet people for American military and material aid. One example from my own experience occurred during the vacation trip which I took in December, 1944, as one of two American passengers on a Soviet military plane. While we were snowbound at a Red Army air base near Saratov, we became acquainted with a twenty-three-year-old aviator colonel and Soviet hero who eloquently described how the appearance of American tanks and planes at Stalingrad had helped to strengthen Soviet morale. Several times I was told by Soviet acquaintances that Russia could not have won the war without American help. Similar statements were made to other Americans.

The golden period in popular appreciation of American and British partnership in the war began after the establishment of the second front in Western Europe. Prior to this, despite popular gratitude for American and British aid, which had helped greatly to maintain Soviet national morale, there had also been an undercurrent of bitterness because of the absence of the second front. This was reflected in many jokes and anecdotes. For example, as I pointed out in Chapter III, American Spam was sometimes referred to as the "second front." But after the Normandy invasion it was quite a common experience for Americans to be congratulated by strangers on the streets or in parks, or by clerks in the stores. I personally recall cases in which Russian acquaintances in the weeks after D Day wept from emotion. All of this good feeling was climaxed in the monster demonstration in Moscow on Soviet V-E Day. This outburst of affection for foreigners was full of tragedy as well as joy, for it symbolized for the Russian people the deepest meaning of the wartime partnership—the hope that at last isolation and fear and suspicion were ending and that they might henceforth live in comradeship with the other peoples of the world. As I have written elsewhere, "V-E Day marked the apogee of a tide which was soon to ebb, leaving the Russian people once again shut off from even the limited communion with the outside world which had seemed to be developing during the war."[1]

Soviet popular opinion of America was reflected perhaps most strikingly in the almost universal deep affection for President Roosevelt. In part this was built up by the Soviet propaganda machine, but the dry, unemotional line of the controlled press could not alone have created the profound admiration and gratitude of the rank-and-file Soviet people for this leader of "capitalist" America. It is probable that the grief experienced—and manifested—among Russians in connection with Roosevelt's death was more genuine and widespread than the popular mourning in America.

Now a cynic might attribute this to the Soviet peoples' associating Roosevelt with lend-lease, with powdered eggs and canned goods, but I think it was far more than that. Not that the material basis for gratitude was unimportant. I remember, for example, that one Soviet girl told an American friend a month or so before Roosevelt's death that she liked Roosevelt because he fed her, but disliked Churchill because he was too cunning. However, it seems to me that what impressed the Russian people most deeply was that in a hard world in which authority was not normally benevolent, here was a powerful leader who had extended the hand of friendship in an hour of need.

The attitude of ideological die-hards toward Roosevelt, including presumably the upper party echelons, seems to have differed from that of the majority. They probably regarded him as a "far-sighted politician" (as one of my Soviet acquaintances, a lawyer, put it in 1946) who was trying to save capitalism. In March, 1949, at a conference of Soviet historians in

[1] Cf. my article "What Russians Think of Americans," in *Foreign Affairs* for January, 1948.

Leningrad the historian Zubok was attacked for ignoring the fact that Roosevelt's efforts to solve the problem of "class collaboration" were made under the pressure of the "masses" and that he was "safeguarding the interests of monopolistic capital." Thus Soviet propaganda, which in prominent editorials on the occasion of Roosevelt's death flatly committed itself to the thesis that he was a great "democrat" and "town crier" of peace, security and international collaboration, has begun openly to attack even Roosevelt, perhaps the last great symbol in the Soviet popular mind of the Soviet-American "coalition."

A number of hints of this inevitable final step in the jettisoning of the coalition line had appeared earlier. Some members of the anti-Varga group in the May, 1947, conference of economists cautiously criticized Varga and his colleagues for a too favorable attitude to Roosevelt and his reforms. V. Avarin's book, *The Struggle for the Pacific Ocean* (*Borba Za Tikhi Okean,* Moscow, 1947), took an unfavorable view of Roosevelt's Pacific Ocean policy. Avarin's views, however, were criticized by S. Deborin in *Voprosy Istorii* (*Problems of History*), for April, 1948. The apparent beginning of an open attempt to deflate Roosevelt is another melancholy manifestation of the expediential and instrumental attitude which the Soviet leaders take toward truth. Truth to them is whatever is useful to Communism. However, the caution and delay displayed in connection with the as yet only partial repudiation, bear out, it seems to me, the deep impression Roosevelt made on the Soviet public mind as a symbol of American humanitarianism, generosity and power.

Thus far I have been describing Soviet attitudes toward Americans as people. These favorable attitudes were accompanied by similar positive attitudes or beliefs regarding various aspects of American culture, life, and institutions. Soviet admiration of American technical achievements was until recently sanctioned even by the Kremlin. It was so deeply rooted in popular opinion that I doubt if the postwar campaign to liquidate it has succeeded, particularly in view of the success of the Allied air lift. It would scarcely be an exaggeration to state that Soviet Russians traditionally regarded the United States as a technological wonderland. I was particularly impressed on the trip which I took on a Soviet naval plane in 1944 by the undisguised and delighted admiration expressed by the Soviet naval aviators who were our fellow passengers for the mechanical aspects of American civilization which they had observed in New York and other American cities. Such things as automats and showers, to mention trifling examples, made a great impression on them. The jeep, which was known in the Soviet Union by the name of "Willys," was a widespread advertisement of American know-how. One could also mention American aircraft, locomotives, and, perhaps most important of all, because of their widespread distribution and the role they played in the great Soviet offensives of 1944 and 1945, American trucks. An intelligent American GI who served at Poltava told me that among the Soviet military personnel there the word "Studebaker" was a superlative term of praise employed by Soviet soldiers even to describe the ladies of their choice. As I have pointed out in Chapter I, Soviet admiration for American technology was nothing new, but the flood of American products which reached the U.S.S.R. during the war confirmed and intensified it.

A similar observation could be made regarding the Soviet impression of the American standard of living. In this area of opinion, the war probably produced even more pronounced effects than in that concerned with American technology. Prior to the war many Soviet citizens accepted the Soviet propaganda picture of America as a country consisting of a wealthy parasitic minority and a poverty-stricken exploited majority. What they learned about the life of ordinary workers and farmers in the countries of Eastern and Central Europe administered a shock to hundreds of thousands, perhaps millions, of Soviet soldiers. They found that the majority of the population in these countries, which they had for years been told were living in misery, enjoyed at least on the material level a better life than they did themselves.

Still more surprising was the impression received by Soviet people who came in contact with Americans whether in the

Soviet Union, in America or elsewhere. Virtually every Soviet person among the several hundred with whom I talked during my war years in Russia was impressed by what they had learned of American material prosperity; perhaps the most striking manifestation of this fact was the frequency with which Soviet people would ask Americans the question: "Things are better in America, aren't they?" I was asked this question by tots in the parks around Moscow, by a Red Army lieutenant whom I met in a Leningrad restaurant in the fall of 1945, by a woman who worked at the air base at which we stayed in December, 1944, by a Soviet Navy lieutenant on my Vladivostok trip in the spring of 1946, and by many others. One of the most interesting places in which this question was put to American visitors was at the rest home near Moscow for children of workers of the newspaper, *Pravda*.

Why did Soviet people ask this question? A few samples of my conversations with Russians may help answer the question. During my trip to Vladivostok in April, 1946, I had a long conversation with a woman official stationed in the Soviet Far North. She described how the people of the little outposts in which she worked had lived all during the war on American food products. Later the same year while on a trip to the Ukraine I talked at length with a Soviet lawyer who had during the war been stationed in the Soviet Far East. He told how impressed he had been at Vladivostok, where he had seen American cigarettes, lemon powder, and even bread arriving from America packed in cellophane and kept fresh and in fine condition. A Soviet actor with whom I talked on one of my trips in 1946 told how one of his relatives had become heir to a small fortune based on property located in America but how he had been unable to receive the proceeds because of Soviet currency restrictions. In the course of this conversation my actor friend said: "Dollars are real money, but rubles are nothing but paper." In the little town of Mtskheta, Georgia, where I was held for questioning for a few hours in February, 1947, the policemen who arrested me, and who freely accepted some American cigarettes, asked me whether it was true that life was so much better in the United States than in the Soviet Union.

One way in which Soviet people indicated their favorable impression of the superiority of the American standard of living was the amazement they so often expressed when told how much the average American worker or salaried employee could purchase per month for his income in dollars. This was not surprising, in view of the fact that while I was in the U.S.S.R. a good suit of clothes cost several times the average monthly income of a Soviet factory worker or clerk.

Another manifestation of the same attitude was the reaction of Russian people to American films. Russians with whom I talked regarding the American films *Mission to Moscow* and *North Star* said that they were "funny" because they showed Soviet villages, towns, and homes which seemed fantastically luxurious to Russian spectators. A well-educated and cultivated Georgian woman, the wife of a Soviet Army officer, who was one of my fellow passengers on the Tbilisi-Moscow plane in February, 1947, said that it was depressing to her to see American movies, because of the contrast in the life they portrayed with that of the Soviet people. She herself appeared to be moderately well-off, but she described conditions of distressing poverty even in Georgia, which seemed to me almost an island of plenty in a sea of want.

In view of all this it is not surprising that many Soviet people with whom I talked expressed a desire to leave the U.S.S.R. and go to America. A clerk in a Moscow book store told me that one of his best friends bitterly regretted the fact that he had not stayed in the United States, where he had been for a time in his youth. A Soviet worker with whom I was casually acquainted for a while expressed the same regret. Rather similar was the experience of another American who with a Soviet acquaintance happened to be in a small factory. When some of the workers learned that he was soon going home to America they excitedly told him how lucky he was and how unlucky they were, "condemned" to spend the rest of their life in Russia. As I have said, such attitudes were expressed by

Soviet people wherever Americans were stationed. I recall a conversation with an American naval officer assigned for a time in 1945 to Khabarovsk. He told me that for a few weeks before Moscow ordered the police to seal off the Soviet population from contact with the Americans, his life was a continuous round of invitations to Soviet homes. In his conversations with the local people, they expressed admiration for the American standard of living. It was obvious that they knew a good deal about it. Some of them asked him whether they thought the Soviet people would ever have such comforts as running water or bathrooms.

I could cite many more examples to illustrate the point, but perhaps enough has been said to indicate the nature of the reaction in the minds of many Soviet people when they compared the gray austerity of their own life with what they had learned about the American standard of living. Of course it should not be assumed that all Soviet people who expressed interest in the possibility of making a trip to America were deeply discontented with Soviet life. Some of them undoubtedly were motivated by a spirit of adventure or by intellectual curiosity. Many would probably have remained convinced of the superiority of the Soviet system even if they had come to the United States. Some would have liked to go to America for educational reasons. I was told at the foreign language institutes and universities which I visited in the Ukraine and Georgia in 1946 that many students and teachers desired to go to America for educational trips. The rector of one institution wistfully remarked that before the revolution travel abroad had been relatively free. A similar sentiment was expressed by several actors and artists whom I met in Moscow.

Thus far in this chapter I may have created the impression that only the material or technical aspects of America appealed to Soviet Russians. This would be an incorrect and one-sided conclusion. There was also much interest in many aspects of American scientific, literary, artistic or dramatic achievement. There was during the war and for some time thereafter, until the Soviet government imposed repressive measures, a great demand among Soviet people for American plays, films, and music. I knew several members of a Moscow jazz orchestra, for example, who were extremely anxious to get scores of American jazz tunes. Some Americans succeeded in getting for their Soviet musician friends a few such scores. Incidentally, the favorite piece in Moscow's leading nightclub, located in the Moscow Hotel, was "Alexander's Ragtime Band." This remained true from the reopening of dancing there in 1944 until I left in March, 1947. Indeed, so frequently was this piece played that guests were likely to become heartily sick of it.

Officials of the Foreign Commission of the Union of Soviet Writers clamored for up-to-date American short stories and novels. Members of the American Embassy's cultural relations and publication sections enjoyed cordial relations with their colleagues in this commission. Insofar as possible, its officials did everything they could to supply us with Soviet literary productions. A similar pattern prevailed throughout the range of contacts among Soviet and American personnel in the cultural relations field, subject of course always to the harassing restrictions imposed by the Soviet bureaucracy. I succeeded for a time in arranging with the director of a Soviet publishing house a profitable exchange of American detective stories for Soviet war posters. In the motion picture field, the Committee on Cinema Affairs displayed at private showings a considerable number of American films. As noted in Chapter IV, these were shown to the Soviet public, including several Deanna Durbin films and such Walt Disney films as *Bambi.*

Concerts of American and British music were arranged by Voks, the All-Union Society for Cultural Relations with Foreign Countries. Yehudi Menuhin's tour of the U.S.S.R. in 1946 was a great success.

All of this and much more reflected, in my opinion, the Soviet intelligentsia's wartime hope that closer cultural relations would follow the war. There was a certain lag of opinion and even policy in the scholarly and cultural field behind official anti-American propaganda. As late as December 28, 1945, *Komsomol Pravda* in an editorial urging the study of foreign languages expressed approval of the interest shown by Soviet young people in the plays of Oscar Wilde. A few months later, Wilde's plays were excoriated as bourgeois poison.

In the field of science, the pattern was similar. An extremely cordial welcome was shown by Soviet scientists to their American and other foreign colleagues during the 220th Anniversary Jubilee of the Russian Academy of Sciences in June, 1945. Soviet scientists invited their foreign colleagues to their offices and presented them in many cases with precious gifts of publications, sometimes extremely difficult or even impossible to obtain. Cordial relations on the basis of correspondence, exchange of publications, and to a certain extent personal contacts, prevailed for some time after the end of the war between Soviet medical circles and their foreign counterparts. I myself had several friendly interviews with officials of medical publishing houses, and succeeded in arranging some valuable exchanges of medical publications. In general, traces of this wartime cordiality in the fields of science and scholarship lingered on for some time, though with diminishing vitality, after the end of the war. As late as the fall of 1946 Professor Corbett of Yale University succeeded in meeting a number of Soviet scholars in the social science field, though as he pointed out in his "Moscow Report" his visit was not so successful as might have been hoped and the contacts he succeeded in arranging were marked by an unnatural constraint.[2]

The reader may wonder whether any of the favorable or even enthusiastic attitudes of Soviet citizens discussed thus far toward Americans and America extended into the field of political institutions or ideology. This question is extremely difficult to answer. To a large extent, those Soviet citizens with whom Americans came into contact were either too simple or too cautious to express opinions (or perhaps to have them) on comparative institutions or ideology. It was always my impression that the vast majority of Soviet people were politically indifferent and apathetic. I often heard ordinary Soviet people

[2] Memorandum No. 22, Yale Institute of International Studies, 1947.

say, "We are little people," or "That is not our affair." As one of my Soviet friends said: "The Party is boss here." I remember with what surprise a Soviet girl telegraph messenger while I was in Vladivostok in May, 1946, answered the questions of one of the Americans there whether the staff in her office had voted on who was to work and who was to have a holiday on May Day. She looked at us in apparent amazement and replied that of course the "bosses" decided such questions.

A similar attitude appeared to prevail with regard to elections to the Supreme Soviet of the U.S.S.R., or to the Supreme Soviets of the various Republics. I discussed the election system with several intelligent young Soviet people. Their opinion seemed to be that they were a carefully arranged demonstration, supervised by the Kremlin, and that voting was a duty rather than a right. Most of them with whom I discussed this question seemed to be highly cynical. I remember how one evening while walking in Moscow with a Soviet friend we came across a poster showing a factory worker candidate for the Supreme Soviet of the R.S.F.S.R. I pointed to this as an example of Soviet democracy, and my friend laughingly said that occasionally a worker was chosen as a candidate but that he would simply shout "Hoorah!" and do as he was told. When I asked another Soviet friend how candidates were chosen, the reply was: "Like recognizes like from afar."

If such opinions reflected the attitude of Soviet people toward their own political life and toward the command-subordination relationship in the Soviet system, and I think they did, it would be too much to expect that these people could have a very clear understanding of Western democracy. I found considerable ignorance and misunderstanding of the nature of the American political system among the Soviet people whom I knew. Rather typical, it seems to me, was the attitude of the pilot of the plane on which I flew to Baku in December, 1944. He assumed that President Roosevelt had been elected for life. One of my Soviet friends told me during the American election campaign of 1944 that many Soviet people were alarmed by the fact that an election was being held in America at all, and thought that it indicated that the United States was about to change its policy to an anti-Soviet one. It was exceedingly difficult for Soviet people to understand that in America, even in wartime, criticism of government policy was permitted. An illustration of this attitude was furnished me by a conversation with a high official of a Soviet publishing house with whom I had done business and whom I met in a convivial mood in a Moscow cafe shortly after V-E Day. We engaged in a long conversation, in which he tried to prove to me that genuine democracy existed in the U.S.S.R. He said, among other things, that one should not judge the policy of the Soviet government by the critical attitude of the Soviet press toward the United States or some of its policies, any more than one should judge America by its jingo press. He attempted to prove that there was considerable freedom of discussion within the Communist Party, of which he himself was a member. Something of the real flavor of his approach to politics was indicated by his statement that people like Herbert Hoover should be "eliminated" to make democracy safe throughout the world.

From these and other observations I came to the conclusion that the Soviet people probably could not fully understand the complicated American political system. However, I also came away with the opinion, which I still hold, that if they did not fully understand political democracy of the Anglo-Saxon type they did have a desire for greater civil liberties and more government respect for the dignity of the individual human being than exists in the U.S.S.R. The widespread terror and hatred of the secret police which any person who really knows Soviet people is aware of is but one indication of these aspirations. The desire to travel, to change one's job freely, to be able to read foreign publications, and many others which are impossible aspirations for Soviet people but are taken for granted by Americans afford further indications. Perhaps I can epitomize this phase of the Soviet common man's attitude toward American freedom by referring to the statement of one of my Soviet friends that I was lucky to live in a country in which a human being could "breathe."

Several Russian friends told me that the reason the Soviet government was afraid to permit free association between Soviet citizens and Americans or free travel of Soviet people to the United States was that, as one of my Soviet friends put it: "Americans don't want to remain here but Soviet people stay in America." I do not know whether knowledge of the defection of such persons as Victor Kravchenko was at all widespread in Russia while I was there, but I do remember being told by several Soviet acquaintances during the San Francisco Conference that some members of the secretarial staff of the Soviet delegation had been hastily recalled because they were incautiously friendly with Americans. In this connection, I was intensely interested in the statement made to me by a high American official after the San Francisco Conference that Sergei Kruglov, who was in charge of the Soviet security arrangements at the Conference, and who later became head of the M.V.D., expressed amazement at the standard of living of ordinary Americans. This is not to imply, of course, that privileged individuals like Kruglov are likely to be tempted by the fleshpots of bourgeois civilization, but it is not illogical to suppose that they are shrewdly aware of its attractions for their less fortunate citizens. Indeed, they and their masters in the Kremlin are far more aware of the almost magical appeal of America to many Soviet citizens than almost any American can be. They realize that for many Soviet people America symbolizes some of their deepest hopes and aspirations.

Of course, even during the highly favorable period of the Anglo-American alliance there were negative attitudes toward the United States among the Soviet people, particularly among the upper strata. Several decades of carefully inculcated suspicion of the outside world, reinforced by the Nazi attack on Russia, could scarcely fail to leave their mark. Moreover, a hungry and harassed people may in some degree at least respond to the efforts of its rulers to divert its discontent and unhappiness against a foreign scapegoat. It must also be remembered that the Russian people, though possessed of much feeling of pride in its power and achievement, and in its capacity for endurance and suffering, has at the same time a certain resentment against the "haughty and conventional West," to borrow a phrase from one of the most brilliant of American experts on Russia. In view of these considerations, it is not surprising that foreigners who have been in the U.S.S.R. have heard many negative comments about Western European and American life and culture.

Even during the war, the possibility of a Soviet-American war weighed heavily on the minds of Soviet people. I remember several conversations in which Soviet friends made such statements as: "Two great forces cannot live in peace," and "You want capitalism and we want communism." A young Russian lieutenant of the Red Army said to me in a Leningrad restaurant in the spring of 1946: "All that we Russians want is to drink, love, dance, and live. The only country we fear is America, but we will fight you if necessary with our bare hands."

This statement was made not long after Winston Churchill's speech at Fulton, Missouri, which, given immense publicity by the Soviet propaganda machine, created the first of the successive war scares with which the Soviet government has kept its people keyed up since 1946. Overnight Churchill lost his wartime popularity, which had never been as great as Roosevelt's and had always been modified by suspicion, but which had, nevertheless, been very real.

I heard considerable comment indicating that the Soviet campaign against President Truman, which did not reach its full proportions until several months after I left the U.S.S.R., was taking some effect. Several Soviet acquaintances even went so far as to tell me that they hated Truman. All of this reflected the astute Soviet propaganda line according to which American policy had become reactionary since the death of President Roosevelt. The alarm expressed by one of my Soviet friends in the fall of 1946 regarding the departure of Henry Wallace from the Cabinet fitted into this general pattern.

But if there were indications that many Soviet people, particularly among intellectuals and party members, thought that war was possible or likely, it seemed clear to me that very few thought it desirable. One well-informed foreign diplomat who traveled in the Ukraine in 1946, did, it is true, report that he had learned that there was a minority faction among the Communist Party members in the Ukraine which believed that the only salvation for the U.S.S.R. was world revolution brought about by a victorious war. Recently a foreign official who left Russia early in 1949 told me that while he was on a trip several Communist Party members had said to him that "force" must be used against Tito. This did not have reference to a possible Soviet-American war, but it might be regarded as a straw in the wind indicating that there are elements in the U.S.S.R. who think in terms of achieving political objectives by the use of military force, even extending to aggressive international war. However, as far as I can determine on the basis of my own experience while I was still in Russia, and such information as I have been able to obtain since then, the vast majority of Soviet people, including probably a majority of party members, dread and fear war, particularly a Soviet-American war. Unfortunately, particularly among the party and armed forces, it is possible that the Soviet government's monopoly of the instruments of communications may have enabled it to persuade the majority of the Soviet people that if there is a war between Russia and America, America must inevitably be the aggressor.

I never met any Soviet people who seemed to take pride in Soviet political or territorial expansion, in pan-Slavism or in the extension of Communist power. However, I did find quite frequently a tendency to assume that the whole world hated the Russians, and that they had no friends. I remember that in one of the last conversations I had with a group of Soviet people it was agreed by the Russians present that no one loved the Russians, that the Russians would one day show the world, and that Moscow would some day be the world capital. Since then, I have been told by several competent foreign observers who have been in the U.S.S.R. since my departure that they, too, had detected similar evidences of a sort of national persecution complex among some Soviet people. This attitude, combined with the national cultural inferiority complex to which reference has already been made, and perhaps with memories among some Soviet war veterans of loot obtained during World War II, might furnish at least some basis for popular morale in the event of another war.

Fear of American aggressiveness and a possible Soviet-American war was not the only negative Soviet attitude towards America which I observed while in the U.S.S.R. Despite the relative political indifference of most Soviet people, it seemed to me that to some extent the anti-capitalist ideology preached to them by their government created anti-American sentiment. Sometimes Soviet people told me that a system in which factories or railroads were privately owned seemed abhorrent to them. The aspect of Soviet propaganda against America which it seemed to me made the greatest impression, however, was American treatment of Negroes, and, in general, racial discrimination in the United States. One well-informed and relatively tolerant Soviet intellectual, with whom I had a conversation in 1946, expressed a typical attitude among Soviet people of his station when he said that the American standard of living was already sufficiently high to satisfy any reasonable person but that the Soviet Union in fifteen or twenty years would have this same standard of living, and the difference then between the U.S.S.R. and the United States would be that all of the people of the U.S.S.R. would enjoy the American standard of living or its equivalent whereas in America it would be denied to the Negroes and other racial minorities.

It should be kept in mind that Soviet propaganda exploits this theme not only and probably not mainly for domestic consumption, but also to discredit the United States in the eyes of the peoples of Asia and Africa, and to win the allegiance of American Negroes. An ironic example of this propaganda theme in action was the permission given to Soviet girls freely to date American Negro seamen at Odessa but to associate with white Americans only at the "International Club," an order which remained in force in 1946. It is interesting to note, incidentally, that here, as so often, the attempt to propagandize Americans boomeranged. Even the Negroes did not "fall" for the line; on the other hand, many of the Soviet girls became bitterly discontented. And not a few became thoroughly demoralized.

Certain other negative attitudes of Soviet people towards American civilization or even Americans as individuals should be mentioned. Despite the materialistic character of Soviet ideology, it did not prevent Soviet people from criticizing American life on moral or even idealistic grounds. Soviet girls, for example, sometimes criticize their American sisters for marrying not for love but for money. In view of their own conduct, this criticism is hardly consistent, however sincere. It stems in part from the ideological indoctrination which holds Western people, including Americans, to be "commercial," "dry" and "soulless."

An extremely intelligent American Army officer who was stationed during the war at Poltava told me that Soviet people often remarked that of course America had a far superior material culture to that of the U.S.S.R. but that Soviet people were spiritually superior. This opinion was sometimes accompanied by condemnation of American culture as commercial. In part these attitudes reflected Soviet propaganda, but at the same time it always seemed to me that they reflected also the reaction of the relatively fresh and simple Russian to what seemed the artificiality of Western civilization. Sometimes this was manifested in trivial or even crude ways. Russians would call Americans "sissies" for eating white bread, although their own officials and bureaucrats tended to prefer white to black bread.

Some Soviet people expressed a certain contempt for Americans because the latter, they said, had too easy a life or had not ever really suffered during the war. This attitude undoubtedly reflected a widespread feeling among the Soviet people that they had borne an unfair share of the war burdens. I remember a conversation in which a Soviet acquaintance told me that Americans were not good fighters but that they had won the war because of their superior technology. Americans, according to him, could never have withstood the hardships endured by the Russians.

I felt, and most of the competent foreign observers with whom I shared my impressions and opinions, agreed, that the positive attitudes of most sectors of the Soviet population toward the United States far outweighed the negative. On balance, it seemed to me that among the masses of the Soviet people there was a great friendliness and admiration for America and Americans. The question now arises whether much or any of this reserve of good will has survived the anti-American campaign of the last three or four years. It is probably even more difficult to answer this question than to appraise Soviet attitudes toward America during the war. On the basis of several types of evidence I believe it is safe to conclude that there has been and still is psychological resistance or at least indifference to the Soviet anti-American campaign. Some of the incidents and conversations which I have cited already in this chapter as evidence of friendly attitudes toward America occurred months after political relations between the Soviet and American governments had deteriorated badly. Let me cite one or two additional examples from 1946 and 1947.

Some six months before my departure from the U.S.S.R., I had what I considered a rather illuminating conversation with a group of Russians. One of them, an intelligent middle-aged working man, expressed both friendliness for America and skepticism regarding Soviet official propaganda. He poked fun at me, for example, when I declared that Soviet agriculture was highly mechanized, declaring that this was propaganda. He said that the workers of the Soviet Union were very friendly to America, whatever might be the attitude of the government. It was agreed among the group that articles by propagandists like Ehrenburg were read only by party workers and possibly factory directors, sitting down to their ample dinners. This was partly because the workers were so tired that they had no energy for reading and partly because it was very difficult for the average man to get newspapers. Even while leaving the U.S.S.R. by way of Leningrad and Finland toward the end of March,

1947, I found my fellow passengers on the trains and those Russians with whom I talked in restaurants and stores in Leningrad still friendly. Characteristically, however, one of the last conversations I heard in the U.S.S.R. was that between a woman passenger on the Leningrad-Helsinki train and a Russian man. The woman was taking her small children to Helsinki to join her husband. She expressed doubt regarding the wisdom of her going, lest the family be caught in Helsinki by a new war.

Since I left the Soviet Union I have talked with a considerable number of persons, both official and non-official, who have been in that country. Some of them left Russia as late as the spring of 1949. They included an American seaman who touched at the port of Poti in the spring of 1948, and who had been in widely scattered parts of the U.S.S.R., and UNRRA personnel, stationed until late in 1947 in the Ukraine or in Belorussia. While of course the evidence they furnished is rather fragmentary and should be used with caution, I believe that the following conclusions can safely be drawn. Apparently there is a continued willingness of Russians, particularly outside of Moscow, to engage in free, frank and friendly conversations with Americans, particularly when the latter are traveling. This tallied with my own impression that on train trips Russians apparently feel relatively safe because they know they probably will not see again the foreigners with whom they engage in casual conversation, and do not feel the constraint which they experience in the capital.

Secondly, there is no doubt that the friendly curiosity of the Russians concerning America continues. It seemed to me, listening to the accounts of my informants, that some of the Russians concerned acted as if there were no political difficulties between the U.S.S.R. and the U.S.A. However, particularly among Soviet citizens of relatively lofty status, the one theme of Soviet propaganda which appeared to be making headway was that which accused the United States of planning a war against Russia. In a conversation in December, 1947, between a relatively highly placed Soviet diplomat and an American, the diplomat argued that certain circles in the United States were seeking to bring about a war against Russia. The American replied that the United States had no motive for war and could not attack the Soviet Union because of the necessity, under the American Constitution, of a Congressional declaration of war, etc. The reply of the Soviet diplomat was typical, it seems to me, of the way in which members of the Soviet ruling group project their own concepts to foreigners. He simply asked the American what he would do if he were ordered to put on a uniform tomorrow. He went on to declare that international relations would be greatly improved if the American government would issue a declaration to the effect that the American press was not representative of the American people. There was an almost wistful note in his attitude, for he remarked that the war had been a "good time," in contrast to the postwar period when Americans were no longer friendly to Russians.

What this Russian had to say about freedom is worth retelling. He admitted that the Soviet conception of freedom differed from that of Americans. It would be impossible, he said, to permit the operation in the U.S.S.R. of an opposition press. The American conception of freedom, he said, was individualistic, and sought the welfare of the individual while the Soviet conception was that of service to the community.

The attitude of this man's wife toward the United States seemed to be a mixture of admiration and resentment. She described America as a "fabulous" country, but said that Americans held nothing sacred, that they were "soulless" people. For example, she criticized what to her was the shamelessness of American "necking" in movies or kissing on the street. She said that the Russians during the revolutionary and early postrevolutionary period had started out to scrap rules in such fields as morals but had found that their people needed to be held in tight reins. Her observation reminded me of the time a Soviet lawyer told me that it was necessary strictly to control the Russian people since they were a simple people whose minds could be easily poisoned by harmful ideas.

An UNRRA official who left the U.S.S.R. in the fall of 1947 told me that the anti-American propaganda confused the people with whom he came in contact but did not convince them. They were impressed, he said, not by the propaganda in the Soviet press but by the tangible evidence of American good will in the form of UNRRA supplies. This official described to me the romantic stories and the generally fabulous conceptions which the Soviet people with whom he came into contact had of American prosperity and power. Incidentally, he said that both the officials and the common people whom he met greatly feared the atomic bomb. His observations tallied in one respect with those of another American who left Moscow about December, 1947. His Soviet musician friends said they were very "confused" when they compared the Soviet press and the "Voice of America" broadcasts on U.S. policy.

An American government official who traveled in the U.S.S.R. in 1948 told me that it was his impression that the anti-American propaganda was taking effect, but very slowly. He described one conversation, which resembled very closely several that I myself had had before leaving Russia. A person whom he had met casually at a museum had said to him: "Your Truman wants war"; then he launched into a description of Russia's sufferings during the war and concluded by saying, "You have seen Russia; you have seen the condition of our cities and you know that we cannot fight." This statement reminded me of my Russian friend who had said to me that Russia was "bled white" by the war and it was ridiculous to attribute warlike intentions to the U.S.S.R.

Some Americans who left the Ukraine in 1947 reported an extremely pro-American attitude in that area. A story which some of them told, and which I myself had heard before I left Russia, perhaps illustrates this point better than any other bit of evidence could. According to this story, many Ukrainians said that Stalin had promised the Ukraine to Roosevelt at Yalta. Was the wish father to the thought?

Some of the Americans who left the U.S.S.R. after I did have written books or articles containing observations regarding Soviet popular attitudes toward the United States. Perhaps the best-known of these is Robert Magidoff, for twelve years a correspondent in the Soviet Union until his expulsion on trumped-up charges of espionage in April, 1948. According to Magidoff the Soviet people

> are offering a powerful, if passive, resistance to the hate-America campaign. Almost in defiance of it, they continue to admire Americans for their prowess in industry, for their keen sense of humor, for their earthy political democracy, as well as for the delightful and bewildering democracy of their everyday behavior. I said bewildering because, their Communist principles notwithstanding, the Russians are most undemocratically conscious of rank and protocol.[3]

An impression rather different from Magidoff's was conveyed by the article entitled "Hate—with Russian Dressing" by the former Moscow correspondent, Alexander Kendrick, in *Collier's* for May 8, 1948. According to Kendrick, "bitter and resentful hostility to the United States is infecting the whole Soviet social structure." Kendrick attributed the mounting hostility of Russians to Americans to "the impact of the United States present foreign policy. . . ." What seems to me to be a well-balanced opinion was presented by Werner Knop in his article, "I Prowled Russia's Forbidden Zone," in the *Saturday Evening Post* for January 1, 1949. Knop was not actually in the U.S.S.R., but he spent several months in late 1948 in the Soviet zone of Germany. According to Knop, "as they saw it, there was on the one hand, the America of Mr. Roosevelt and Mr. Wallace, the America of oppressed Negroes, enslaved workers and shackled intellectuals fighting for democracy. On the other hand, there was the semi-fascist America of Marshall and Wall Street. . . ." Knop was particularly struck by what he calls the "half wistful, half frightened way" in which Russians talk about America. According to him, "even when they castigated it, you saw how, to them, America was out of this world—a mixture of monster and fairy prince. Something greedy, cruel, decadent, and voluptuous, but also something so rich and efficient, so inventive, glittering and daedalian." These remarks referred to conversations with Soviet Army offi-

[3] *In Anger and Pity,* Doubleday, 1949, p. 72.

cers. In evaluating them, it should be remembered that the Soviet Army is perhaps the most heavily politically indoctrinated of all major segments of the Soviet population; this is particularly true of the officer corps. His impressions corresponded rather closely with those which I had formed in my own contacts with Soviet Army officers inside the U.S.S.R., with the qualification that the unfriendly component in the attitude of Soviet officers was in its early stage in my experience.

Since I have treated, at least briefly, the Soviet popular reaction to atomic energy in Chapter VIII, I shall not deal specially with this subject here, except to point out again that the atomic bomb undoubtedly heightened the awe of American technology and "know-how" already so highly developed in the Soviet popular consciousness. It was undoubtedly one of the factors which motivated the postwar Soviet campaign alleging Russian superiority even in technical fields to the United States and the Western world.

A reservoir of evidence regarding Soviet attitudes toward America which it would be very valuable to tap is the experience gained by American officials and military personnel who have had contact in Germany, Austria and other occupied countries with their Soviet opposite numbers in the postwar period. I have talked to a number of these people, and have always questioned them regarding the attitudes toward the United States of the Soviet personnel with whom they came in contact, but my sample is certainly too small to offer a basis for generalization. A few broad observations can, however, probably safely be ventured.

The initial phase of Soviet-American relations, particularly among military personnel, in the occupied areas was on the whole one of great cordiality. The early meetings of Russian and American soldiers and officers, from the lowest to the highest rank, were friendly and sometimes uproarious. There was a good deal of informal contact in the early stages. An American Army colonel told me that in the period from August to October, 1945, he almost lived with some of his Soviet friends, sharing experiences, going to parties together, and freely discussing political and military affairs. In a word, he enjoyed a genuine warm human relationship with his Soviet colleagues. The friendly relations between Marshal Zhukov and General Eisenhower and General Smith and other high American military leaders are well known. It is possible that Zhukov's friendliness to Americans may have had something to do with his postwar eclipse. Certainly the Kremlin's decision to refuse to allow him to accept General Eisenhower's invitation to visit the United States, which he had indicated he would like to do, was one of the many Soviet actions in the months following the end of the war which reduced the great good will in America which had been built up toward Russia during the war.

The initial stage of close, relatively unsupervised, and friendly relations in the occupied countries was all too brief. Gradually, restrictive measures which almost entirely sealed the Soviet military and official personnel from contact with all foreigners, particularly Americans, were introduced by the Soviet authorities. Yesterday's allies were turned into potential enemies anxiously guarding frontiers stretching halfway around the world. It was inevitable that ill will would develop. The nature of the relationship which grew up was symbolized by the Soviet Berlin Blockade and the Anglo-American Air Lift. There have been minor incidents involving the shooting of Americans and Russians.

Most of the conversations I have had with Americans who came in contact with Russians in Germany and other occupied countries date back to 1945. They reported the usual mixed picture of Soviet attitudes toward America, predominantly friendly but marred by the stereotypes regarding American capitalism drilled in by Soviet propaganda. It would be idle to suppose that the highly friendly attitude of this period has not been altered by propaganda and still more by the tense situation existing in the occupied areas between the Soviet Union and the United States. However, some of my informants have told me that even in 1947 and 1948 Soviet military personnel with whom they happened to have conversations and who were apparently loyal Soviet citizens nevertheless expressed a very friendly attitude toward America. Apparently, a Soviet soldier or officer would occasionally use a conversation with an American to get grievances off his chest even though he remained basically loyal to the U.S.S.R.

According to several former American Army officers, the legend of America was still very strong among the Soviet people with whom they talked. Soviet military personnel, particularly enlisted men, were amazed by what seemed to them the democratic spirit in the American Army. They were also impressed by the uniforms, the good food and other features of life in the American armed forces. One former American Army officer who knew well several hundred Soviet officers and enlisted men, with whom he had business in connection with his work in Austria, Czechoslovakia, and Germany, told me of a conversation with a Soviet officer who was being sent back to the U.S.S.R. Although apparently unfriendly to America judging by the tenor of most of his remarks, the officer nevertheless took leave of the American with the words: "I want you to know I wish I had been born in America too."

One final observation should be made here regarding Soviet-American relations in the occupied areas and accompanying mutual attitudes. As a general rule, at least until the development of the cold war, an open-minded or friendly attitude toward the Russians was more likely to be found in the higher rather than the lower ranks of the American Army or other government services. On the Soviet side, a quite different distribution tends to prevail. Hostility and suspicion of America appear in general to increase with elevation in rank.

We turn now to another source of information regarding Soviet attitudes toward America, the Soviet DP's and escapees scattered throughout Europe and many other parts of the world, but concentrated mostly in the American and British zones of occupation in Germany. It seems probable that Soviet refugees are inspired mainly by negative rather than by positive considerations in leaving the Soviet Union or Soviet government service. They are attempting to escape from intolerable conditions. However, one reason these conditions seem intolerable is that they are contrasted with what is known to these people about the existence of another and better life outside of Russia. The whole subject of Soviet DP's and refugees has been very little explored and only the most cautious observations are in order with respect to it. It seems clear to me, however, on the basis of wide reading in the writings of former Soviet citizens both in English and in such American Russian language publications as the *Novoe Russkoe Slovo* and *Sotsialisticheski Vestnik,* conversations with some of the people and with persons who are familiar with their attitudes, and from other sources, that an important factor in the decisions of many of them to break with the U.S.S.R. was the appeal of the West, particularly America. This factor stands out quite clearly in the escape of such persons as Igor Guzenko in Canada or Mrs. Kasenkina in New York. Victor Kravchenko, perhaps the most famous of all Soviet escapees, tells in his book *I Chose Freedom* that he had decided to escape before he came to the United States as an official of the purchasing commission. However, it is clear from parts of his book that contact with the American scene had an alluring and disturbing effect on him and some of his fellow Soviet officials in America. Thus he describes how even before the group of Soviet persons en route on a Soviet freighter had reached the United States, their first sampling of Americans on a Pacific island caused them to be "lyrically enthusiastic—the boys' looks, their friendliness, their humor touched our hearts." [4]

According to the excellent article by Marguerite Higgins in the *Saturday Evening Post* for June 4, 1949, "Now the Russians are Fleeing Russia," knowledge about America is an important factor impelling these flights. She interviewed one nineteen-year-old Russian peasant boy who said to her: "Soldiers coming back from Germany to my village said that American soldiers—even enlisted men—ate well and had much more freedom than the Russian soldier. They said it was not true

[4] *I Chose Freedom,* Scribner's, 1946, p. 454.

that American soldiers treated Russians badly." According to Miss Higgins, "intelligence interrogations show that most of the Russian flights westward were stimulated by this glimpse of an alternative to postwar lives that, according to the stories of the Russian refugees, are filled with incredible toil, fear and in some cases semi-starvation." *Newsweek* for October 25, 1948, listed as one of the important reasons for Soviet desertions the "fantastic ideas" most of the deserters entertained about the United States. "They believed all Americans rode in big automobiles, lived in luxurious houses and smoked Chesterfields all day long." My study of the evidence which has come to my attention regarding the attitude pattern of Soviet DP's and refugees has led me to conclusions substantially similar.

The existence of attitudes at variance with the official propaganda line and therefore considered harmful or dangerous by the Kremlin is, finally, indicated by much material contained in Soviet propaganda itself. The virulence, intensity, and volume of the anti-American propaganda discussed in this study constitutes in itself a striking indication of this fact. It is a safe rule in evaluating Soviet propaganda to assume that the volume devoted to a particular theme is a key to the resistance which it encounters among the Soviet public. The postwar propaganda effort against the West indicates the magnitude of the task faced by the Soviet Communist Party in attempting to eradicate respect, admiration, and friendliness toward America from the Soviet popular mind.

It is not necessary to confine oneself to purely deductive reasoning of this character to find in Soviet published statements impressive evidence of the appeal of Western, particularly American, life and ways for the Soviet people. One of the first and most striking of a series of Soviet press items of this nature was the pair of articles sent from Bucharest to *Pravda* September 24 and 26, 1944, by Leonid Sobolev, leading Soviet writer and war correspondent. Sobolev warned the Soviet people, particularly military personnel serving abroad, not to be deceived by the "tinsel" and "glitter" of bourgeois culture. In addition to reflecting concern regarding the sometimes demoralizing effect upon Russians of contact with the West, Sobolev's articles were tinged with a moral indignation which perhaps reflected the injured pride of the Soviet leadership contemplating the susceptibility of the heavily indoctrinated and well-shepherded Soviet masses to the sinful influence of alien ways and ideas. Among other things, Sobolev wrote: "True culture comes with you. It is our love for humanity, our torment experienced for it. . . ."

Subsequently, numerous other items in *Pravda, Red Star* and many other Soviet periodicals, echoed Sobolev's warning to Soviet people not to be seduced by the false and theatrical façade of bourgeois culture. Even Stalin's order of the day of May 1, 1945, published in all Soviet newspapers and circulated among the Soviet armed forces, contained the injunction to Soviet military personnel: "While you are beyond the borders of your native land, be exceptionally vigilant." Placed in the context of other press items and statements of the period which warned against the influence of a "private property" culture, this exhortation appeared, in part at least, to be a vindication from the highest quarters of Sobolev's warnings.

Among the most amusing of such items was one published in the Soviet humorous magazine, *Krokodil,* shortly after the great popular demonstrations in Moscow of friendliness toward the Americans and British on V-E Day. Entitled "The Hypnosis of Pearl-grey Trousers," this concerned a young Russian disguised as an American who listened for a whole evening to Soviet girls praising such manifestations of Americanism as the Lindy Hop and gangsters. At the end of the evening he revealed that he was after all a Russian and that though on May 9 he had tossed an American and embraced an Englishman, he was proud to be a member of a nation to which other peoples were grateful not for cigarettes but for liberation.

The reference in this story to what was probably the first genuine popular demonstration in Moscow since that of the Trotskyites on Red Square in 1927 indicated concern in the Kremlin regarding popular cordiality toward the Western Allies. And from the xenophobic point of view of the Kremlin, such concern was justified. This was a time when among Soviet students, particularly young women, the study of English was "the mode." Even such trivial things as admiration for American cellophane packaging were indicative of the trend. When I was in Georgia in February, 1947, some people from Tbilisi, whom I had met on a trip to Gori, invited me to their home in Tbilisi, and I was amazed not only by their extreme friendliness but by their delighted admiration of the wrapper and package of some American cigarettes I had with me.

Kalinin, in his important speech to party secretaries in August, 1945, touched at some length on the problem of the influence of foreign culture on Soviet people. Kalinin was talking here about the influence of German culture, but the arguments which he used were soon to be applied with far greater heat to American and Western European culture. The culture of the "German burgher and kulak" with which many Soviet people had come in contact during the war, including people who were returning from Germany, Kalinin characterized as "a culture purely external, empty—not plumbing the depths of the human soul, a philistine culture. . . ." Numerous items in the Soviet press in the summer and fall of 1945 and the spring of 1946 echoed these remarks.

Perhaps an even more impressive, though more guarded indication of the preoccupation in high Soviet quarters with the influence of foreign culture on Soviet people was given by Molotov on November 6, 1945. He stated among other things: "Of course, acquaintance with the way of life of other people is beneficial to our people and widens their horizons. It is interesting, however, that Soviet people return home with a still more burning feeling of devotion to their motherland and the Soviet power." [5]

Some indication of the significance of these statements may be derived from an article in *Sputnik Agitatora* (*Agitator's*

[5] For the above quotation from Kalinin's speech see *Propaganda i Agitatsiya*, Leningrad, No. 18, 1945, p. 8; the Molotov quotation is from the Russian edition of his speech published by the State Publishing House for Political Literature, Moscow, 1945, p. 23.

Companion), No. 18, 1945, entitled "Talks with Repatriated Soviet Citizens." This article instructed agitators to correct the impression, widespread among repatriated citizens, that "the Red Army won because of the Allies." Molotov's and Kalinin's remarks must also be examined critically in the light of the fact that many thousands of Soviet soldiers and officers deserted from the Red Army in 1944 and 1945 at least in part because of the allure of the life of what had been portrayed by Soviet propaganda as the backward, decadent and poverty-stricken countries of Eastern Europe. In this connection, one recalls the often-quoted statement that one of Stalin's greatest mistakes was to let the Soviet people see Europe and Europe see the Soviet Army.

In the light of the foregoing the cultural purge which began on a grand scale in 1946 and has been pressed with increasing intensity ever since, is understandable.[6] It would require a book, or at least a series of articles, to deal comprehensively and systematically with this subject. I shall confine myself here to indicating briefly the attention devoted in this gigantic ideological reconversion operation to the eradication of Western influence on the thinking of Soviet people, particularly intellectuals. The whole tone and texture of the basic documents and the voluminous stream of supporting material employed in this great drive indicates the stubborn tendency among many Soviet people to "kowtow to bourgeois culture," a tendency which has over and over again been denounced as one of the most harmful and vicious "survivals of capitalism in the consciousness of the people."

The most important document of the postwar ideological housecleaning was Zhdanov's "report" on the magazines *Zvezda* and *Leningrad* and the city of Leningrad, delivered in August, 1946, to the assembled writers of Leningrad and to the active group of the Leningrad Communist Party organization. It set the main lines and tone of the campaign, with particular applica-

[6] For translations of the major documents of this campaign see *The Country of the Blind*, by George S. Counts and Nucia Lodge, Houghton Mifflin, 1949.

tion to literature. Zhdanov employed the technique of selecting two scapegoats to illustrate his thesis that Soviet literature had fallen into an evil state of indifference to politics and susceptibility to harmful ideas. These scapegoats were the popular humorist, Zoshchenko, and the middle-aged poetess, Akhmatova. Although neither of these writers was a Communist, and the literary output of both was certainly open to criticism from the orthodox Communist point of view, they had been permitted to publish freely during the war and had even been highly praised in special literary journals and in the general press. In fact, the *Pravda* publishing house had put out a special edition of some of Zoshchenko's best short stories only a few months before the official denunciation of the two writers. Perhaps there was even some ground for Zhdanov's charge that Zoshchenko had become the literary dictator of Leningrad.

After denouncing these two writers for indifference to politics, for "un-Soviet" views and ideas, Zhdanov made this significant statement:

> It is no accident that in the literary magazines of Leningrad they began to be attracted by the contemporary low grade bourgeois literature of the West. Some of our literary people began to regard themselves not as teachers but as pupils of bourgeois-philistine literary men, and began to adopt a tone of subservience and obeisance to philistine foreign literature.

These and similar statements scattered throughout Zhdanov's long report, which occupied more than two pages, over half of the entire space in the Soviet daily newspapers for September 21, 1946, suggest that the Soviet reading public was surprisingly susceptible to "alien" influences and moods. With characteristic lack of humor, Zhdanov accused Zoshchenko of portraying the life of a monkey (in his sketch "The Adventures of a Monkey") as better than that of free Soviet people. After damning Akhmatova as a museum piece and a carry-over of decadent pre-revolutionary traditions, Zhdanov flayed her for her disastrous influence on Soviet youth and asked, somewhat naïvely, how the Soviet people could be interested in her antiquated ideas in the twenty-ninth year of the Soviet revolution.

Zhdanov's speech had been preceded by a resolution of the Central Committee of the Communist Party of the Soviet Union on literature. This was soon followed by a Central Committee resolution on the drama. One of the chief demands of this resolution was the removal of bourgeois plays from Soviet theatrical repertoires. Press articles published both before and after this resolution of late August, 1946, made it appear that the popularity of foreign plays was so great with Soviet theatrical audiences that they were threatening to crowd new Soviet plays off the boards. In 1947 Soviet economists and philosophers were condemned for allowing themselves to be influenced by Western concepts. In February, 1948, the Central Committee issued a decree on music, one of the most significant themes of which was condemnation of Soviet composers such as Shostakovich and Prokofiev for reflecting foreign influences in their works. In August, 1948, a long campaign against Soviet biologists like Zhebrak, followers of the "anti-popular" and harmful "Weissman-Morgan-Mendel tendency in biological science" was climaxed by the intervention of the Central Committee on the side of T. D. Lysenko, chief exponent of the Soviet party line in biology. This was followed by the dismissal or demotion of a number of leading Soviet anti-Lysenko biologists.

In hundreds of articles, in millions of words, in dozens of administrative actions involving rebukes, demotions or disgrace, and in some cases personal ruin of leading intellectuals, the Kremlin has carried out its campaign to eradicate the taint of Western influence from the minds of Soviet people. Scarcely any field of art, science or scholarship has been left untouched. The campaign has mounted in fury. In late 1948, particularly in connection with the purge of biologists, the propaganda campaign was increasingly superseded by administrative measures involving in some cases dismissal of ideological offenders from the Communist Party. At the same time, particularly in connection with the denunciation of Soviet dramatic and musical critics for "cosmopolitanism," the tone of the language employed against the victims has become more threatening. A good example of this is afforded by *Sovetskoe Iskusstvo* (*Soviet Art*) for February 26, 1949, which reported an "all-Moscow meeting of dramatists and critics" at which "homeless cosmopolitans" were flayed under the banner front-page headline: "Smash completely the anti-patriotic group of theatrical critics." The campaign was even extended to Soviet astronomers, who were called upon to fight relentlessly against "bourgeois cosmology" and relativistic conceptions which "should be regarded as a manifestation of cringing before the reactionary science of the bourgeois West." [7]

The anxiety of the Kremlin is nowhere better illustrated than at the meeting at which the Cominform was founded in 1947, where G. M. Malenkov, now perhaps the most powerful man in the Soviet Union next to Stalin, devoted a large part of his "informational report on the activity of the Central Committee of the All-Union Communist Party (of Bolsheviks)" to the "decisive struggle with various manifestations of kowtowing and obeisance to the bourgeois culture of the West" which, he said, enjoyed "a certain distribution among certain strata of our intelligentsia." [8] This and many supporting statements in the daily press over the past three years, if taken together with similar expressions of anxiety regarding the influence of alien ideas on Soviet youth, are significant. Many statements by leaders of the *Komsomol* (the Young Communist League), have accented the harmfulness of permitting bourgeois ideas to infect Soviet youth.

M. N. Mikhailov, the head of the *Komsomol,* in an article in *Bolshevik,* Number 23-24, 1946, referred to a mood of "demobilization" among Soviet youth, and to the danger of permitting "spontaneity" in the training of youth because this "opens the door to the infection of youth by bourgeois ideology which is foreign to us, and leads to a situation in which the feeling for the new and the enthusiasm for the new threatens to

[7] New York *Times,* July 14, 1949, p. 1.

[8] *Pravda,* December 9, 1947.

wither." The fact that Mikhailov is also a member of the Central Committee and the powerful Organization Bureau of the Communist Party lends significance to his statement and bears out the remark a twenty-five-year-old Russian made to me to the effect that the Kremlin had lost faith in the ideological purity of Soviet youth and was relying for its future strength on Soviet children.

In the postwar period the *Komsomol* press has published a number of items excoriating "formalism" and ideological indifference. In reading these items I am reminded of stories which I heard while I was still in the U.S.S.R. to the effect that many youths, including even *Komsomol* members, were irritated by the constant propaganda bombardment to which they were subjected. An indication of this attitude, which might be called a sort of Soviet anti-clericalism, may be gained from an anecdote related by one of my friends, who described her fellow students as referring contemptuously to a woman teacher of "dialectical materialism" as "diamama."

In combating popular moods and attitudes which it considered dangerous, the Kremlin in the postwar period did not confine itself to purely negative methods. These it supplemented by tightening censorship and virtually hermetically sealing off the Soviet people from contact with foreigners. In this connection, one need mention only the law of February 15, 1947, forbidding marriage of Soviet citizens to foreigners, to give an idea of the barbaric extravagance of the postwar Soviet campaign of isolation. When foreign diplomats sought exit visas for Soviet girls married to nationals of their countries, Vyshinski replied that the U.S.S.R. government felt all Soviet citizens should bear their share of the hardships of building the new order.

Although resorting to campaigns of excoriation and intimidation, the Kremlin has also sought to appeal to Soviet national pride as a weapon against foreign influence. Like so many features of the postwar Soviet scene which became conspicuous to the outside world only in 1946 or 1947, the inculcation of a chauvinistic nationalism dates back to the war years and even to the prewar period. The main features of the Messianic Soviet nationalism, which perhaps as much as its Nazi counterpart deserves the name of "National-Socialism," are emphases upon the superiority of Soviet to bourgeois culture and of the Soviet man to his bourgeois counterpart. Wartime developments of this trend included the introduction into the Soviet higher educational curriculum of nationalistically tinged courses on "Russian Classical Philosophy." In these courses, and in a flood of newspaper and magazine articles on Russian philosophy and Russian culture in general, the groundwork was laid for the postwar campaign denouncing as vicious the previously accepted idea that Russia owed much in its cultural development to foreign influences.

One among many wartime harbingers of things to come in this field was a pamphlet by the distinguished Soviet linguist, Professor D. V. Vinogradov, published in 1944 by the "central newspaper courses under the Central Committee of the All-Union Communist Party (of Bolsheviks)," entitled *The Grandeur and Might of the Russian Language*. This publication abounds in such phrases as "the superiority of the Russian language to all European languages. . . ." In the postwar period, Soviet cultural Messianism in the linguistic area has gone so far as to assert that Russian is the coming universal world language.

As for the cult of the Soviet man, one can trace this back to such press items as the Sobolev articles referred to earlier in this chapter. Zhdanov's speech to the Leningrad writers gave impetus to the campaign to inculcate this concept. Zhdanov asserted that the Russians of today were vastly different from those of 1917 and that Soviet people, the product of a superior social order and a superior culture, were in a position to teach "a general human morality" to the other peoples of the world. Doubtless one purpose, or at least one major implication, of the re-emphasis on the idea that acquired characteristics can be and are inherited, which was a major feature of the biological purge, was the idea that a special superior breed of human beings was being created in the socialist Soviet Union and that these people could pass on their socially determined superiority to their children. It was this implication of the purge in the field of biology which caused the noted American geneticist, Herman J. Muller, to resign from the Soviet Academy of Sciences and to charge that the Kremlin was seeking to inculcate a master-race mentality in the Soviet people.[9]

Postwar Soviet chauvinism and the emphasis of Soviet propaganda on the "rottenness" of the West reminds one of similar trends in nineteenth-century Russian thinking. It is difficult to escape the conclusion that now, as then, frantic assertions of superiority reflect, in fact, the inferiority complex of an elite which is not sure of itself and is still less sure that its values and aspirations are shared by the masses whom it rules by bureaucratic controls, police terror, and propaganda myths. In this connection, the observations of Alexander von Schelting in his recent book *Russland und Europa in Russischen Geschichtsdenken* are extremely pertinent. He points to the resemblance between the "national vanity" and Messianism of the nineteenth-century Russians and the similar sentiment of the Jews of old in bondage. In both cases, these feelings, far from reflecting a positive situation, were compensations for misery and humiliation and arose from a desperate need to palliate the misery of the moment by belief in a glorious future.[10]

With some qualifications, von Schelting's observations are as applicable to the Russia of Stalin and Malenkov as to the Russia of Nicholas I and his famous minister of education, Uvarov, who performed for his master, Nicholas I, the same function as Stalin's high priests of Communism do for him, namely, that of attempting to shield the minds of Russians from the disintegrating effect of knowledge of or contact with foreign ways and people. Like the czars, the Soviet rulers must contend against what can probably be accurately described as a deep-rooted cultural trait of the Russian people, namely, an almost abnormal

[9] See text of Muller's letter of resignation as published in *Science* for October 22, 1948 (Vol. 108, No. 2808), pp. 423-24.

[10] Alexander von Schelting, *Russland und Europa in Russischen Geschichtsdenken*, Bern, 1948, pp. 307-8; my attention was drawn to this book by a review in *International Affairs* for April, 1949.

curiosity about and tendency to admire things foreign. While this is nothing new in Russian or Soviet history, the effects of the Second World War were to increase the troublesomeness of this problem for the Soviet rulers.

There is probably nothing in Russian history quite comparable to the effect upon the Russian people of the wartime breach in the Iron Curtain, except possibly the intellectual ferment produced among Russian officers by similar contact with Europe during the period of the Napoleonic wars, which led to the Decembrist Uprising of 1825. Not only the objective facts of a vast differential in living standards between Soviet Russia and most of Europe but also the psychological factor of the shock produced when products of such a closed intellectual system as that of the U.S.S.R. come into contact with realities differing sharply from the propagandist stereotypes with which they have been indoctrinated, seemed to render the Soviet people particularly susceptible to what the Soviet press and radio stigmatized as alien influences.

I am convinced that this susceptibility is ultimately in large measure the result of discontent among Soviet people with the conditions of life in the U.S.S.R. Obviously, this discontent cannot be measured. Its extent and intensity must remain imponderable. But that it exists and is many-faceted is revealed by the same sources as indicate the attraction of the foreign world for many Soviet people. The existence of an all-penetrating police network, the ban of the Soviet government on emigration from the U.S.S.R., the constant warnings in the Soviet press against the sinister plots of foreign powers and their agents who are declared to be operating within Russia—all these and many other actions and policies of the Soviet government itself attest to the existence of serious tensions in Soviet society. They certainly indicate that the Kremlin has much to conceal. My own personal observations and those of other foreigners who have had experience in the U.S.S.R. lead me to believe that there still is, as I am convinced there was when I left the country, widespread apathy, cynicism about official propaganda, and in many cases despair among Soviet people.

One indication of these moods is the fondness of the Soviet people for grimly humorous political jokes, or, as they call them, "anecdotes." Despite the fact that telling such stories may easily lead to a concentration camp, they appear to be widespread. One story I heard just before I left Russia illustrates an attitude which was widely prevalent at that time regarding the Soviet standard of living. According to this anecdote, Lenin came back to life and visited Stalin in order to discuss the situation of the Soviet Union. Stalin assured Lenin that things were in good shape and that the people were following him. Lenin asked for facts and figures on housing, transportation, industry and other data. Finally, he requested figures on food rations. When he had listened to these, Lenin said: "If this keeps up the people will soon be following not you but me." I was informed that a student who told this story to a group of his fellows was sentenced to six months in prison.

Another anecdote which I heard late in 1946 indicated the skepticism of many Soviet people regarding official propaganda. A man with the title of hero of the Soviet Union went to heaven, where he saw a group of beautiful girls. He requested the "authorities" to arrange for him to meet the girls. The authorities told him that he must have been dreaming. If he wanted to meet girls and drink wine he would have to go to hell. Accordingly, he asked to be transferred there. However, after he had been there a few days he complained that he had not met the girls. Again our hero was told that he had made a mistake. This time the authorities said to him: "You must have been in an Agitpunkt." An Agitpunkt is a place in which professional agitators operate. This story takes on added interest when it is recalled that it was told during the campaign for the election of deputies to the Supreme Soviet of R.S.F.S.R. It thus illustrates a widespread attitude toward the election system, as well as toward Soviet propaganda in general. I heard dozens of such anecdotes while I was in Russia. Perhaps the best-known of them all is one which describes how Stalin, Roosevelt and Churchill while riding, presumably at Teheran, found their automobile blocked by a cow standing in the road. Neither

Churchill's eloquence nor Roosevelt's persuasiveness was of any avail in inducing the cow to leave the road. Stalin, however, simply walked up to the cow, whispered quietly in its ear, and the cow darted off. When asked how he did it, Stalin replied: "I told her I was going to put her in a collective farm."

I heard many comments from Soviet people which reflected moods similar to those crystallized in these political jokes. One would ask a Soviet friend when communism would be achieved and sometimes he would reply, in a tone of irony, "In a thousand years." One of my friends was told by a Soviet girl, a member of the *Komsomol*, that she was not a "Marxist" but a "democrat." According to this girl, most Soviet students doubted the official party line, but because it was dangerous to express their doubts they learned to pay lip service to it. When asked how she had arrived at such ideas, despite the fact that she had been brought up on Marxist teachings, she replied: "From life." Such a conclusion was after all not so surprising as it may seem. Even without knowledge of conditions in foreign countries, there was and is much in Soviet life to create doubt and discontent. Not only the hardships of life and the cruelties of the police and forced labor system, but also the appalling contrast between these realities and the professed ideals of the official ideology must stimulate ironic reflection.

In this connection, I am reminded of what I saw in 1946 in the little town of Ushumun, 7,647 kilometers from Moscow, where on one side of the railway station there was displayed a quotation from one of Molotov's speeches regarding the "superiority of Soviet democracy," while on the other side there was a sign reading "third class waiting room." This is symbolic of the inequality in the distribution of goods and social status which has flourished under Stalin but which seems to many Soviet citizens to be contrary to the teachings of Lenin.

If one adds to these basic factors the temporary but extremely serious difficulties resulting from a frightfully destructive and grueling war, it is not surprising that popular morale in the U.S.S.R. was at a low ebb in the first postwar years. The ruthless determination of the Soviet government to press on with its program of forced draft industrialization, in which the people's comfort and welfare were sacrificed to the Kremlin's power, together with the fear of war induced by Soviet anti-Western propaganda, added to the general gloom pervading the outlook of most Soviet people. In the months before I left Russia, I heard from several well-informed sources that popular morale was at the lowest ebb in the history of the U.S.S.R. In particular, according to these informants, the morale of intellectuals was at an all-time low.

In the two and a half years that have elapsed since those days the Soviet standard of living has improved somewhat, although it appears still to be below the level reached in the middle and late thirties, which in turn was not as high as that enjoyed in the N.E.P. Of course even a slight rise in living standards is gratefully received by a population accustomed to such a Spartan life as the Soviet Russians. No doubt the Kremlin counts on this factor, together with the fading of memories among the several million Soviet citizens who caught a glimpse of the outside world, as positive factors in its effort to improve morale. It also relies heavily on arousing a patriotic reaction against the alleged foreign foe. It would be idle to dismiss these factors as insignificant.

Moreover, and here again we are confronted by a fateful imponderable, we should not underestimate the attraction for youth of the opportunities for careers offered by the expanding Soviet economy or the impression of progress and power generated by what the Soviet press often refers to as the "pathos of construction." To be sure, many Soviet refugees maintain that even the majority of the Communist Party members in the U.S.S.R. are lukewarm or even hostile in their attitude toward the regime. Even if this were true, however, and there were only one or two million, or perhaps even only several hundred thousand ruthless, fanatical, ambitious politician-administrators of the Malenkov type directing the U.S.S.R., it would still be a formidable machine.

It must be remembered that the Soviet leaders, perhaps to an extent greater than any other elite in history, have dedicated themselves to the arts of power. With them, politics is literally a full-time and a life-time occupation. They are highly skilled in such techniques as the differential distribution of rewards and punishments in the interests of the power of the Soviet regime. Their absolute power, free from the distractions which prey on the nerves of democratic statesmen, confers upon them great advantages of flexibility in tactics. This concentration of power, combined with the massive machinery they have built to canalize and mobilize national energies, enables them to recruit most of the ablest elements in the population in the service of the Kremlin. They command absolutely the body and brain of the nation.

But the negative attitudes generated by this system, to which attention has been drawn in this chapter, together with their accompanying yearnings for a freer, more humane life, constitute limiting factors on the Kremlin's drive for world power. These factors can be positive assets on the side of democracy and peace if America and other democracies can fashion and proclaim policies which have a stronger appeal to the intellect and imagination of the peoples of the world, including those of the U.S.S.R., tnan the fatal but deceptively logical solutions to its problems offered to a confused and troubled world by the master of the Kremlin. In the next and concluding chapter of this study I present some reflections on the implications for American policies of the pattern of attitudes discussed thus far.

XII. Facing Up to the Soviet Problem

WHAT are the implications for American foreign policy of the pattern of beliefs and attitudes analyzed in this study? We have seen how in the strange realm of Soviet political mythology America resembles more closely the horrid fantasy of Orwell's *Nineteen Eighty-Four* than the country we know. The America of Soviet propaganda is ruled by force and fraud. Its handful of rulers pull the strings to which their subjects dance like puppets. Its domestic policy is one of exploitation and oppression, and its foreign policy is characterized by deception and aggression.

This nightmare vision derives partly from ideology, partly from political cunning, and partly from the projection by the isolated and provincial Soviet rulers of their own motives, concepts, and characteristics to what they regard as their American counterparts. Hovering physically and spiritually behind fortress walls, the masters of the Kremlin look out like the prisoners of Plato's cave upon a world of shadows.

But the fantastic Soviet image of America is a very real and powerful factor in world politics. It is both a determinant and a rationalization of Soviet policy. It is a salient feature of the ideology of world communism. It is a potent weapon of the propaganda by which the Kremlin and its agents seek to gain dominion over the minds of men.

The obstructive, hostile, and even sinister behavior in which these Soviet and communist attitudes have been expressed has constituted a very real threat to the values basic to Western and American civilization. If these values are to be maintained and enhanced, and if civilization, and perhaps even human life itself, are to be preserved, it is essential that the Soviet challenge be correctly understood and accurately appraised.

Either underestimation or overestimation of the imminence or intensity of the danger might well have dangerous consequences. Failure to resist Soviet pressure leads inevitably to political subjugation and moral extinction. A hysterical overreaction could lead to vitiating the values in the name of which resistance was undertaken. Let us not forget that anti-communism can cover a multitude of sins. Let us always keep in mind the fact that however important it may be, defense against Soviet imperialism is only a negative and—I hope—in the long run, a minor aspect of the struggle to maximize human achievement which should be the ultimate end of all policy. Let us seek earnestly to attain the balance and perspective afforded by objective historical and political analysis. It is one of the hopeful signs of the times that such a study, on a truly vast scale, is now well under way. As its fruits become available, there should be greater understanding of the problems resulting from the co-existence in a shrinking world of socialist Russia and capitalist America.

But in the meantime these problems, protean in complexity and sobering in gravity, demand the attention of decision-makers and public opinion. It seems to me that the tasks which they pose and have posed since the pull of rival interests and ideologies dissolved the wartime coalition, fall into three main categories. The most urgent, immediate, and obvious is the containment of Soviet and Soviet satellite armed power. The urgency and difficulty of defeating Soviet-engineered satellite aggression has of course been highlighted by events in Korea. At the same time, the Korean developments have emphasized the enormousness of the infinitely greater problem which would be presented by direct, all-out Soviet military action. Equally important and, I believe, even more complex and difficult, is the waging of what Professor Robinson in his brilliant article in *Foreign Affairs*, July, 1949, called the "ideological combat." Finally, an aspect of the second problem, so special in its importance and characteristics that I shall treat it as a third point, is that of establishing communication between ourselves and the people of Russia and the "new democracies."

Each of these sets of problems has its own peculiarities, determined by such factors as the targets of Kremlin operations in each area and the weapons available for them. The solution of each one, therefore, requires a special, appropriate complex of counteroperations. At the same time, all these problems are interdependent since they derive in so large a measure from the same source and since the forms of power, especially in the case of the Soviet dictatorship, are so largely interchangeable. The solution of any of them may well be impossible unless at least a considerable degree of success can be achieved in the solution of the others.

It would seem that in coping with the hostile intentions and vast military capabilities of the Kremlin, the statesmen of the West adopted a sound policy. They perceived clearly that Soviet power was multiform and must be countered by a blend of physical and moral force. They understood that unlike the Nazis, especially Hitler, the Soviet rulers were sufficiently rational to be prepared to postpone if not to abandon objectives when confronted by effective opposition. Guided by this understanding they avoided the pitfalls of appeasement and of preventive war. Either of these courses of action might have had fatal consequences for the values which constitute the essence of the Western moral and political tradition.

Had we indulged in the folly of permitting our wartime policy of accommodation to degenerate into appeasement of Soviet imperialism, the Kremlin would in all probability now enjoy the hegemony of Europe, Asia, and Africa which eluded the grasp of Napoleon and Hitler. This result would have made a mockery of American efforts and sacrifices in World War II. It would have involved incalculable and very probably fatal risks to American national independence. For in the unlikely eventuality that America could have looked forward to continued existence over the years as an island of resistance in a predominantly Soviet world, she could have done so only by becoming a garrison state, morbidly preoccupied by problems of security. Thus, ironically, appeasement would have led to the surrender of the democratic values it sought to preserve.

It is—or was—somewhat easier to argue for preventive war than for appeasement. The case had a certain superficial logic. It is said that if we had utilized our superiority of power perhaps we could have eliminated a threat which was likely to become increasingly dangerous with growing Soviet strength, especially in atomic weapons. But could we? At the time when a preventive action might have been most feasible militarily, perhaps shortly after V-E Day, it would have been politically and morally impossible.

The moral and political arguments against it have remained convincing and its military feasibility has tended to diminish, especially since President Truman's disclosure regarding an atomic explosion in the U.S.S.R. Whatever the arguments may have been—and in view of presumed continued American atomic superiority may still be—the military possibilities of successful preventive war must be weighed against what seem to me overwhelming counterarguments. Would it not unite the Soviet people and perhaps all peoples against us? What would be our plight as international gendarmes? What program of world organization could have a chance of success in the shattered, embittered postwar world, assuming, of course, that civilization was not completely destroyed? At the least would not the internal political measures necessary for prosecuting a preventive war, and after the war, for maintaining a "preventive peace," destroy our free institutions and lead to results opposite from those envisaged by its proponents?

Fortunately American policy-makers, supported by enlightened public opinion, refused to be impaled on either horn of this dilemma. They kept their heads and adopted a policy characterized by the *Economist* of London, January 22, 1949, as one of "resolute and concerted defense, political, economic and strategic, combined with a careful avoidance of provocation." Perhaps this characterization somewhat idealizes the American and British dual policy of containment of Soviet power and rehabilitation of the area behind dikes. There have been some fumbling and weakness on the one hand and some unnecessary bluster on the other. But on the whole it would seem that an appropriate answer to the Soviet challenge has been found.

The policy embodied in such instruments as E.R.P. and the North Atlantic Treaty made sense in terms of the main primary value shared by the Kremlin and the West: a common interest in survival, both physical and political. For while it did not pose the threat to their existence which might have goaded the Politburo into desperate adventures, this policy made it clear that Moscow might have to pay a prohibitively high price for continued expansion of the kind so cheaply obtained in the early and easy postwar period. Soviet behavior in the face of the West's policy since 1947 has confirmed the analysis set forth by "X" in his now famous article in *Foreign Affairs* for July of that year. The old belief that time and the "laws of social development" were on their side has apparently remained a powerful determinant of Soviet conduct. And so the West's policy achieved the gain of precious time during which a wide range of measures designed to promote recovery and stability was inaugurated.

But was anything fundamental accomplished as a result of General Marshall's bold initiative? Did the course which he charted set the world on the path toward a stable peace?

Prior to Moscow's unleashing of outright aggression in Korea my answer was a carefully qualified but confident affirmative. Our policy of course involved a risk of war which, though it could be carefully calculated, could not be eliminated. It was clear all along that this risk would continue to haunt a world in which ideological cleavage, especially on the level of official Soviet-American relations, and other basic factors, militated against the early establishment of the community of values and interests upon which alone a genuine world society can be built. However, it seemed just possible that our policy, if patiently adhered to and wisely implemented, might furnish a framework for a *modus vivendi* between the U.S.S.R. and the West which might eventually evolve toward a more cordial relationship than the present armed truce.

Must we, in the light of developments in Korea, discard this estimate of the world situation? I do not think so, but I think these developments force us to revise upward our estimate both of the risk which the Kremlin is willing to run to achieve its aims and of the scale of Russian mobilized power. We must resolve, if need be, to use all necessary power if the West is to deter Soviet aggression and preserve the peace. The Korean operation may have been motivated mainly by a desire to pinch off a particularly vulnerable and unguarded salient of the world-wide frontier. If so, the move was at least in part a blunder, since it has set in motion a mobilization of the West which will make further Soviet and satellite aggression still riskier.

Or Korea may be a combined feint and demonstration with a twofold purpose: first, to drain off Western power from the indubitable main target of Soviet expansion, Western Europe; second, to terrorize the Europeans, particularly the Germans, by the specter of Communist power and Western weakness. The move may have several other implications, but of course the most alarming interpretation of all is that it reflected a Kremlin estimate of the timing of current history considerably at variance with the one which had hitherto seemed most probable. Was Korea intended to be the Kremlin's version of Hitler's swallowing of Czechoslovakia, to be followed perhaps soon by an operation against Berlin or Yugoslavia roughly parallel to Hitler's invasion of Poland?

Whatever the answers may be to these questions, it is increasingly clear that the Korean gambit, besides re-emphasizing the necessity of first-rate military-political intelligence, also underscored the necessity of building up and maintaining in instant readiness for action adequate American and U.N. armed forces to cope with such possible developments as a satellite attack on Yugoslavia or an East German "police" operation against West Germany.

But the existence in the West of sufficient military power to deter further Soviet aggression is only part of the answer to the problem of stopping and eventually rolling back the Communist tide. In fact, excessive preoccupation with it might have very harmful consequences, whether the future brings a continuation of the cold war, its transformation into all-out military struggle, or something in between. Military and internal political strength must provide the shield of security and freedom from fear behind which the work of economic, social, and psychological rehabilitation can proceed.

The Soviet ideological challenge is likely to prove more troublesome in the long run than Moscow's armed might. The U.S.S.R. is the embodiment of a social philosophy, and its ruling Communist Party might be called an ideology in arms. Its most potent weapons are its propaganda and its techniques of political organization, including, of course, its secret police and its apparatus of conspiratorial subversion.

The ignorant, the gullible, and the discontented of all lands and cultures fall prey to these weapons. Their application, like the power horizon of the cunning and ruthless zealots who direct their use, is universal. No military defense can be total proof against them. Only a healthy society, economically strong and psychologically well-integrated, can withstand Soviet ideological pressure. That this is true is indicated by the history of the Soviet impact on the non-Soviet world. Countries relatively weak physically such as Finland have certainly been far more successful in resisting Communism than have potential great powers such as China. The postwar American policy of containment has been most successful in Western Europe, where there were still internal ideological forces of resistance. When these were lacking and efforts to revive or create them were not made or were unsuccessful, it has failed.

The moral of this record is clear. The United States must intensify its efforts to strengthen the ties of common interest and purpose binding together the members of the non-Soviet community. It must convince the peoples of this community that they have a better chance of solving their problems and achieving a decent life under free institutions than under the harsh total organization of Communism. This is no small task. Its accomplishment requires a whole range of positive policies too vast even to be suggested here. It seems to me that in general it requires more emphasis on the "rehabilitation" component in our foreign relations and less relative emphasis on the "containment" element, vital though the latter be. It obviously requires the avoidance of such shortsighted expedients as allying ourselves with reactionary forces or regimes merely because they are anti-Communist. There may be desperate situations in which such tactics are necessary, but they should be avoided if possible, and if they must be employed, this should be done in such fashion as not to alienate democratic world opinion.

Is it too much to hope that America may be able to nurture democratic cadres who can cope with the Communists in lands where the outcome of the ideological combat hangs in the balance? A world-wide network of parties embodying the Communist ideology is Moscow's greatest weapon. Too often we have depended on dollars while the Communists have concentrated on people. Their doctrine has fired many with zeal to refashion the world according to a revolutionary blueprint. It has filled the spiritual vacuum left when patterns of thought and belief have collapsed unreplaced by a new vision of life's meaning and purpose or by the reaffirmation of sound but dormant philosophies.

Dynamic democracy must recapture the initiative from Communism. Why not a world-wide "people's deal," bringing to peoples menaced by Communism not merely a technology superior to Moscow's but the freedom and respect for human dignity which Soviet police socialism destroys? Such a program will be expensive and difficult. It will require not merely the technical assistance envisaged in Mr. Truman's Point Four but a vast co-operative effort by the free nations to pool their resources of knowledge, good will, and world community responsibility. It will require, among other things, a great deal of attention to the education of democratic citizens and of leaders drawn from their ranks, responsible and responsive to their peoples. Above all, the carrying out of such a program will require intense rededication to democratic values by the citizenry of America. Only this can generate the enthusiasm, patience, and courage needed to meet the terrifying but exhilarating tasks ahead.

But if we are successful, we cannot merely dam the surging tide of totalitarianism but eventually must roll it back. For in the long run a dynamic democracy is both a more revolutionary and a more satisfying philosophy than communism. Democratic success in the competition of cultures will exert a magnetic force on the peoples of the world, including those fenced in by Kremlin walls.

Despite its tragic aspects, the Korean crisis offers an opportunity for the West to regain, in part, the political initiative lost to the Communists in Asia, provided that America proclaims as one of its main war aims a broad program of social reform and social welfare for the Korean people.

The problem of finding a common language and of appealing to the aspirations of the submerged people of Russia presents very special difficulties. The most obvious of these is the physical problem of communication. I do not propose to discuss this problem here, except to observe that the physical imprisonment of the Soviet people is both symbolic of and instrumental in their spiritual enslavement.

In addition to this question of physical communication there is the less primitive but almost equally difficult problem of making ourselves understood by a people with a background radically different from our own. This difficulty should not discourage us. It is by no means insuperable. We shall be encouraged if we keep in mind what to me seems the obvious fact that the similarities of peoples are greater than their differences. Bertram D. Wolfe, in the *New Leader*, March 26, 1949, has phrased the problem concisely: "Indeed, the major problem of democratic statesmanship today is that of reaching the Russian people, both through their leaders and over the heads of their leaders, with the message that we mean them and their country well, and that our intentions are peaceful and friendly."

The results of American attempts in the postwar period to pierce the curtain between the Soviet people and the truth about American life and policy offer encouragement. By far our most important medium has been the "Voice of America" radio broadcasts. Also worthy of special note is the Russian language magazine, *Amerika*, which began circulation in the U.S.S.R. in March, 1945, with 10,000 copies, and increased in June, 1946, to 50,000. In addition to these media, vigorous efforts have been made by the United States government as well as by private organizations to introduce or foster other forms of cultural relations such as exchange of persons, publications, and artistic performances.[1]

On the whole our information program has followed what I feel is the correct line of fostering in the Soviet audience a sense of identity with Americans in facing similar problems, sharing similar interests, and striving for similar achievements. It seems to me we shall be wise to follow a positive approach in our propaganda. We must include in it factual material designed to correct the distortions of the Soviet press and radio, but I feel that we should avoid a merely polemic tone. It is only too easy to injure the pride of the receptive and curious, but extremely touchy, Soviet audience. It is important to make it clear that we respect Russian cultural achievements. It is equally important to tell the story of American cultural achievements and to correct the historically rooted Russian impression that Americans are a narrowly materialistic people indifferent to spiritual values. We must also keep in mind a certain solemnity and ceremoniousness in the Soviet character which contrasts with American informality. Despite their craving for a release from official regimentation, to which we can appeal, Soviet Russians react unfavorably to what they are prone to regard as the frivolity and lack of seriousness of Americans. They can endure what seem to us stiff and heavy lectures, theater, and radio programs.

I believe that our radio programs are meeting these requirements. Perhaps occasionally we have yielded unwisely to the temptation to score a debater's point or achieve a flashy short-term result, but it should be remembered that the whole problem is a thorny one, and that our experience, though increasingly rich, is relatively limited.

Now, of course, no matter how honest, sensible, and tactful our information program may be, we must recognize that the Soviet regime will inevitably be highly suspicious of it and its purposes. They will regard it as an attempt to drive a wedge

[1] On this subject see Department of State Publication 3840, "Cultural Relations between the United States and the Soviet Union," released in April, 1949.

between the Kremlin and the Soviet people. We cannot expect an early abatement of this suspicion—and should not be deterred by fear of intensifying it. However, it seems to me that insofar as possible we should make it clear to the Kremlin, as well as to the Soviet people as a whole, that it has nothing to fear from America if it eschews military or ideological aggression.

Impressive evidence has come to the attention of the State Department indicating the effectiveness of our information program and, in particular, the "Voice" broadcasts. When Madame Kasenkina leaped from a window of the Soviet Consulate in New York on August 12, 1948, news was beamed almost immediately to the U.S.S.R. General Smith, then American Ambassador to the U.S.S.R., reported that this news became common knowledge in Moscow within a few minutes. Very significant was the statement made in January, 1949, by a Soviet propaganda official at a meeting of lawyers to the effect that since the B.B.C. and the "Voice" began their broadcasts it had become much more difficult to indoctrinate Soviet people in the Marxist-Leninist ideology.

Much similar evidence is available. Far more impressive, however, is the Soviet government's reaction to the "Voice." Beginning in the summer of 1947 with a sharp attack by the famous writer Ehrenburg, the Soviet press and radio has carried a steady stream of vitriolic criticism and depreciation of the "Voice" and also of our magazine. After fairly small-scale preliminary efforts, there began on April 24, 1949, a gigantic "jamming" operation. According to official American estimates, this operation even at its beginning employed more transmitters than were available at that time to the "Voice." These Soviet reactions testify eloquently to the interest of both the Soviet public and the Kremlin in our broadcasts. They lend force to the statement made by the U.S. Advisory Commission on Information in its first semi-annual report to Congress, dated March 19, 1949: ". . . the 'Voice' is heard and it is effective. It is effective partly because it tells the people the truth . . . mainly because it brings hope and encouragement." The report added: "The Voice of America reaches millions of Russians today . . . without these media [Voice of America and *Amerika*] our battle would not be a contest, even a losing one. We would lose out entirely and only too quickly. . . ." [2]

I do not agree completely that without our information media we would "lose out entirely." They are vital and we should do everything to improve them so that we may with increasing effectiveness bring to the Soviet and other peoples the American message of the pursuit of happiness and the dignity of the individual. But I feel that even without them the battle of the mind would not necessarily be won by the totalitarians. As long as America and other free nations flourish, the submerged peoples of the world will not despair entirely. The Soviet propaganda machine is immensely effective, but truth is still more powerful. If the faith of the Soviet peoples in the truth of their rulers' word continues to be sapped, and if the target of the Kremlin's attack refuses to behave like a predatory monster, the Soviet regime will remain ideologically vulnerable.

The desire of the Soviet people for peace, prosperity, and a more humane life will continue to constitute a bridge between them and us in the difficult years ahead. They will, I believe, continue to offer psychological resistance to propaganda against an America whose power they respect and whose achievements symbolize many of their own aspirations.

The West has thus far not done all in its power to enlist the aid of former Soviet citizens, now refugees from the Soviet Union, in bringing its message of peace and welfare to the peoples of Russia. Soviet refugees understand the Soviet system, particularly its most evil aspects, better than any people can who have not been brought up under it. They can assist us in our task of accurately defining the aspirations of the Russian people and convincing them that we wish to help them to fulfill their hopes. They can conduct valuable research on Soviet Russia. They can furnish help in the field of propaganda, particularly in radio broadcasting, and can be of service in other ways.

The value of the Soviet refugees to the cause of peace and freedom has thus far been limited by the failure of the Western

[2] See Department of State Publication 3485a, released in April, 1949, for full text of the Commission's report.

nations, particularly the United States, to adopt a bold and humane program of assistance to them in resettlement and building new lives in the Western world. Assistance to such refugees would furnish striking proof of the sincerity of American professions of political idealism; it would go far toward undoing the harm caused by our return to the Soviet authorities in 1945-46 of thousands of Soviet citizens who wished to remain abroad.

Within the limits defined by the foregoing, we should not neglect any opportunities, however slight, to narrow the chasm of mistrust between us and the Soviet leaders. The fading of Wendell Willkie's bright, but premature, dream of one world should not discourage future efforts in the same direction. Infinite patience and profound study of both Soviet and Western thought and culture will be indispensable prerequisites for these efforts. There is no longer as much danger as there was of overlooking the great Soviet-American ideological differences, particularly regarding the nature of political power and the political process. The greatest stumbling block to mutual confidence is the Soviet doctrine that compromise, consensus, and mutual satisfaction cannot be achieved in the struggles of classes or nations. Ideologies, however, are in large measure reflections of experience. Is it too utopian to suggest even today that a democratic capitalist world which refuses to collapse but refrains from aggression could cause even Communists to modify their ideology? At any rate statesmen and scholars should study underlying trends with an eye for this and the other contingencies the future may bring.

Other possible lines of future development perhaps deserve mention. One, a partial step toward the hopeful possibility I have just suggested, was mentioned in the article in the *Economist* to which I referred earlier in this chapter. "The Soviet rulers," stated the *Economist*, "may adjust themselves in the long run to a world which restricts their opportunities for expansion, yet permits them to enjoy unmolested the power and wealth which a new social order in a vast empire has bestowed on them."

Another possibility, that of the disintegration of the Soviet

Union, was suggested by "X." The history of absolute states offers relatively little support for this hypothesis, but it must be remembered that the Soviet combination of despotism and utopianism has few or no parallels in history. Perhaps the death of Stalin might set in motion processes leading toward eventual disintegration. While I feel that his passing may weaken the Soviet system, I think its effects will be fully manifested only after some time when quarrels among the elite and the difficulty of replacing Stalin's political genius have produced their effects.

No social order is static. As the Soviet industrial revolution matures, new social formations will emerge. It is possible that the developing Soviet technical and scientific intelligentsia may break out of the strait jacket of ideological conformity and party supervision and even that in some manner, now difficult to foresee, new forms of freedom may emerge from the neo-feudalism of Soviet totalitarianism as they once did from the breakup of the feudal order in medieval Europe. If not, deprivation of the stimulating exchange of ideas with the West and of domestic freedom of discussion imposed upon the Soviet mind by the Kremlin may lead to intellectual dry rot in the new Muscovy.

It is certainly worth while to couch our propaganda to the Soviet Union in so far as possible in terms of the conflict of interests between the Soviet intelligentsia and the Communist Party apparatus. Judging by the testimony of some of the most intelligent Soviet refugees, the new Soviet intelligentsia favors a measure of restoration of private property or at least of economic initiative, resents party interference in science, the arts, and scholarship, and fears the consequences of the Kremlin's adventurous foreign policy. We should, with the aid of Soviet émigrés, undertake a systematic analysis of Soviet society with a view to the most effective presentation of America's message to its various audiences within Soviet Russia.

The future is hazardous, but not hopeless; if we face it with patience and common sense, even the problems posed by Soviet-American relations in the atomic age may eventually be solved.

Index

P

R

S